D0941875

MAR 1 7 1987	DATE DUE		
FEB 03 1988			
OCT 1 4 1989			
JUL 0 1 1990			
DEC 2 8 1993			
NOV 2 2 1994			
AUG 1 9 1996			

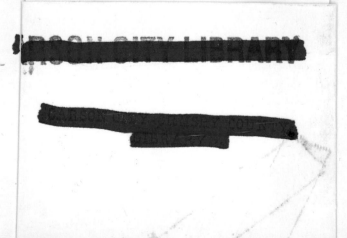

BOOKS BY OSCAR LEWIS

SILVER KINGS (1947)

THE LIVES AND TIMES of Mackay, Fair, Flood, and O'Brien, lords of the Nevada Comstock Lode.

THE BIG FOUR (1938)

THE STORY of Huntington, Stanford, Hopkins, and Crocker and of the building of the Central Pacific.

BY OSCAR LEWIS AND CARROLL D. HALL

BONANZA INN: *America's First Luxury Hotel* (1939)

A PAGEANT of San Francisco life in the colorful era when the Palace Hotel was the crossroads of the world.

THESE ARE *Borzoi Books,*

PUBLISHED IN NEW YORK BY *Alfred A. Knopf*

BONANZA INN

Artist's Sketch of the Palace Hotel, 1875

From the *San Francisco News Letter*

BONANZA INN

America's First Luxury Hotel

BY

OSCAR LEWIS

&

CARROLL D. HALL

1967

ALFRED A KNOPF
NEW YORK

PUBLISHED DECEMBER 1, 1939
REPRINTED SEVEN TIMES
NINTH PRINTING, MARCH 1967

CONTENTS

ILLUSTRATIONS

Illustrations

BONANZA INN

SHOW PLACE

1

SAN FRANCISCO housewives, standing on little drifts of sand, leaned over backyard fences the better to hear details of the passing of Mary Ann Whalen, who had died of being run down by a horse-car. On breezy street corners gentlemen twirled their mustaches in dismay as they pondered the fate of Mr. Lankman, brought to his end by a beer-glass accurately hurled by Ellen Londaine — and were reassured when the city's supervisors passed an ordinance excluding women from saloons after nightfall.

There was other news. Screened behind huge pages of the morning's *Alta*, citizens read that Arnold Smith, a local ancient, had discharged his gun at a gang of hoodlums and that the ball had killed Joseph Demas, innocent bystander. Down at Hunters Point drydock a sailor named Dutch Charley was kicked to death by Antonio Hidalgo in a quarrel of unknown origin. Newspapers announced that a fund for the relief of victims of Nebraska's grasshopper plague had reached the round sum of eight thousand dollars, and a night or two later sneak-thieves broke into Senator Latham's house and stole three thousand dollars' worth of jewels and bric-a-brac.

Off on her first voyage to China, the *City of Pekin* steamed out the Golden Gate, leaving half a dozen slow-moving grain clippers bobbing in her wake. Soon crowds reassembled at the Pacific Mail dock to wave *bon voyage* to another steamer inaugurating the Australian run. The *Alta's* readers learned of the organization of the Underwriters' Fire Patrol of San Francisco and, with more interest, read of the demise of William Kelley, killed by a fall from his carriage. These traffic accidents were growing far too numerous.

The year 1875 advanced and presently three events jarred the city from its placid routine. On August 20 the Bank of California, largest financial institution on the Coast, crashed about the ears of its founder, William Chapman Ralston, with a din heard with particular distinctness in far-off Virginia City. The next day Ralston himself was dragged unconscious from the bay and expired on the sands at North Beach while inexpert bystanders applied methods of resuscitating the drowned. The entire state divided on the question of whether Ralston had died by accident or by design. The debate was still raging two months later when the doors of the most magnificent of the dead man's creations were opened to the public.

It was the Palace, " the world's grandest hotel."

2

THE NEW hotel would be at least four times too large for its period and place, but the town had never had a

4

sense of proportion and no one was disturbed. San Francisco was less than thirty years old. Population numbered 191,716, if one counted the Chinese, of whom there were close to thirty thousand. In most directions houses had fanned out more than a mile from the cluster of shacks about the Plaza. The four nearest hills, Telegraph, Rincon, Nob, and Russian, were built up to their windy tops. Rows of wooden houses and new plank sidewalks were pushing out from the edges of the fan — literally hundreds of little rectangular boxes, each with its bay window and a brave showing of millwork beautifying its façade. Nearly two thousand new buildings were put up in the active year 1875, and by no means all had been these workingmen's cottages on the remote sandhills beyond Tenth Street. There was talk of hard times and of a shortage of cash, but those who complained had to raise their voices to be heard above the din of carpenters' hammers and the rumble of trucks piled high with building-materials. Along Montgomery Street and on California, Sansome, and Pine, construction was so active that half the time citizens had to walk in the muddy streets because sidewalks were blocked with heaps of bricks, stone, and marble, kegs of lime, and troughs of mortar. Dozens of the forthright iron-shuttered buildings put up in the '50s were being demolished and replaced by business houses in keeping with the city's present — homely, pretentious structures with exteriors as ornate as wedding cakes.

Visitors from conservative Eastern centers found at least half the population suffering from delusions of grandeur. In the boastful '70s every American was expected to believe his own state or city or crossroads village the geographical center of God's universe, but few could compete with the San Franciscans in the matter of civic pride. Newcomers were often puzzled to know what the boasting was about. To unprejudiced eyes the town was crude, noisy, unkempt, its sidewalks littered and in wretched repair, its streets lined with buildings reflecting the worst features of the debased architectural taste of the period. In the downtown area every third structure was said to be an eyesore; on the newer residential streets the percentage was much higher.

That San Francisco was unlike Boston, Charleston, or Philadelphia need not have surprised the strangers. The town had been in existence less than three decades; of course it had neither background nor taste. It had grown far too rapidly; too much had happened in too short a time. By the middle '70s the spare simplicity of the frontier village had given place to the ostentation of the suddenly rich. Consequently the place was full of contradictions, not only in its physical aspects but in the behavior of its citizens. Captains of industry in stove-pipe hats and Prince Alberts were known to scrawl their illegible signatures to checks made out in six figures, then carefully wipe the pen-point on a leg of their beautifully tailored trousers. Grand ladies five years removed from washtub or boarding-house kitchen paraded down fashionable Kearny Street, holding the trains of their Paris-made dresses above the sidewalk while jets of muddy water fountained upward between the planks at each descent of their ample feet. Citizens picked their way through streets filled with mud-holes and littered with horse-dung, entered a bank that was an inexact copy of a Venetian palace, and in the marble and bronze office of its president discussed the art of Edwin Booth in sentences sprinkled with oaths. Ex-teamsters married the daughters of brothel-keepers and shouldered their way into society, while men with degrees from ancient universities scoured cuspidors in Pacific Street dives, and women of refinement tended the tables of squalid boarding-houses.

Whatever his station, each citizen of the town was sure of its future, and of his own. The result was a mass restlessness, an urge to be up and doing that struck strangers as too intent and taut to be normal. It was, in short, a gambler's atmosphere; here gambling had flourished from the beginning. But the faro tables of '49 and '50 had given way to a more exciting game. The Comstock Lode was discovered in '59. Fifteen years later, speculation in Nevada mining stocks had become San Francisco's major industry. The spirits of the entire city rose and fell in unison with the daily quotations on the board at the Mining Exchange. Rich prizes had been won in the Comstock lottery and were still being won. Not only had it converted a score of saloon-keepers, pick-and-shovel miners, shoestring brokers and bankers into millionaires; it had elevated thousands of others to affluence. Fortune had smiled impartially on judges and hack-drivers and servant girls, on housewives and prostitutes, ministers and ex-jailbirds. For years local gossip had been brightened by countless success stories. A speculator down on his luck might pass a few shares of valueless stock over a counter in exchange for new soles on his boots. Three months later a dizzy ex-cobbler would be seen driving down Montgomery

7

Street in his own carriage. A broker might give his chambermaid a tip on the market and in a few weeks find her owning the rooming-house and lecturing *her* chambermaids on the evils of gambling. Such incidents became so numerous that the stories lost their novelty, but never their interest. Few citizens did not personally know someone — no smarter than himself — who had turned a profitable deal in Comstock stocks; fewer still resisted the temptation to get some of the easy money for himself. The result was San Francisco's gambling fever of the '70s, a malady so widespread and acute as to impress every stranger who came to town.

Of course the speculators lost as well as won. At fairly regular intervals the dominant group of professional gamblers, the new Comstock millionaires, were able to manipulate the market to the end that thousands of shoestring operators were wiped out. But the latter could always see clearly where they had made their mistakes. As soon as they were able they were back in the market intent on new fortunes.

The Comstock was, of course, more than a mere gambling device. Mines were being operated on the slopes of Mount Davidson, at Gold Hill, Austin, White Pine and the dozen other boom towns. Many were startlingly rich. Through the '70s new wealth was being hoisted from the Nevada mine-heads in greater volume than at any other period of history. Consolidated Virginia and California produced a total of $133,000,000; Ophir, $15,000,000; Gould and Curry, about the same amount; Savage, $20,000,000; Hale and Norcross, $11,-000,000; Chollar-Potosi, $14,000,000 — and there were dozens of others. Nearly all this immense production

8

was crowded within a period of less than a decade, and nearly all found its way to San Francisco. Naturally, visitors thought the town a bit erratic; its pockets were bulging with bright, new-minted gold and silver, and no one doubted that the streams of easy money would continue to flow for years. With virtually the entire population speculating, the price of seats on the mining board skyrocketed from $100 in '62 to $40,000 twelve years later. Brokers who had to keep their office forces late to enter the day's orders, nightly treated two dozen clerks to the best dinners the town could provide, with unlimited champagne. Carriages of the recently rich jammed the fashionable figure-eight driveway in Golden Gate Park, and on mild evenings the Cliff House bar was crowded three deep by those who could afford the best and who insisted on having it. When Barrett or Booth came to town, hundreds of choice seats were snapped up (usually at a premium) by lordly ex-paupers who habitually bought for every performance, matinee and evening, of the entire engagement.

Whatever was worth doing at all was worth doing on a grand scale. Citizens of all degrees considered themselves personally responsible for the confused, helter-skelter metropolis that had sprung up at the bay's edge. They boasted that no other city in history had grown from nothing to a place of such importance in twice as many years. But it was only a start; the town was just hitting its stride. What might it not accomplish in the next five years, the next ten? The whole Coast was awakening — not alone its mines, but its agriculture, lumber, transportation, manufactories — and San Francisco *was* the Coast. Did anyone doubt that a great city

9

was in the making? Arrogant, boastful, teeming with energy, the town was eager for any grandiose scheme that might suggest itself.

It was in this mood and atmosphere that the Palace was planned.

3

THE TOWN already had as many hotels as it could support, some of them quite good. From the beginning private residences had been comparatively few in San Francisco and an uncommonly large number of the inhabitants had lived in furnished rooms and taken their meals at restaurants or boarding-house tables. That custom changed but slowly. As late as the '70s visitors were still impressed by the number and variety of eating-places, the solid blocks of boarding-houses (some quite elegant and expensive), and the many hotels. Visitors were likely to observe, too, that hotels played an unusually important part in the social and commercial life of the town. Thousands of citizens never outgrew, or wanted to outgrow, their early habit of looking on a hotel room as the logical place to conduct one's business affairs, to consummate deals, meet friends, entertain visitors, hold poker sessions or, lamentably, *affaires d'amour*.

By the end of the '60s Montgomery Street was lined with pretentious hostelries: the Lick House and the Occidental, on opposite corners of Sutter Street; just beyond, the Russ House, extending the block from

Bush to Pine; farther down Montgomery, near Pacific, stood the Commercial. These had been the leading hotels of the booming '60s. Two others, both imposing houses, had been newly finished: the Baldwin and the Grand. The former, put up by " Lucky " Baldwin, stood at Market and Powell; its cost, with the Baldwin Theater under the same roof, was $800,000. The Grand was admired for the intricacy of its exterior decorations. It was its misfortune to be overshadowed soon by the lofty walls of the Palace, directly opposite.

San Francisco had no real need for a new hotel of any kind, much less for a mammoth structure of eight hundred rooms. No matter — it was to be the largest and most luxurious hostelry in the universe; that distinction would be worth whatever it cost. And the cost was not niggardly even by the expansive standards of the Bonanza era. First and last a round five millions went into its building and furnishing. Moreover, the average citizen's pride in this new civic monument was enhanced by the knowledge that it would not cost him a penny. Like the amphitheaters and baths and commemorative arches of another imperial city, it was being provided for his enjoyment by the benevolence of a wealthy patrician. The comparison is not altogether inept; there was more than a touch of Roman emperor about William Chapman Ralston.

Better than any other citizen Ralston typified the city's flamboyance, its headlong ambition to accomplish this year, or next, what prudently might be delayed a decade. Self-assured, energetic, brash, he never doubted his power to do whatever he set out to do — and to do it a bit more splendidly than it had been done before. His liking for the theater was significant; few men had a more highly developed instinct for self-dramatization. Ralston's own career was as exciting a melodrama as many he had ever seen in the big play-house he built on Bush Street. A former ship's carpenter and ex-clerk on Mississippi river boats, he reached San Francisco in 1853 with the rear guard of the gold-seekers, as agent for a New York steamship line. When his employers presently went into banking, he drifted into finance as a resident partner. In the gyrating town of the '50s banking was no more stable than other businesses, and the firm passed through a rapid series of partnerships. The New York connection was cast off; Fretz and Ralston survived until '58 and were succeeded by Donohoe, Ralston & Company. That firm lasted five prosperous years before Ralston withdrew to organize, with ample backing, the Bank of California, the largest financial house yet projected in the West.

During the next dozen years Ralston's career reached its gilded height. As the bank (conservative D. O. Mills remained president until 1872, but Ralston was always its mainspring) grew in power and prestige, so did the ambitions of its treasurer. The establishment of agencies at Virginia City and other Nevada boom towns gave the bank control of some of the richest mines, and its owners a share in the profits. Ralston's personal riches grew with those of the bank. At the time, there seemed little need to keep the two fortunes separate.

With seemingly unlimited money at his disposal, Ralston became the acknowledged leader of the city's bumper crop of promoters. Any man with a plan for a new factory, a new colonization scheme or subdivision or civic improvement, hurried to the banker's office, knowing that the warmth of his reception would depend on how spectacular he could make his conception sound. Ralston listened with delight to each gaudy proposal. A very large number of them received his backing. Through the late '60s and early '70s hundreds of thousands of dollars of his and his bank's money were poured into buildings and machinery designed to make the Coast independent of the Eastern manufacturers. California raised thousands of sheep; why ship wool to New England and buy back blankets, flannel shirts, and broadcloth? The Mission Woolen Mills (cost: $250,-000) were to change all that. Citizens of so progressive a city needed carriages in their stables, tables and chairs and corner what-nots in their front parlors, watches in their vest pockets. Ralston set out to supply them all, and money in volume was expended on the Kimball Carriage Factory, the West Coast Furniture Company, the Cornell Watch Factory. Between times he financed irrigation schemes to aid the spread of agriculture, helped build a drydock for the encouragement of ocean traffic, planned ironworks and car-building plants to provide rolling stock for the state's scores of projected railroads.

A man of such large activities was expected to live ostentatiously, and Ralston did not disappoint. His San Francisco house, on Pine Street, near Leavenworth, was one of the show places of the city; its cost was estimated at $140,000. This was easily eclipsed by his country home at Belmont, twenty miles down the peninsula.

Ralston bought the place, a modest villa on a wooded hillside, in the late '60s. He at once began to improve both house and grounds. Construction went on for years; before he had finished, it was by far the largest residence on the Coast. In 1871 a visitor compared it to a huge, sprawling country hotel. As usual, expense was no object. Ralston cheerfully expended $10,000 to provide an additional water supply; a gas plant cost $50,000; the stables a like amount. No one bothered to guess how much the new wings and ells and galleries had cost, or the acres of landscaped grounds, or the private wharf extending far out into the bay. Belmont's entertainments set standards of hospitality never since equaled in the West. Fifty guests were not unusual; on special occasions two hundred might sit down to meals that — even in an era when dining was both an art and an endurance contest — aroused admiration by their length and complexity. At such times special trains carried the guests to and from the city. On his daily trips to town, however, Ralston found the railroad too slow. He traveled by coach, driving at top speed over dusty roads while his guests clung to their swaying seats. In order that he might " beat the train " on these breakneck journeys, he kept fresh horses waiting at the halfway point and men trained to change the teams with only a few seconds' delay.

By such spectacular extravagances Ralston cemented his reputation as San Francisco's most conspicuous citizen. Of course his name led the list of subscribers to charities, and his big affable figure was to be seen everywhere: at social and civic functions, at the speakers' table at banquets, in the foremost box on first nights.

Show Place

In the public mind Ralston's prodigal support of
local enterprises and his personal expenditures were
regarded as evidence that the resources of his bank were
limitless. The belief was strengthened when the money
stringency of the early '70s — which caused dozens of
lesser institutions to shorten sail drastically — had no
effect on the banker's lavish career.

But the most convincing argument of all was his immense new hotel. Surely no sane man would have undertaken *that* unless his pocketbook was bottomless.
For upwards of two years not only San Francisco but
all California watched " the largest building ever projected in the West " take shape and substance. Since
early in 1874, its walls, only slightly less than a quarter
mile in circumference, had been rising, story on story.
By the beginning of '75 it was already the city's most
conspicuous landmark, a great angular mesa looming
above the surrounding plain. It was *seven stories* high.
It was to contain *eight hundred* rooms. Citizens under-
scored the words each time they repeated them. No
other city had anything to compare with it.

It was not a matter of size alone. Ralston had planned
the Palace as a symbol of San Francisco's coming of age.
It was to mark the closing of one era and the beginning
of another, the end of the transition from mining camp
and raw boom town to established city. As such it must
be not only big but elaborate, a model of convenience
and luxury and taste. It must be built for permanence,
of the finest materials and by artisans of superior skill.
It must also be the last word in modernity. Everyone
then admitted that America's inventive genius had
reached full flower in the early '70s. The Palace must

15

contain every one of the new mechanical marvels that were becoming the pride of Americans and the envy of foreigners. Finally, the Palace was Ralston's most grandiose conception. It was to be a fitting apex to his career.

4

THE MANNER in which he acquired the property was characteristic. In the middle '60s Asbury Harpending, having made a modest fortune by the sale of lots in a forgotten mining camp in southern California, arrived in San Francisco and looked about for another speculation in real estate. After a shrewd survey of the direction of the city's growth, his interest centered on the region south of Market Street, opposite the end of Montgomery. Montgomery Street was then the main business thoroughfare. It was solidly built to its end at Market, and it was logical to assume that it must some day be extended to open up the growing region south of Market. The extension of Montgomery Street had been discussed before, but nothing could be done. Part of the land through which it must pass was owned by the Catholic Church, and the Church planned to erect an orphanage there.

Harpending concluded that if Montgomery were to be cut through it would have to be, not on a straight line, but at an angle. That would avoid the Church property; and it would also provide a direct route for traffic between the middle of town and the Pacific Mail

16

docks. Accordingly, he quietly picked up various parcels of land along the proposed route. He presently owned a broad strip extending two blocks from Market to Howard. The land was mostly unimproved sand hillocks, with a few small cottages. The neighborhood was not particularly desirable; most of his purchases were at bargain prices.

Inevitably the speculator hunted out Ralston and outlined his plan for Montgomery Street, South. Before he left the banker's office Ralston had bought a half interest in the property and they had jointly organized the Montgomery Street Land Company. Work got under way. Montgomery Street, South was duly opened as far as Howard Street. At once the group of former backyards became valuable business property. Beyond Howard, property-owners refused to sell and the plan of extending the street to the bay had to be abandoned; to this day New Montgomery Street ends at Howard. Meantime Harpending had become involved in other speculations and needed cash. Ralston accommodatingly took over his holdings in the Montgomery Street Land Company.

Between Market and Mission the new street had been cut through a high sandhill. A steep bank had been left, and during the next few years the property remained unimproved, while children of the neighborhood amused themselves by sliding down its sandy slopes. Some years later the Spanish-Californian, General Vallejo, chatting with Adelina Patti in the hotel that went up on the site, recalled that as a young man in the '30s he had shot a grizzly bear on that very hill.

Ralston held the property and gradually extended its

17

area. With his friend Maurice Dore acting as agent, he presently acquired the adjoining Church property; later he completed the block by paying a round $50,000 to the owner of a cottage at a far corner. Meantime the city's business section had continued to move in that direction, and even his last purchase proved a sound investment. The entire block cost him $400,000. He presently refused an offer of a million dollars for it. The prospective buyers wished to build a group of wholesale warehouses there, and Ralston believed the district should logically become a retail shopping area. Besides, he had already formed other plans.

His decision to build a hotel on his sandhill was reached in 1872. The announcement of the plan surprised no one; that the banker was fascinated by large construction enterprises was already widely known. In ten years he had put up at least a score of substantial structures: the California Theater, the Grand Hotel, a series of big factories, two elaborate residences. He had kept the town's leading building contractor, Henry L. King, almost continuously busy for years. His association with King had begun when the latter took a contract to do carpenter work for a new building for the Bank of California. King estimated that the job would take six months; his bid was $1,600. It took him nearly two years and Ralston voluntarily increased his compensation to $5,000. King once built a ballroom over the garden of Ralston's Pine Street house, completing it at dusk on the evening of the ball. At dawn the next morning he and his crew began demolishing it. Ralston one day called the contractor to his office and announced that he had decided to build a carriage

An Early View of the Grand Court

View of the Palace Office

LEFT: *William C. Ralston*
RIGHT: *Warren Leland, First Manager of the Palace*
From the *California Spirit of the Times*

factory. The two got into the banker's carriage and drove to the site, at Fourth and Harrison streets. There Ralston pointed out where he wanted the buildings placed and with characteristic impatience insisted that King start work " at once." The latter managed to complete the two large brick buildings in seventy days.

When Ralston decided to build a hotel on his Market and Montgomery street property he of course called in King. He had already engaged an architect, John P. Gaynor, and Gaynor had gone East to study the construction of leading American hotels: the Palmer House and Grand Pacific in Chicago, New York's Sturtevant House and New Windsor — all far smaller structures than this was to be. Early in 1873 a high board fence was thrown up about the property and the excavation of the site began — a huge task, for there was to be a basement and sub-basement covering the entire block, including the sidewalk areas — an area of two and a half acres.

While a procession of carts carried the sand to the bay-shore, citizens learned something of the building that was soon to rise on the site. Its general plan was to follow that of certain hotels in Vienna. It was to be in the form of a rectangle, with the long sides, 350 feet, on New Montgomery and Annie streets and the shorter, 275 feet, on Market and Jessie. Three large courts would supply light and air to the interior rooms. The largest of these, and the hotel's chief architectural ornament, would face the main entrance in the center of the Montgomery Street side. This central court — 84 by 144 feet — was to have a circular driveway opening on the street; thus arriving guests would be driven inside the building and deposited on a marble-paved floor in the midst of a forest of potted trees and plants. Extending upward on all four sides was to be a series of seven galleries and, surmounting it all, a great domed roof of opaque glass. Advance descriptions of the grand court were borne out by the reality; within a few years after its completion this vast chamber was famous all over the world.

Other features of the hotel were as noteworthy, though less spectacular. Its walls overshadowed not only its close neighbors but the entire central part of the city. A year or two after its completion a traveling Scotchman described its exterior as " more monstrous than elegant," a remark that was locally ascribed to plain jealousy. Vertical banks of bay windows completely covered the great façades, giving an effect that natives proudly described as " typically San Franciscan." For these angular projections, designed to catch a maximum of sunshine in a fog-ridden climate, had long been an almost universal feature of the local domestic architecture. In the original design the bay windows were to extend only to the fourth floor; Ralston vetoed that plan and ordered that they be continued to the top. It was his aim to make every room equally desirable. If some were to have the distinction of a bay window all must have it. From a purely artistic standpoint the result fell far short of perfection, but for a full generation few looked for the first time on the great parallel rows of windows without feeling something akin to awe.

The Palace ran not only to size but to massiveness. Its outer walls, of brick, averaged two feet in thickness.

These rested on massive foundations of masonry, twelve feet in depth. For still greater solidity, the walls were reinforced every four feet by double strips of iron, bolted together, forming continuous bands from end to end. The ends of the bolts were visible on the outer surface of the walls. When the building was finished the exterior was painted white, all except the bolt-heads, which were gilded, and these parallel lines of gold dots extending horizontally around the building had a curious effect. For greater strength, the mortar binding the bricks had an uncommonly high proportion of cement to lime. When in later years it was occasionally necessary to cut through one of the walls, workmen were astonished to find that the mortar was as hard as the bricks themselves. Not only the outer walls but the miles of inner partitions were of the same materials. During construction, there were often three hundred bricklayers at work, each of whom laid about 1,500 bricks per day. About 300,000 bricks were required daily and the task of supplying that many taxed the capacity of every brickyard on the Coast. One Saturday morning the supply ran short and Ralston, arriving on one of his frequent rounds of inspection, found half the bricklayers idle. He hunted up King and ordered that the idle men be sent home. King refused. Bricklayers, he told the banker, were sensitive about such matters. If he laid the men off, half of them would fail to return on Monday. Building was active all over town and there were plenty of other jobs. Both men lost their tempers and Ralston stalked off. But on Monday morning he found an ample supply of bricks on hand and the full crew at work, whereupon he sought out his building superintendent and restored friendly relations.

Ralston's occasional interference and his characteristic impatience of delay were by no means King's only problems. The magnitude of the enterprise drew heavily on the resources of the state, and there were periodical shortages of both men and materials. King was never able to find enough skilled workmen. Consequently he was forced to hire scores of untrained men, with the delays and waste and confusion that naturally resulted. Occasional strikes were a further complication. One visitor during the latter stages of construction was astonished to find the rough plastering was being done by crews of boys in their teens. These and other problems, however, were taken in stride. The work went forward.

Those who planned the building took unusual precautions to guard against fire and earthquake, for these dangers were less remote in San Francisco than in most cities. In 1868 a severe earthquake had exposed a number of weaknesses in local construction methods. Cornices had been shaken loose all over town; brick walls had cracked and in some instances fallen into the streets. In the Palace this danger was guarded against partly by increasing the thickness of the walls and the strength of the mortar, but mainly by the liberal use of reinforcing iron. Three thousand tons of iron strips were built into the walls. It was more than thirty years before the efficiency of such devices was put to a really severe test.

Precautions against fire were equally thorough. It was stated that Ralston's insistence that the big struc-

ture be made as nearly fireproof as was humanly possible added a half million to its cost. It was money well
invested. San Francisco's fire record was not encouraging to a man who contemplated putting up one of the
most expensive structures ever built. In less than a
quarter-century the town had had seven major con-
flagrations. An eighth was a by no means remote possibility, for wood was still the most widely used building-
material. The local fire-fighting equipment had been
brought to a high degree of efficiency, but two serious
dangers remained: frequent strong winds and a water
supply that was sometimes — at the end of the long,
dry summers — shockingly low.

To give the hotel a water supply independent of the
city's mains, a series of artesian wells, with a capacity
of 28,000 gallons an hour, was drilled on the site. A
storage reservoir holding 630,000 gallons was built in
the sub-basement, under the grand court, and seven
tanks with a capacity of another 130,000 gallons were
placed on the roof. This assured an ample supply in
the event the city's reservoirs went dry. There remained the matter of making it available in time of
emergency. This was accomplished by building a separate distribution system, independent of that which
supplied wash-basins and toilets and bathtubs. It consisted of *five miles* of pipes, ranging from three to eight
inches in diameter. There were 350 outlets, to which
were attached 20,000 feet of fire hose. Three pumps in
the basement maintained the pressure at a hundred
pounds to the square inch; the pumps automatically
started when one of the fire plugs was opened. Other
ingenious devices, " automatic fire detectors," were

placed in each room, and, as a final precaution, watchmen patrolled every part of the building at thirty-minute intervals day and night. On their rounds they were required to touch an electrical apparatus at each of seventy-nine stations; should they miss one the fact was registered at a central control room.

These complicated precautions proved effective. In the thirty-one years of its existence the hotel had numerous small blazes, for the building was put up before the day of central heating, and fires were usually burning in the fireplaces of hundreds of the rooms. From the day of its opening until mid-April of 1906 the big building was believed to be safe from major damage by fire.

5

BY THE spring of 1875, construction had reached a point where it was possible for visitors to visualize the future wonders of the place. On Saturday afternoons Superintendent King piloted groups of citizens through the spacious chambers of the ground floor. The sightseers looked with wonder at the grand court, its seven tiers of galleries rising to the lofty dome, and passed on to other rooms: a marble-flagged office 65 by 55 feet, with a 25-foot ceiling; a ballroom of the same dimensions as the office; ladies' and men's reception rooms, each 40 by 40; billiard room, barber shop, and bar (all on the Jessie Street side) of the same generous proportions; and a main dining-room 150 feet long, incomparably the largest in the West.

Features new in hotel design were not lacking. On the Montgomery and Market Street sides provision had been made for eighteen retail stores. Each had two entrances and two sets of show-windows, one facing on the streets, the other on long galleries within the building; guests would thus enjoy the luxury of doing their shopping — or of merely admiring the displays — without the inconvenience of stepping outdoors.

Inventors were then putting electricity to a variety of clever uses, and many of the devices were installed for the convenience of the Palace's guests. A hundred and twenty-five miles of wires permitted the functioning of electric call buttons in each room, of telegraphic instruments providing communication between the service pantries on each floor and the main office or dining-room, and of what was perhaps the greatest novelty of all: electrically operated clocks — ". . . sixteen large and handsome time dials, running in perfect unison, and controlled by Field's patent electric regulator." Telephones and electric lights were still too crude for practical operation (both were installed a few years later), but gas fixtures were modern as well as elaborate, with burners of an improved design, and in the public rooms they were so arranged that a hundred jets might be regulated by the turning of a single master key.

Other interesting gadgets charmed a mechanically minded generation. Each floor had its own "tubular conductor" to carry outgoing mail direct to a central box in the office. Another system of pneumatic tubes conveyed incoming letters, messages, or even small parcels, to a score of stations, requiring only a few seconds to reach the most distant parts of the building. Each of the 755 water closets — made by Maddock & Sons, Burslem — boasted "an arrangement by which the water is carried off without producing the horrid noise one usually hears." Bathtubs and wash-stands had devices that prevented overflowing should faucets be carelessly left running. There was even a primitive air-conditioning system, with more than two thousand vents connecting with each room, closet, and bathroom, and thirty-three ventilating boxes. "Hot coils placed in these boxes rarefy the air, drawing all the foul air out and admitting fresh air at will."

Five hydraulic elevators provided access to the acres of upstairs rooms. The elevators were described as luxurious and spacious, with mirror-faced walls, and seats upon which passengers might recline at ease while being whisked noiselessly to the dizzy height of seven stories. The upper floors contained 755 rooms, with accommodations for 1,200 guests. By modern standards the rooms were large. Most of them were twenty feet square and none was less than sixteen by sixteen. Ceilings were uniformly fifteen feet high. Hallways and the arcades fronting on the main court were on a like scale. The arrangement of the rooms about short, lateral hallways, and a system of intercommunicating doors, permitted a wide variety of grouping. "The connections and approaches are such that an individual, a family, or a party of any size can have a suite of any number of rooms, combining the seclusion of the most elegant private residence, with its own private toilet, ample clothes-closet and fire-grate."

When rough construction was completed and hundreds of workmen began installing the interior fittings, new wonders greeted the Saturday afternoon crowds of visitors. So great was the amount of marble used that contracts had to be made with fifteen different firms, for 804 mantels, 900 wash-stands, 40,000 square feet of pavement. Finishing woods came from many parts of the world: mahogany, East India teak, primavera from Mexico, rosewood, ebony. Much of it was elaborately hand-carved, all was highly polished. Painters applied finishing coats to walls, inside and out. The color of the public rooms was a delicate pink, " somewhat resembling the peach blossom " — a shade described as " showy in the highest degree, but not at all offensive. . . ." The exterior was even more striking; it emerged from behind the scaffolding a dazzling white, with gold trim, sparingly used. Some observers were reminded of a gigantic wedding-cake. But San Francisco's staple fuel was then a low-quality California coal, which gave off as much soot as heat. Within a few months the hotel's snowy walls were visible only in memory.

Most of the furnishings were locally made. This was in line with Ralston's policy of encouraging manufacturing on the Coast. A factory was bought specially for the purpose — a typical Ralston gesture. It was one example of the banker's way of doing things on a big scale. There were others. Because a considerable amount of oak flooring would be needed for the hotel, he purchased a large ranch in the Sierra foothills, near Grass Valley. The ranch contained hundreds of oak trees. Not until after the deal was made did he discover that they were not the variety of oaks from which flooring could be made. Such feats presently caused misgivings even among Ralston's empire-building friends. William Sharon was one of those who protested: " I said to him: ' If you are going to buy a foundry for a nail, a ranch for a plank, and a manufactory to build furniture, where is this going to end?' He said: ' It does look ridiculous to you?' 'Yes,' I said, '. . . it looks pretty bad.' "

Nonetheless, Ralston went ahead with his furniture project. As usual everything had to be done in a hurry. His factory was presently humming with activity, filling in the short space of a hundred and twenty days " the largest contract ever undertaken by any furniture manufactory." New machinery had to be installed and new men trained, but that was the sort of thing Ralston liked best. For four months two hundred and fifty men worked from seven in the morning until ten thirty at night — but skeptics were confounded and the contract was filled on time, down to the last table and chair. The furniture was of the " East Lake " style, then at the height of its vogue. It was made of natural finished woods — primavera, golden mahogany, and tomano — with austere decorations consisting chiefly of parallel grooves, gilded, extending vertically along the head and footboards of beds, on the legs of chairs and bureaus.

This was for the regular guest chambers; the public rooms and de luxe suites were on a grander scale. For the downstairs chambers there were huge rugs specially woven in France, fragile and befringed French furniture of the ladies' reception room, leather-upholstered chairs for more masculine chambers, and for the parlors two grand pianos " ornamented with inlaid foreign woods." California's school of landscape painters enjoyed a period of unprecedented prosperity, and scores of views of Yosemite, Lake Tahoe, the Golden Gate at sunset, and clipper ships under full sail, ornamented the twenty-five-foot-high walls of the ground floor.

As midsummer approached and furniture and equipment were installed, San Francisco papers printed new columns of statistics. Of dishes there were enough to supply an army, although they were not of army quality: 9,000 plates, 8,800 " side " and 8,000 " vegetable " dishes, 4,000 cups and saucers. These had been made, on special order, by C. F. Haviland, France. There were also 9,000 cuspidors, maker unspecified; 2,000 knives (silver plated, with ivory handles) ; forks, spoons, tea and coffee jugs, cruets, silver serving dishes in quantity. The catalogue of Irish linens was so lengthy that " the Belfast warehouses must have been stripped as bare as Mother Hubbard's cupboard," and to supply and install the acres of carpets the firm of W. & J. Sloane, of New York, established a local store and so went permanently into business in San Francisco.

6

MEANTIME PREPARATIONS for the opening got under way. In midsummer of 1875, local papers announced that the Palace had been leased to Warren Leland, of the then famous family of hotel men. " Wherever civilization is known or appreciated the name of Leland is preeminent," stated the *Alta*, and went on to list the hotels that had enjoyed the privilege of being operated by one or another of the five Leland brothers: the Sturtevant, Clinton, and Metropolitan, New York; the Delavan House, Albany; the Clarendon, Saratoga; the Ocean Hotel, Long Branch; and the Leland, Springfield, Illinois. Their uncles owned the Eutaw House in Baltimore.

Leland was born, appropriately enough, in a Vermont tavern. He was genial, suave, dignified, pleasantly smiling; in San Francisco Ambrose Bierce promptly nicknamed him "Blandlord" Leland. When Ralston sent the architect of his projected hotel on a tour of inspection of American hotels, Leland — who had lived in San Francisco in the '50s — was one of those to whom he presented letters of introduction. Of the scores of hotel men interviewed, he had offered the soundest advice, advanced the most practical suggestions. Later Ralston had renewed their acquaintance in New York and was favorably impressed. Here was a man of imagination and ideas, one who could visualize a hotel of unprecedented size and luxury and who recognized that it must provide guests with services appropriate to the splendor of their surroundings.

Leland reached San Francisco several months before the scheduled opening and set about selecting his staff and training the personnel. George Smith, formerly of the Occidental, was made chief clerk; known to thousands all over the Coast as "the Count," Smith had to an unusual degree one of the prime qualifications of a hotel man: the ability to remember names and faces.

Leland's son, Van, came out with his father and was given a minor job that he might learn the business and so carry on the family tradition. Two other experienced hotel men were added to the staff: M. D. Main, of the Windsor Hotel in New York, and Charles F. Dodge, from Chicago's Gardner House.

For his operating personnel Leland introduced the novelty of Negro waiters, porters, and chambermaids. There were then few Negroes in San Francisco and almost no Negro domestic servants; the Chinese had long had a monopoly in that field. In most hotels and restaurants guests were served by white men, and the service was usually far short of perfection. This was particularly true in the middle '70s, for the whole Coast was booming and jobs were plentiful. Even the lowliest citizen was likely to regard waiting on table as a temporary expedient useful only to keep the wolf at bay until something better turned up. For was he not also playing the Comstock? And might he not tomorrow, or next week, be ordering his dinner at the most expensive restaurant in town, his napkin tucked grandly under his chin? Just such things were constantly happening and they admirably illustrated the workings of a democracy — but they did not help the service. Leland's announcement, accordingly, was greeted with pleasure. Whatever their shortcomings might be, Negro waiters were sure to be " a vast improvement upon the impudent ' white trash ' who have exchanged the hod for the napkin, but still retain the manners of their native hovels." There was an approving word, too, for the chambermaids. " We noted . . .

some of the prettiest kind of colored girls . . . in nice, clean dresses, and felt very much inclined to take a suite of rooms in consequence."

July passed, then August, while hundreds of workmen swarmed through the structure applying the finishing touches. The opening date was fixed — October 2 — and the tempo quickened. Plasterers, painters, carpenters, plumbers, gas-fitters, electricians, stone-setters completed their jobs and moved out with their paraphernalia, to be succeeded by new crews who laid carpets, hung curtains, moved in and placed the numberless drayloads of furniture. Night after night gaslights burned into the small hours as crates of dishes, linens, silverware, kitchen and laundry and bar equipment, were unpacked and put in place, as cellars were stocked with foods and wines, and " Blandlord " Leland drilled his staff of three hundred in the intricate business of operating the world's greatest hotel.

Meantime the local papers, which for three years had been describing the future wonders of the place, blossomed out with new enraptured descriptions, new statistics. But by that time the appetites of local readers had begun to be jaded. For the moment they had heard quite enough of the new hotel; the time was ripe for satire. The latter was duly provided by " Derrick Dodd " in the pages of a local weekly. The entire town read what he had written — and roared its approval:

The statistician of the *News Letter* estimates the ground covered by the Palace Hotel to be eleven hundred and fifty-four square miles, six yards, two inches and ha'penny farthing, or say a space equal to the states of Wisconsin and Rhode Island, and the right-hand half of Senegambia. . . . The weight of the entire edifice, that is, when full, is eighty-six billion nine hundred and forty million, six hundred and four thousand, two hundred and one tons, and eleven pounds. . . . This ponderous weight accounts for the recent singular bulge noticed in the earth near Shanghai, China, within a few months past. The extreme height of the building is twenty-two thousand and twenty-eight feet, six and three-quarters inches, or just forty-six and two-sixteenth times as high as the dome of St. Peter's, and nearly twenty times as tall as the Bunker Hill monument. A contract is already given out for the construction of a flume from the Yosemite to conduct the Bridal Veil fall thither, and which it is designed to have pour over the east front. . . .

From the dizzy height of the roof can be seen the most astonishing expanse of territory. On the one hand tower the majestic Rocky Mountains, while on the other stretches the illimitable vastness of the sea. Far down below lies the bay, the Golden Gate, the line of the crested beach, and, but a little way off we can descry, in the changing glory of the heaving waters, the distant Farallones, nestling in the deep like three chinches slumbering on a velvet cushion. (The above simile must be returned, if used by private parties, as it is to be stuffed for the Centennial). Alcatraz and Sausalito are in the immediate shadow of the great pile, but Santa Barbara is concealed by a high hill to the south. Arrangements have just been made, however, to have the hill removed or the town jacked up into the scenery, which will then be perfect. . . .

The Palace Hotel, as is well known, contains 66,000 rooms, each containing 13½ more cubic feet of space than Platt's Hall, not counting the closets, of which there are 42 in each room, all of them about the size of the dining room of the Lick House. The beds are made with Swiss watch springs and stuffed with camel's hair, each single hair costing eleven cents by the wholesale. Over each bed is a silver tube, through which hot tea or gruel can be forced up from the kitchen by means of a solid silver force pump, exclusively for the benefit of invalids. Every bed has a highly ingenious clockwork arrangement connecting with the main office, by which, at any desired hour in the morning, the sleeper is gently tilted out into a mother-of-pearl bathtub, filled with milk of roses, which, in turn, boosts him over into a most admirable invention, which rubs the guest dry and combs his hair in less than eight minutes. . . .

The carpets for the entire hotel cost $32 a short yard, and it is thought, by a man specially employed to think it over, that if they were all raveled out and wound round the earth from northeast to southwest, there would be enough to make the globe look like a ball of yarn in eight years and forty-two days. . . . It is more than probable that this noble idea will be carried out during the Centennial. . . .

All the entrees will be sprinkled with gold dust, and the native oysters will be carefully done up in tin foil to avoid leaving an unpleasant taste in the mouth. By a happy idea of the younger Mr. Leland, everybody ordering wine will receive a large chromo, and every ninth pie will contain a pearl as large as a hen's egg (*wren's* egg, probably. — Ed.), which, of course, belongs to the prettiest girl at that particular table. . . . Each table accommodates four persons and a boy, and is waited upon by two picked waiters, one of whom is attired in a superb swallow-tail coat, cut bias, and a Frodsham watch, and who brings in the solid gold dishes; while the other is arrayed in the costume of a 14th century troubadour, and accompanies the conversation on a mandolin. . . . On a raised dais in the center of the room a troupe of 60 beautiful Persian dancing girls, specially selected, will dance during the meals the Saraband, or Eliza-band, if preferred. . . . Professor Herman has been engaged as hat taker, and will produce a rabbit and a hoopskirt from each and every hat before returning it to the guest. Just before the conclusion of dinner, Mr. Leland and Mr. Smith will enter at opposite ends of the dining salon, mounted on solid bonanza silver velocipedes, and will make graceful curves around each table, handing every waiter at the same time a new trade dollar. This will obviate the necessity of feeing the waiters, and is a truly thoughtful convenience to the public.

The mail facilities are as perfect as can be devised. Any lady in the house failing to receive a letter, one will be immediately written by a corps of talented young Complete letter-writers, kept for the express purpose, and at once sent up on a silver salver. There are thirty-four elevators in all — four for passengers, ten for baggage and twenty for mixed drinks. Each elevator contains a piano and a bowling alley. . . .

CHAPTER TWO

SULTAN AFTER SULTAN

1

" It is indeed true that across twenty-five centuries the spirit of Pericles whispers through every architrave and pilaster and angle of the beautiful structure in which we assemble tonight; but Pericles could never have ascended on an elevator, or banqueted by gaslight."

LAUGHTER and a scattering of applause rippled down the length of the big, bright room. Layers of cigar smoke floated upward from the long tables and eddied about three hundred gaslights, burning in brilliant clusters of twenty-five. Two hundred and sixteen guests sipped cognac or benedictine or chartreuse from diminutive glasses of cut crystal, ran fingers around the tops of collars, and surreptitiously loosened the tight upper buttons of trousers. It was close to midnight and they had been dining and speech-making since eight. But the Honorable Thomas Fitch showed signs that his oration was nearly done and interest focused again on the head of the table.

" I have endeavored — I feel very indifferently — to convey the idea that we are a very great people, and when that is said, all is said — except, perhaps, that in the near future we are destined to be still greater. . . ."

A very great people? Who could doubt it? One had but to look at this roomful of men, at the room itself, and recall the ragged huddle of shacks that had been San Francisco twenty-five years earlier. With so much already accomplished, what might not the future hold? Imagination played nimbly about coming triumphs, for the long banquet had not lacked liquid accessories: Château Yquem, Château Lafitte, champagne, punch à la Romaine, a variety of liqueurs. Two out of three of these men in stiff shirts and broadcloth had swung picks for a livelihood in the recent past, or had tended bar, or had served customers in little canvas and sheet-iron stores. Like the town itself they had come up with a rush, and now they claimed their privilege as self-made men to be complacent and boastful and mildly arrogant. They had fought their way through to power and possessions; their offices and stores and factories covered the recently leveled flats above the former cove, and their big wooden residences were shooting up like mushrooms on the slopes of Nob and Russian hills.

All evening the Fourth Artillery Band had played in the grand court while the wives and daughters of the new aristocracy had promenaded around the galleries or, with little cries of simulated alarm, had approached the railings and peered down at the circle of musicians among the palms. Imagine! This immense cavern of light and beauty was in San Francisco! Fully half these jeweled ladies could remember when the town had lacked the simplest conveniences; when one bathed in a wooden tub on the kitchen floor, in water delivered (in five-gallon cans) by a peddler each morning, and patiently heated above a wood fire. Only a scant twenty years separated that day from the present. And this transformation had been brought about because some mines beyond the Sierra had exceeded everyone's expectations and so had brought prosperity to everyone who held the right stocks.

Back in the dining-room the guest of honor, Lieutenant General Philip Sheridan, lamentably short of stature, had to stand on a table that all might see as well as hear. His short speech was in key with the city's mood:

". . . But there has been a greater pleasure . . . in seeing the development and progress which has come to this coast since I was here before. Still it does not seem to me that it should be a matter of astonishment when I find that . . . your mountains are filled with that kind of mineral which makes up the standard currency of the world. I may remark that it is very hard for any imagination I possess to picture what may be the future. . . ."

But even prophecies of coming greatness grew dull from too much repetition, and faces broke into anticipatory smiles as George Bromley rose to propose a toast to the ladies:

" When I left my domicile this morning and the partner of my joys and sorrows inquired affectionately what I expected to do besides eat and drink . . . I very frankly told her it was expected I should respond to the ladies. And she very anxiously inquired what ladies I was going to respond to. That was a very unfortunate confession on my part, Mr. President. In order to convince her that the ladies were entirely imaginary, it took the whole time that I had expected to devote to preparing this speech. . . ."

Smiles broadened and the cares of the empire-builders slipped away. Not for nothing had Uncle George
become unofficial jester to the court of King Comstock,
always on hand with a flow of pleasant nonsense when
the business of producing and expanding millions grew
a bit too serious.

" Now, Mr. President, we have reason to feel proud of
this magnificent monument of enterprise and skill erected
in our midst. Solomon's Temple . . . might have got
ahead a little in the day time, but in the illumination of
the night, Solomon's Temple was like a farthing rush-
light to the two-penny candle; and just imagine her Majesty, the Queen of Sheba, coming from the East, flashing over the continental railroad, crossing our magnificent
harbor in the most magnificent ferryboats that ever floated,
seated in a voluptuous carriage . . . and whirled into this
majestic port, brilliantly illuminated, bewildered and
overwhelmed by the sight, and suppose her falling into
the arms of the jocose Leland, and saying, ' Oh Warren,
the half has not been told me! ' "

The rambling discourse went on, punctuated by
explosions of laughter. The sophisticated splendors of
the Palace dining-room had not dulled the town's taste
for frontier humor.

" And now, Mr. President, I would that I had some
war reminiscences that I could relate appropriate to this
occasion but . . . my military experiences were confined
to two nights at Camp Schofield. I was placed in the guard-
house in consequence of being found disgustingly sober
after taps, and those soldiers refused to let me out unless
I sang myself out, and this is the song I sang, and they all

39

joined me in the chorus, and it is to be hoped that the boys
here will do the same:

> Happy are we tonight, boys;
> Happy, happy are we;
> The hearts that we delight, boys,
> With us may happy be."

This banquet to Sheridan, the hotel's first major
social event, took place on the evening of October 14,
1875. The Palace's official opening, twelve days earlier,
had been celebrated by a less formal gathering. On that
day, October 2, the reorganized Bank of California had
opened, happily ending weeks of uncertainty. Ralston's death and the collapse of his bank had brought
none of the dire consequences many had predicted. A
relieved and reassured throng had crowded the public
rooms and paraded through the long, bright corridors,
to the strains of the *Poet and Peasant Overture* and the
Blue Danube waltz, played by Chris Andre's orchestra
in the grand court. Later, from the second-floor balcony, William Sharon had addressed the throng. The
dapper little Nevada Senator had succeeded Ralston
in the ownership of the hotel, yet his speech was a model
of self-effacement:

"... In the crowning hour of victory, in the presence
of this grand witness of your skill in the mechanic arts, in
this glorious temple of hospitality amid all this flood of
light and music, I experience a sense of almost overwhelm-
ing sadness. I miss, as you do, the proud and manly spirit
of him who devised this magnificent structure, and under
whose direction and tireless energy it has been mainly
reared. I mourn, as you do, that he is not with us to enjoy

this scene of beauty, and I offer here, with you, the incense of respect and affection to his memory. . . ."

Sharon's speech went on, and presently ended in a polite patter of applause. Guests drifted away from the gallery rails, the orchestra struck up another waltz, and Sharon bowed and withdrew. In the chronicles of the Palace he was to reappear many times, but not always would he find the circumstances so pleasant.

2

ALL THROUGH the first years guests streamed into the hotel in picturesque variety, for a spacious era was unfolding. In 1876 the nation rounded out its first hundred years. Black Friday receded in the distance and a wave of confidence and heightened patriotism swept over the land. Visitors from every corner of the nation thronged the courts and galleries of the Centennial Exposition at Philadelphia to see at first hand what, by a century of effort, an enterprising people had accomplished. Editors and preachers and platform orators joined to assure the nation that it had just begun to grow, and confidence again became the national byword. Gradually purse-strings relaxed, industry revived, and with well-founded optimism speculators launched new schemes to recoup their losses. The nation swung into the later '70s, currents of booming trade flowed outward from the centers, stimulating production and renewing enterprise everywhere. As the expectation of easy rewards began to be realized, activity piled on activity, while thousands drove ahead to accelerate still further the development of the country's resources and to claim their share of the spoils.

One of the results of the quickened tempo was a mass restlessness that sent the real and potential empire-builders moving over the country. California, Nevada, and the awakening Northwest exerted a growing attraction. Here was territory with resources still hardly touched, vast untapped reservoirs of wealth. Sawmills, fisheries, railroads, gold and silver mines, cattle ranges, manufactories, agriculture — all these awaited the capital and energy of men accustomed to gamble for big stakes.

The early pages of the Palace register contained the signatures of dozens of currently eminent figures in the country's upbuilding: bankers, railroad-owners, steamship and mining magnates, lumbermen, promoters of every hue. A free-spending, hard-drinking group, " self-made " almost to a man, they used the hotel's best suites as a base of operations. There they laid plans, heard reports, and worked out the details of their operations, then set off to look over mining or lumber properties, the proposed routes of railroads, vast cattle and grain ranches. Between times reporters interrupted poker games in their Palace rooms or sought them out in the crowded bar, then returned to the newspaper offices and wrote interviews in which the empire-builders pronounced the country sound, and pointed out that in America it was still possible for a man of ideas and energy to get ahead.

The dawn of California's vogue as a tourist center

brought, too, little groups of the industrial aristocracy, rolling westward on mere pleasure jaunts in new private cars. With their families and groups of friends they took in Yosemite, the Big Trees, and the fashionable Napa County watering-places. At the Palace many such groups occupied the presidential suite — a series of spacious chambers on the second-floor corner, overlooking both Market and New Montgomery streets. The rooms were furnished in ebony and ash, with tables of quartz and rare woods. Antique Egyptian stands stood in the recesses of the bay windows, and on the walls were landscapes by the admired California artists Bierstadt and Julian Rix, and a view of Gloucester Harbor by Julund. There a succession of illustrious groups lived in remote seclusion, taking their meals in the private dining-room of the suite and permitting themselves to be seen only when they emerged for an afternoon drive in the park, for an evening at the theater or a trip through certain quaint opium dens that were maintained in Chinatown for the express benefit of tourists.

These traveling social and financial leaders took the Palace in stride. An immense luxury hotel on the far edge of a country where buffaloes and Indians were still at large? Curious, yes, but theirs was a nation and an age in which positively nothing was impossible. Witness their own amazing careers. After contemplating that miracle they remained permanently beyond surprise.

3

TYPICAL OF the lavish era was Jarrett and Palmer's Lightning Express — " the most dramatic event of the Centennial year " — which charmed the country a few months after the Palace opened.

The exploit was the inspiration of Henry C. Jarrett, co-manager of Booth's Theater, New York. In May 1876 Lawrence Barrett and his company were concluding a New York run, and Jarrett and Palmer were preparing to send them on a country-wide tour. Something was needed to draw attention to the tour and fill the houses along the way. Jarrett, already known as " the Barnum of the footlights," now proved his right to the title, for what he proposed was nothing less than to send the entire company on a headlong dash across the continent. Barrett was to conclude the New York season with a performance of *Henry V* on a Wednesday night — and to open with the same play in San Francisco on the following Monday.

The exploit perfectly symbolized the century's progress. In 1876, railroads had captured the popular imagination to an extent hard to realize today. The locomotive was conceded to be the premier creation of the age of mechanics. What, then, did the Lightning Express lack in the way of popular appeal? To send a luxurious special train racing against time, with the tracks cleared from coast to coast and with a matinee idol and his company inside the swaying Pullmans, was the ultimate in showmanship.

By regular schedules the journey from coast to coast

over the seven-year-old transcontinental line took seven days. The Lightning Express would attempt to do it in four. Besides Barrett and the company, sixteen paying passengers were to make the trip. Each ticket — " encased in sterling silver covers of exquisite workmanship and superb finish " — entitled its holder to a passage to San Francisco on the Lightning Express, to meals en route, to a week's board and room at the Palace, and to a first-class return passage to New York.

The entire country read descriptions of the express, made up and waiting at Jersey City: the Pennsylvania Central's fastest locomotive, the *Governor Tilden;* a baggage car; then a hotel car, the *Thomas A. Scott;* finally, the sleeping car *Yosemite.* As the date of the departure drew near, guards patrolled the space about the train to keep the crowds at a distance and to prevent attempts at sabotage. There was reason for these precautions. All over the land arguments were in progress over how many days and hours the journey would take. Pools had been formed and thousands of bets placed. Without the vigilant guards someone might yield to the temptation to throw sand in an axle-box and so lengthen the journey by hours. Along thirty-five hundred miles of track other precautions were taken. The newest locomotives of five railroads were put in condition, checked and inspected as carefully as a racehorse being trained for the Derby. Six thousand dispatchers and signalmen rehearsed plans to speed the express on its way, to make sure the tracks would be clear and the green lights showing over the entire distance.

The evening of May 31 arrived. While Barrett and

his company gave a final performance at Booth's
Theater (with their trunks packed and hacks waiting
for the race across the river), other members of the
party gathered in the pressroom of the *Herald,* saw
fifteen thousand copies of the June 1 issue run off for
distribution four days later in San Francisco, then repaired to the Astor House for a late supper. Meantime postal employees were tossing sack after sack of
mail into the Jersey City baggage car; a hundred thousand letters had been written for Pacific Coast delivery
via the Lightning Express.

Promptly on schedule the special rumbled out of the
Jersey City train-shed, and the epic race began. Not
since Lincoln's body had been returned to Springfield,
eleven years earlier, had the progress of a railroad train
aroused so much interest. Crowds gathered at every
town and crossroads along the route, while those at a
distance congregated before newspaper offices to cheer
bulletins reporting its rocket-like progress across
Pennsylvania, Ohio, Indiana, Missouri and over the
Mississippi at St. Louis. When the prairies of
the Middle West were reached, speed approached the
phenomenal; the seventy-five-mile run from Boone to
Council Bluffs was made in seventy-nine minutes.
Nearly a mile a minute! Time and again on the western half of the trip progress approached the sixty-mile-
an-hour mark — a truly reckless speed considering the
light cars and rails and the uneven roadbed. But engine and coaches luckily remained on the rails and the
record-breaking journey continued.

Thursday and Friday passed, and in San Francisco
preparations for an elaborate welcome got under way.

Sultan after Sultan

On Saturday afternoon, at a stop in central Nevada, Jarrett received a telegram from Warren Leland:

> Informal breakfast will be served immediately on your arrival. Leading citizens, members of the press, theatrical profession, army and navy officers, leading railroad officials, and the mayor of San Francisco will be present. . . . On your arrival at the wharf, thirteen guns will be fired from the roof of the Palace, and when you reach the city the flag will be hoisted. . . .

At Reno that night, bonfires blazed and bombs were set off, but the special roared down the main street at such speed that passengers saw only a blur of light, heard a series of muffled " booms." Well ahead of schedule, the express strained to the Sierra's summit, coasted down the spiraling west slope, and, as tracks flattened out on the valley's floor, hurtled onward at top speed.

From Ogden on, the Central Pacific's veteran engineer, Hank Small, was in charge. Small occupied the driver's shelf of engine Number 149 continuously during the 883-mile run. The express stopped only for water and fuel. On the way down the west side of the Sierra the brake-shoes became so worn as to be nearly useless, but Small refused to pause for repairs. Beyond Sacramento another complication arose — the conductor's bell-cord broke. The engineer tied the cord to his arm and continued. " If we had wanted to stop we would have had to yank him out of the cab," recalled a railroad official. The run from Ogden to Oakland pier, via Stockton and Niles, was made in twenty-five hours and forty-five minutes, by far the fastest

47

passage on record. " On the finish from Livermore to Oakland," reported the *Bulletin,* " there was a fine exhibition of speed . . . a run of four miles was made in four minutes."

Crowds became continuous as the express neared the end of its run. There was a brief pause at Oakland. Lawrence Barrett, the stubs of four days' beard covering his face, spoke a few sentences, and the ceremony was concluded (it being Sunday morning) by a singing of the doxology. The *Bulletin* reported: " The first line was sung standing, but a lurch of the coach sent the singers to their seats and the remainder . . . was omitted." A short run to Oakland Mole followed; the party descended and pushed through a dense throng to the ferry *Oakland.* As the boat reached the Market Street wharf the cannon on the roof of the Palace began a thirteen-gun salute. Through crowds of spectators a line of hacks dashed up Market Street, took the turn at New Montgomery on two wheels, and seconds later clattered into the cheering confusion of the grand court. " At the desk the excursionists were scarcely able to register their names, owing to the immense crushing to which they were subjected by the curious crowds. At two minutes before 10 o'clock the name of Mr. Jarrett . . . was inscribed on the hotel register."

The passage from ocean to ocean had been accomplished in 83 hours, 59 minutes, and 16 seconds — twelve hours less than the advertised four days. Newsboys wormed their way through the throng selling the *June 1* issue of the *New York Herald* — and this was the morning of the 4th! Members of the party were prevented from reaching their rooms by circles of inquisitive citizens. " Well, how did you stand it? " " Aren't you tired to death? " " What part of the trip did you like best? " A reporter commented: " Had they been remnants of the Six Hundred no more attention could have been paid to them."

Not until half past eleven did the hungry crowd of a hundred sit down to breakfast. Luckily, the meal was worthy of their appetites:

Salmon Grille à la Maître d'Hôtel

Tom Cod Frit.   Sauce Tartare

Cucumber Salad

Filet Bœuf.   Sauce Bernaise

Côtelettes d'Agneau, Sauce Soubise

Escalope de Veau, à la Guennoise

Pomme de terre, Maître d'Hôtel

Rognon Sauté au Champignon

Poulet Grillé au Cresson

Œufs Brouillés au point d'Asperges

Œufs Frites au Temben

Pré-Salé

Omelettes au Rhum

Apricots   Raspberries   Strawberries   Cherries

It came time for speeches. Mayor Bryant voiced the city's welcome, and Jarrett responded for the adventurers. His remarks were not offensive to civic pride:

" Twenty-six years ago I landed at the foot of Sacramento Street. . . . At that time your city lay prostrate in the dust by the great conflagration of the 14th of May, 1850. Soon after, she rose from her ashes, and through the indomitable energy of her citizens she has become ' gladsome to the heart and beautiful to the eyes.' On the very spot where ships rode at anchor twenty five years ago, today I find streets innumerable, splendid buildings, and all the surroundings of a great commercial city; where once was heard the dipping of oars, the rolling of the tide, now ' civilization on her luminous wings soars Phœnix-like to Jove.' "

The welcoming committee had not neglected to have Uncle George Bromley on hand, and he spoke next:

" In connection with this occasion, I may relate an incident: I had the honor of being connected with the first railroad enterprise in the state. We determined to have a trial of speed on the road between Sacramento and Brighton. We invited General Sutter to make the trip. He had never seen a railroad before. He was much impressed — especially with the conductor. I was the conductor. In order to give you an idea of the speed we travelled, I will mention that we accomplished the four miles in eighteen minutes! The event was not celebrated as it would have been had there been a hotel at Brighton. However, the General was so much struck with the velocity with which we travelled that, when asked to return, he replied that he lived only two miles off, and he guessed he would walk."

On the night of June 5 Barrett and his company opened in *Henry V* at the California, where he had appeared on a momentous evening six years earlier when the theater had been opened to the public.

The house was jammed to the doors and remained so nightly to the end of the run.

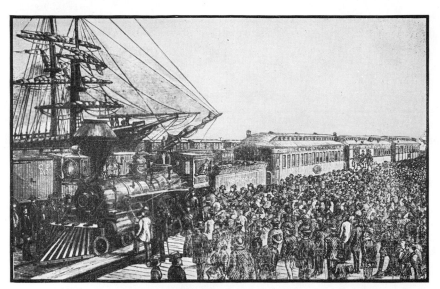

Arrival of Jarret & Palmer's "Lightning Express" at Oakland Wharf

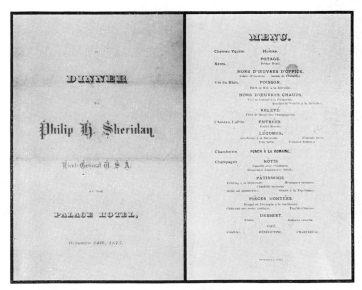

Menu of the Banquet to General Sheridan — the first important function at the Palace

The Palace from Market Street, Showing, at left, the Bridge Connecting it with the Grand

Negro Chambermaids and Porters on the Upper Balcony of the Grand Court

4

ONLY A few weeks before the arrival of the Lightning
Express, the Palace had been the scene of another notable event. Dom Pedro II, Emperor of Brazil, the first
reigning monarch to visit the United States, arrived in
April 1876, and of course put up in one of the de luxe
suites at the new hotel. He had visited the Centennial
at Philadelphia and then had started on a tour of the
country. The announcement that his itinerary would
include San Francisco caused Warren Leland to set in
motion elaborate plans for welcoming the first royal
guest to the Palace.

While the Emperor's party traveled westward, San
Franciscans learned from their newspapers that Dom
Pedro stood six feet three inches in his royal socks, and
that his kingly bearing was enhanced by a dignified
white beard. He had abolished slavery in his realm,
encouraged the arts and sciences, and was said to speak
Portuguese, French, German, Spanish, and Italian as
well as English. The city's preparations for an extensive public welcome had to be drastically revised when
the Emperor sent on a request that functions in his
honor be simple and few.

Dom Pedro's entrance into California was not without incident. On its descent of the western slope of the
Sierra his train paused at Cape Horn, the lofty shelf
chipped out of granite by Chinese railroad-builders ten
years before. Dom Pedro stepped down from his car to
admire the view. He was conversing with John Mc-
Cullough — manager of San Francisco's California

Theater — when the train started down the grade without them. There being nothing else to do, the pair started to walk. They were trudging over the ties when the train backed up for them, and the embarrassed conductor offered his apologies.

At the Palace the Emperor was given the suite formerly occupied by Governor Stanford. On the evening of his arrival he was serenaded in the grand court by Gilmore's Band, after which he appeared on the second-floor balcony and bowed to the applauding throng. Following his scholarly bent, the visitor spent the next day or two inspecting the University of California, Bancroft's Library, the Mission Dolores, and the Chinese Theater. At Synagogue Emanu-El he was shown some ancient scrolls, and impressed onlookers by translating their Hebrew text. At the theater he was offered varied dramatic fare, ranging from *Kit, the Arkansas Traveller* to *King Lear*. In Wade's Opera House he heard *Lucrezia Borgia*.

Between times he remained in seclusion at the hotel. Its size and luxury caught his eye, and he was said to have stated to Mayor Bryant that " nothing made him ashamed of Brazil so much as the Palace Hotel." During his stay there Dom Pedro's privacy was invaded by a young woman autograph-hunter, who followed the royal party in the elevator to their floor. Her perseverance was ultimately rewarded. Expecting, at best, his secretary to secure the autograph for her, she was overcome by the sudden appearance of the Emperor himself, who graciously granted her request.

Dom Pedro was not the only reigning sovereign to

stop at the Palace. Nearly sixteen years later, toward the end of 1890, a middle-aged, dark-visaged man in a Prince Albert and tall silk hat disembarked from the cruiser *Charleston* at the Clay Street dock, while naval guns boomed and the Fifth Artillery Band played patriotic tunes. The visiting celebrity, who had been ill, was carefully escorted to a waiting barouche and driven up Market Street to a reception at the Palace.

The visitor was King David Kalakaua of Hawaii. San Franciscans held divergent opinions concerning the ruler. Some smiled, not too discreetly, at " King Calico " and his " toy kingdom "; others hastened to the royal suite to pay their respects. Governor Waterman and Mayor Pond headed the official callers.

Meantime the city recalled the visit, in the spring of 1887, of Kalakaua's consort, Queen Kapiolani, who had come from Honolulu with Princess Liliuokalani, the King's sister and heir apparent to the throne. That visit had proved embarrassing to the town's fire chief, David Scannell. Some days before, while he was on duty at a fire, a can containing some chemical substance had overturned and its contents had showered down on the chief, changing his grizzled locks to a soiled emerald color. The chief was in his office in the old City Hall when Mayor Pond, who was escorting the Queen on a tour of inspection of public buildings, entered with his royal guest. Scannell, trying to remember his speech of welcome, forgot his green hair, doffed his hat, remembered the dye, and forgot his speech.

There was a round of social engagements for the ailing King. He accepted an invitation to dine at the

Bohemian Club, another to attend a charity ball of the Woman's Exchange; and he lunched with John D. Spreckels, who was interested in Hawaiian concessions. At the Palace he bestowed the Order of Kalakaua on several officers of the *Charleston,* then continued his tour. But his health grew worse and at Santa Barbara his condition caused alarm. He returned to San Fransico, where, against the advice of his physicians, he attended two other social functions. These were his last public appearances. The King took to his bed and grew steadily worse. On January 20, 1891 he turned to his aide-de-camp, Colonel Baker, and said: " Well, I am a very sick man " — and lost consciousness. He died the same day.

The Hawaiian flag above the Palace was lowered to half-mast. Inside the hotel, members of the dead sovereign's staff, in relays, stood above his body, slowly waving palm leaves during the next several days. On the day of the funeral six stalwart Negro porters of the Palace lifted the casket and, followed by a guard of honor, bore it down the main stairway to the Jessie Street entrance. At Trinity Church fifty police were hard pressed to hold the vast crowd in check, and after the services an estimated sixteen hundred persons were in the cortege as it moved to the waterfront, where the body was carried on board the *Charleston.* Operators of excursion boats found their enterprise profitable. Minute guns sounded from the *Charleston,* from Alcatraz and Black Point. At four forty-five that afternoon the cruiser steamed through the Golden Gate toward the setting sun, carrying the remains of the last of Hawaii's kings.

Sultan after Sultan

The procession of distinguished guests continued as long as the Palace itself stood. Their names constitute a catalogue of the great and near great, the eminent and the notorious, of the last quarter of the nineteenth century — such dissimilar figures as the Grand Duke Boris and Bob Fitzsimmons, the Nabob of Rampur and " White Hat " McCarthy, Henry Ward Beecher and Bob Ingersoll, Carry Nation and the daughter of Queen Victoria, James J. Jeffries and the Prince of Siam. At one time or another the Palace housed such industrial titans as Rockefeller, Morgan, Carnegie, Pullman, Huntington, Studebaker, Swift, Wanamaker, Vanderbilt, and a dozen others; such public figures as Presidents Hayes, Harrison, McKinley, Theodore Roosevelt, and William Howard Taft; W. J. Bryan, Champ Clark, Nicholas Longworth, and Chauncey Depew; foreign notables in profusion, among them Prince Albert of Belgium, Prince Louis of Savoy, Prince Poniatowski, Ferdinand de Lesseps, Prince Napoleon Louis Joseph Jerome Bonaparte, Lord and Lady Randolph Churchill; social lights like Mrs. Stuyvesant Fish and Mrs. William K. Vanderbilt, Jr., and Mrs. Harry Payne Whitney; virtually every dramatic and opera star of the period; scores of authors and journalists, dozens of Civil War generals; diplomats, clergymen, scientists, explorers, and unclassified notables without number. In short, during the thirty-one years of its existence the old Palace played the role of lavish host to practically every distinguished traveler who reached the Pacific Coast.

5

BEFORE THE Palace had been open two years its reputation as one of the world's great hotels was established and secure. Before it had been open half that time a less welcome fact was driven home. Financially the place was a white elephant and would probably remain so for decades.

The trouble was merely that the hotel had cost too much and that there was too much of it. When Ralston had conceived the project the banker was at the height of his career, obsessed by his Napoleonic delusion that whatever he touched must be on an epic scale. By that standard his creation was everything he may have hoped. It was big, luxurious, showy, just the sort of spectacular display to delight a boastful and civic-minded community. But the community had less than a quarter of a million population. It was already well supplied with hotels, and the rest of the Coast was thinly populated and growing less rapidly than the optimists had hoped. When the hotel was projected Ralston, like everyone else, had expected the transcontinental railroad and the new Pacific steamers to carry a heavy traffic between the Orient and Europe. This traffic had never materialized. The Suez Canal was completed in 1869 and the majority of travelers between Europe and the Far East chose that shorter (and less expensive) route. For years the Australian and China steamers plied the Pacific with half their cabins empty.

The consequence was that a great many of the Palace's eight hundred rooms were tenantless and seemed likely to remain so for a long time. Before the place had been open a year the matter of trimming expenses was receiving close attention. In July 1876 Senator Sharon appeared before the city board of equalization and petitioned that the building's assessment of two million dollars be cut in half. He stated that the hotel was not worth more than a million and that receipts were falling much below expenses. The hotel was not paying five per cent on a million dollars and probably would never pay that amount on the whole investment.

Sharon testified that the building had probably cost five millions. Its foundations had been far more expensive than anyone had expected, and the cost of materials and labor had been very high. " The amount of money that it cost to build the hotel is no criterion of the value of the property." He added that the Palace was a public improvement and an ornament to the city, and that his plea for a reduction of taxes should be considered on these grounds.

The board discussed the matter. Assessor Badlam thought the two-million assessment was low enough. Mr. Gibbs thought the city could well afford to make the reduction. Mr. Roberts moved to allow it. Mr. Boyce suggested a million and a half. Mr. Strothers objected: " I don't see why any difference should be made in favor of a rich man against a poor man." Mr. McDonald said: " I know that Sharon has got to give his check each month to pay expenses of that hotel." Mr. Wise was convinced that the property would never pay " as long as the world stands." He added that he considered its building a " fancy idea."

The question was balloted on. The assessment was reduced to a million and a half. The vote was seven to two.

It was but one of the long series of attempts to shorten sail financially. Another was a drastic reorganization of personnel which a new manager, Captain Samuel F. Thorn, made in the fall of 1888. Thorn's successful operation of the Grand, the Palace's neighbor and satellite (which had recently been connected with the larger hotel by a bridge over New Montgomery Street), had won him the promotion. He speedily proved himself no believer in half-way measures. One of his first acts was to dismiss thirty cooks. Another was to discharge the Negro waiters who had been a fixture of the Palace since its beginning. The whole Coast was scoured for trained men to take their place. Colored bellboys to the number of twenty-six were retained, as were seventeen porters and bootblacks. Presumably the colored chambermaids, whose pert uniforms and demure manner had charmed early guests, were also allowed to remain.

Of course these wholesale dismissals caused repercussions. The *Alta* explained that the trouble began when Manager Thorn issued an order requiring that the dining-room and kitchen help be searched when they went off duty. " It is said that before the colored gentlemen knew of the order some of them, taken unaware, were caught carrying home tenderloin steaks, fruit, chickens and even silverware." The employees denied the charges and countered with a threat to strike. One of their spokesmen stated:

Sultan after Sultan

"We think the record of hotel management in the United States will substantiate us in our claim that colored help, male or female, has proved to be fully equal in honesty and fidelity to white help. . . . We will not, even in self-defense, make use of information in our possession that the white help employed in the Palace Hotel has been deficient in integrity. . . ."

But Thorn proved unyielding; his dismissal order stood, and the dining-rooms of the Palace knew the familiar black faces no more.

Not many months later a new difficulty arose. This time it affected not only the Palace waiters but those of other hotels and of such restaurants as the Poodle Dog and the Maison Riche. It was no less than a world-wide agitation in favor of whiskerless waiters. The movement had originated in Europe and was already acute in the East. Now it was sweeping inexorably westward, and local members of the craft became apprehensive over the possible loss of their handle-bar mustaches and other prized hirsute adornments.

Their fears were well grounded. The management of the California Hotel one day posted an order requiring waiters to report for work clean-shaven. Not only the waiters themselves but the public joined in the controversy. For days the pros and cons of beard-less waiters were debated all over town.

The spokesman for the Palace proved pro-mustache:

" In the leading European hotels a waiter cannot wear a mustache, and the swell establishments in New York are imitating this fashion, but it will not do here. There is this

59

difference: in Europe a man once a servant is always a servant, but in America the servant of today may be a millionaire tomorrow.

" We wouldn't try to enforce such a rule at the Palace. We have trouble enough without trying to bring it on. The waiters would not submit to it, and when they strike we can't replace them."

But the speaker was arguing a lost cause. The movement gained force steadily and it was not long before the Palace was forced to fall into line. When the order was issued, the waiters protested to the head steward, Victor Reiter. Reiter was adamant. Rules were rules and must be obeyed. Waiters must wear white jackets and black pants; turn-down collars always; black ties for breakfast; white ties for lunch and dinner; *and* no beards or mustaches at any time. Determined to make a last stand, the waiters took their plea to the manager, John G. Kirkland. Reiter countered by addressing a formal statement to Kirkland:

" It has been the wish and instructions of the owners that all the waiters in this hotel who serve guests be clean shaven. All the first-class hotels, or those which give first-class service, now require waiters to be smooth shaven. The reason is plain and sensible.

" I take the liberty to quote from *The Hotel:* ' It is impossible for a man to eat or drink who has a mustache without soiling it, let him be ever so careful. . . . Was there ever a man who did not unconsciously handle his beard or mustache? Your waiter hands you a plate, he places bread on it in your presence with a fork, but in the serving room the hands are less troublesome and perform this duty quicker than the fork. He reaches you a spoon, turning it so that you can take it by the handle. He performs the little duties of his office. You turn around and find him stroking his mustache . . . but why further . . . ? Where this has been tried there has been at the start more or less opposition by the waiters, but intelligent men will soon see the sensibility of such a course. This custom, so prevalent in foreign houses, is one more American proprietors could adopt to advantage. . . .' "

Of course the Palace staff was forced to yield. Grumbling, the waiters resigned themselves to the inevitable and paid fateful visits to their barbers.

Even the settlement of this controversy did not make relations between the management and the staff uniformly cordial. Efforts to pare expenses were fairly constant during the first years and these brought periodical protests from the employees. In 1893 occurred another major revolt. Senator Sharon had meantime died and the ownership of the hotel had passed to his heirs, with his son-in-law, Frank Newlands, in active charge. Newlands, who was in Washington, sent out two men to institute economies wherever possible. One was C. F. Johnson, ex-manager of a Washington boarding-house; the other was an early-day efficiency expert, G. Bauman.

The *Chronicle* commented:

These gentlemen had no fixed positions assigned to them, but their letter from Mr. Newlands to Captain Smith was to give them *carte blanche* to look into every detail of the hotel's management.

Smith . . . accepted their suggestions as fast as made; not that he always felt them advisable reforms, but simply that he hoped to let them get to the end of their rope. C. F.

Johnson reached his inside of five months, and when his dictation to the engineers caused forty men to walk out and leave nearly two thousand incandescent lights unlighted and the elevator stopped, Frank Newlands called him back to Washington.

Bauman, however, remained. It was his attempt to economize in the grillroom and bar — the best-paying departments of the hotel — that aroused the most opposition. One of his innovations was to charge bartenders full prices for such meals as they ate at the hotel; another was to install check clerks in the grillroom to prevent waiters from " knocking down " on patrons' checks. This last was particularly offensive to the chief steward, P. A. Warnock, known as " Steward Scotty."

" What a farce that move was," he told the *Chronicle.* " If my men wanted to do what was not right all the checkmakers Bauman wanted to put on couldn't stop them. Now, for instance, it is their duty to report to the checkman the amount of the patron's bill. If they said you ate only tea and toast the check would be made out for twenty-five cents, and the checkman would not have the slightest idea that you were walking out with a broiled chicken under your coat. . . ."

Bauman's drastic paring of the staff in other departments caused a new series of complaints. Jack Hayes, the broiler, was indignant because there was not enough help to peel potatoes. The housekeeper, Mrs. Butters, complained that she was unable to get a proper supply of clean towels. The management admitted that the labor-saving washing machines recently installed had proved too efficient; they so thoroughly cleaned the towels that they carried away their texture as well as the dirt. All that was bad enough, but when Bauman dismissed most of the grillroom waiters, Steward Scotty felt that the limit had been passed.

" Think of it! When I came here I had eighteen waiters — just about enough for a first-class place of this kind — and now they want me to get along with four. I'll not stand for it. . . . I can't with that number serve between six hundred and eight hundred gentlemen every day."

Scotty resigned his post forthwith. In a day or two, papers reported that he had " found haven in the Palace bachelor quarters of Judge Mesick, lawyer and epicure, as a caterer and ' gentleman's gentleman.' "

6

SUCH ECONOMY waves usually coincided with the cycles of business depression, when hard times caused a dropping off of patronage and the owners found themselves facing operating deficits. As the years passed, however, the situation slowly changed. The population of the city and the Coast grew steadily; the annual influx of tourists increased from a thin trickle to a broad, lucrative stream. Honolulu began its rise as a tourist center and trans-Pacific travel was stimulated by the introduction of new and faster steamers.

Gradually the acres of bedrooms, scantily populated for years, began to fill up. A new local movement helped. It became the fashion for prosperous older citizens, many of them pioneers of the city's beginnings, to close their houses on Nob Hill or in the Western Addition and to lease one of the compact Palace suites. By the middle '90s the colony of permanent guests solidly filled the top floor, and the overflow was housed on the floor below. There were even times when the management, after struggling for years to fill hundreds of vacant rooms, faced a less disturbing problem: that of finding accommodations for old patrons when the house was jammed to the doors.

After nearly two decades Sharon's white elephant began to belie its name. San Francisco finally became able to support a luxury hotel. As the revenue grew the owners were at pains to preserve the hotel's prestige by periodical overhauling. The opening of George C. Boldt's Waldorf in New York in 1893 had set new standards of hotel luxury and service, and throughout the land other houses imitating its features were springing up. Newlands and the other Sharon heirs made it a matter of family pride to see that the Palace kept up with the parade. From the middle '80s remodeling of one sort or another was fairly constant.

Extensive alterations were in progress during most of the year 1890. Since the hotel had been built, the direction of the city's growth had been toward the west and south. By the end of the '80s the retail shopping district was centered in the triangular area formed by Market, Sutter, and Powell streets. To provide more direct access to the hotel for patrons from this district, a new entrance was opened in the center of the Market Street front. Both the grill and the bar, which had originally been at the far end of the hotel, were moved to the Market Street side. Another entrance was opened on Annie Street, from which a handsome corridor with stained-glass roof and Belgian marble walls led to the grill; the American-plan restaurant was across the grand court. The grill itself was " done over " in François I style; its colors were white and gold. One end of the hundred-foot chamber was covered by three immense French mirrors in ornate frames; in the center of one wall a fireplace with a handsome French mantel was built. The gaslights were supplanted by a profusion of incandescent bulbs. " In this apartment alone there are no less than three hundred and twenty electric lights." At night this brilliantly illuminated room seemed to be transformed by the mirrors into a chamber of epic proportions. Even seasoned globe-trotters were moved to exclamations of delight.

In printed descriptions of the improvements, the bar received (and deserved) a paragraph to itself. Mahogany and red African marble successfully gave the room the desired air of luxury. It was in Empire style, with marble floor, bronze fixtures, and a vaulted roof. The lighting was particularly admired. The room was at the bottom of one of the inner courts, and the light, filtering through amber-tinted glass, shed a glow not inharmonious with that dispensed at the bar. " In order to maintain the soft light at night powerful arc electric lamps are hung above and outside the stained glass roof."

The upper floors were not neglected. The bathrooms were brought up to date; the old-style metal tubs were replaced, wooden floors and wainscoting were supplanted by tiles, and bright nickel fittings were in-stalled. Many of the suites were done over in the fashionable Louis XV style, with walls in cream, ivory, and pearl tints, and furniture and hangings in har-mony.

As the new century opened, plans were being dis-cussed for the construction of hotels that might chal-lenge the Palace's long-standing supremacy. Of course it was inevitable that the Palace must some day be sup-planted. Although it still held its place in the affection of the town, most citizens under fifty had become aware that its big rooms, high ceilings, and bay windows and its huge hydraulic elevators were beginning to have a distinctly old-fashioned appearance. San Franciscans returned from stays at the new luxury hotels of the East and discovered with a shock that the Palace had some-what the air of a crowded and well-kept museum. Even the local papers, although they refused to concede that the hotel was surpassed anywhere in luxury and con-venience, began to make occasional references to the " historic " and even the " venerable " Palace.

The town grew reminiscent and a shade sentimental when, soon after 1900, a notable change in the grand court was announced. The famous circular driveway was to be torn up. The major reason was the growing popularity of the horseless carriage. By then the brief battle between the horse and his mechanical rival had already been won; even the old-timers recognized that henceforth the automobile was to be the chosen means of locomotion for the wealthy and fashionable. There were prophets who stated flatly that soon even men of moderate means would be scurrying about in the ill-smelling contraptions; that every man who could afford a horse and carriage would some day own an automobile.

The sight of workmen tearing up the macadam in the grand court was evidence enough of how rapidly this was coming to pass. The automobile of the day needed a large area in which to turn, and the circumference of the circle was too small for them to execute the maneuver. Besides, their engines set up a deafening noise in the big enclosed court, and the fumes they emitted proved unpleasant to loiterers on the upper balconies. So the old driveway disappeared. The space it had occupied was covered with marble tiles; the court became another lounge and no longer knew the pleasant clatter of hoofs.

7

FROM THE middle '90s onward the Palace grillroom came to be regarded as the premier restaurant of the Coast. Toward the end of the century this famous room again underwent alteration and modernization, and the *Chronicle* thus commemorated the event:

Comparison? Well, there is none, for the reason that the grill room has no competitors; it has only imitators. The Palace grill room came first . . . then the globe trotters discovered it, and they carried its fame to the four corners of the earth . . . and the imitators fell into line.

The Palace grill is the *fin de siècle* in café, restaurant, cuisine in America. It has no peer, and the zest of the grill

room steak would bring Chateaubriand from his grave.
. . . Over its silver-framed tables and beneath its white
ceiling and glittering chandeliers the great world meets to
eat, to drink and talk. It has brought famine to half the
club dining rooms. . . .

In its grillroom the hotel reached its gastronomic
zenith, but by then the Palace had been catering to
the town's gourmands for more than twenty years. It
had opened just at the time when Americans were
growing aware of subtle distinctions in the meaning of
the words " eating " and " dining," and when here and
there all over the land groups of the newly affluent had
begun to question the naïve belief that the chief function of food was to sustain life.

Their number grew rapidly. A prosperous era was
unfolding and it was being impressed on the pluto-
crats — often by their wives — that while the rules for
accumulating wealth remained pleasantly lax, those
governing its proper expenditure were steadily becoming more complex. It was another result of the rich
American's rediscovery of Europe and of the belief,
which thousands came to share simultaneously, that an
annual crossing of the Atlantic automatically elevated
one above the ranks of the mere money-grubbers.
These casual contacts with an older civilization had
impressed many with the cultural shortcomings of the
raw cities and towns from which they had sprung.
Once their conviction of America's superiority in all
things had been shaken, scores of patriots went to the
other extreme and assumed roles of extreme humility.
An era of exaggerated and uncritical worship of everything European got under way. European clothes and

architecture, European art and literature, and, when it could be managed, European husbands, became the goal of thousands who hoped thus to surmount the handicap of having been born in a culturally barren land. And of course Americans who seriously wanted to be cultured had to give up the quaint idea that one ate because one was hungry.

The opening of the Palace did much to further the new movement in San Francisco. The theory that a good chef is a necessity to a good inn was here given its first local test, with eminently satisfactory results. The hotel's first chef, Jules Harder, became the Coast's authority on all matters pertaining to food and its serving. Harder's reputation had been fairly earned. He had been ten years with Delmonico, and before that at the Union Club, New York, and the Grand Union at Saratoga. In all, he had had twenty-six years' experience as chef in hotels, clubs, and restaurants.

The town looked to the chef for light on the question of how San Franciscans might acquire proficiency in what was beginning to be called the art of dining. The hotel had not been open long before Harder was submitting to an interview. The reporter asked what effect a European trip might be expected to have on a man's dining habits.

The chef rattled off a comprehensive answer:

"All Americans who have the natural capacity of learning how to dine develop the capacity quickest by a trip to Europe, presuming they spend some time in France. . . . Of course there are some people who, no matter what their advantages may be, never learn how to dine. But generally the improvement is very great. . . . I have had people right here at the Palace who were what we know as pork-and-bean livers, who have returned from a trip abroad so benefited by their opportunities for learning that I have noticed the improvement the very first dinner they ordered. I need only one order from a man to know what kind of a liver he is."

Harder was asked about the dining habits of some of the hotel's distinguished guests. General Grant had been a recent visitor; what of his eating habits?

" General Grant is a good diner now."

" Was there ever a time when he was not? "

" Oh, yes. He has improved very much by his travels abroad. I first remember Grant at the Grand Union at Saratoga. That was before the time he was first made President. He really did not know much about dining then. When I had him here after his trip around the world he showed great improvement."

" What kind of a diner was President Hayes? "

Harder shrugged his shoulders. " Well, you know Hayes never drinks wine with his dinners . . . and a man who drinks no wine with his dinners never cares much what he eats. I don't recall preparing a dinner for any big man who drank no wine. . . ."

Emperor Dom Pedro of Brazil was classified as " a plain good diner," and another guest, Alphonse Rothschild, was pronounced " one of the best." Rothschild breakfasted *à la fourchette* at eleven o'clock and ate " a very intelligent dinner " at six. Princess Louise and the Marquis of Lorne dined in the English style; Harder scored a professional triumph by serving them some English dishes they had never got in England.

The Princess had brought her cook with her and that had put Harder on his mettle. The result was an anchovy paste that brought the cook to the Palace kitchen with the Princess's request for the recipe. "When she returned from British Columbia the first thing she did after coming into the house was to order the same dish." The Marquis was not so good a diner as the Princess. It is a mistake, said Harder, to assume that ladies know less of the art than men. "There are some California ladies here in the hotel who appreciate my most careful work."

Many of San Francisco's first citizens knew how to order a good dinner, Harder continued, and others were learning. Isaac Friedlander, grain merchant, led the list; he was one of the best livers the chef had ever known. Leland Stanford had entertained lavishly during the months he had lived at the Palace, and had always consulted with Harder about the menu. Nicholas Luning's dining habits had gained the chef's stamp of approval, as had also those of A. N. Towne and General W. H. L. Barnes. Barnes, leader of the local bar, drank only champagne with his dinner, an eccentricity he shared with James Gordon Bennett. But many of the town's eminent figures remained pork-and-bean diners in spite of all Harder had done for them. "The most discouraging experience I have is to get up something extra in the way of a sauce or flavor for some big man, and to have him accept it as the regular run; have it make no more impression than a baked potato. . . ." But he had noticed one encouraging sign: an unusual number of Palace guests had their dinners served in their rooms. A man who did that was certain sooner or later to develop a discriminating palate.

Harder gave his views on the eating habits of other famous Americans. Chester Arthur was the most accomplished diner of any President. " Arthur was not particularly known as a good liver as I remember him at the Union Club and Delmonico's. But he knew how, else he could not live as well as he does now. . . . You see, a man must have a great deal of intelligence to appreciate a good dinner, or else he may live all his life like Hayes, and not know what it is to eat a good meal." Jay Gould was a good diner; a chef who knew his tastes might serve him a year without an order, whereas Colonel Vanderbilt insisted on ordering every meal. Asked if that was an unusual procedure, the chef replied that it was. " If a man who is a *bon vivant* comes here . . . he sends for me. I go to him and have a little talk. I discover his tastes, his general preferences, and his usual hours; and he never orders a dish after that if he stays a year. But Vanderbilt is eccentric."

The interview with Harder took place in 1883. Sixteen years later another Palace chef, Fred Mergenthaler, returned to the subject. Mergenthaler, born in Strasbourg and the son of a noted chef, had learned the elements of his art in Paris. While he was still a young man he had prepared dishes for such eminent persons as the Queen of Holland, the Grand Duchess of Russia, and the kings of Württemberg and Prussia. Coming to America in the early '8os, he repeated his triumphs, and in July 1885 Senator Sharon had persuaded him to come west and preside over the Palace kitchen.

For the next fifteen years Mergenthaler catered to the varied appetites of scores of world-famous figures. To an *Examiner* reporter he confessed sadly that old-time Californians, the empire-builders of the '6os and later, had for the most part remained pork-and-bean diners to the end. John W. Mackay, despite the advantages of a dozen millions and a socially ambitious wife, remained a plebeian at table; his tastes never rose above the standards of the Virginia City boarding-houses where he had lived while he was making his pile. Senator Sharon, lean and sickly, cared nothing for food. With the entire resources of the hotel's larder and wine cellar at his command, he habitually dined frugally, washing down his simple fare with weak tea. " James G. Fair," continued Mergenthaler, " never seemed to care what was placed on the table, and so I could go on indefinitely, if I chose, to speak of other men similarly noted who are and were among the builders of the Pacific Coast."

There had been some progress, none the less. The sons and daughters of the empire-builders, profiting by trips to Europe and by education in the select colleges and seminaries in the East, could be counted on to choose with discrimination from the Palace's complicated menu. And of course there were always a few local *bon vivants* on whom the chef could practice the more subtle phases of his art. It had been a slow, uphill struggle, but before the century ended, victory was in sight.

Mergenthaler continued:

" In the last twenty or thirty years wonders have been accomplished. Prior to that they threw all the beef into the bay, except a few choice steaks. The heart, the lungs, the tripe, and the sweetbreads, all went overboard. Pigs' feet and lambs' feet went the same way. The people had not learned to make magnificent dishes of these things. Their palates had not been educated.

" Today all these things command a very high price and are the luxuries of the table. We can't get enough sweetbreads. Take frogs, for instance. Now there is such a demand for frogs that it is a favor to us to get them for $5 a dozen. California oysters are beginning to be very much liked. California oyster cocktails are now famous all over the world. The canvasback, mallard and teal that are found here are magnificent. The same may be said for the Mongolian pheasant, quail and other birds. As for vegetables, ours is the richest market in the world. . . ."

The Palace was mainly responsible for spreading abroad a knowledge of distinctly Californian foods. Mountain and valley quail were often on its menu, as were also duck, venison, and, in the earlier period, grizzly steaks. Rainbow trout was for years a specialty, along with sole, bass, and, presently, abalone. The small, native California oyster, with its characteristic faintly coppery taste, became a favorite of gourmands who first encountered it in Palace cocktails or omelets. The California oyster omelet was probably the first production of the Palace kitchen to attain wide renown. Many guests carried the memory of its highly individual flavor with them on their travels, and so spread its fame. It was the creation of Ernest Arbogast,

74

one of the chefs of the early Palace, and was long a favorite breakfast dish in the ladies' grill. A breakfast of California oyster omelet, toast, and fragrant coffee in that mirror-walled room constituted a meal that still lingers pleasantly in the memories of early-day San Franciscans. Not until much later did another Palace creation, oysters Kirkpatrick (named for Manager John C. Kirkpatrick), come to rival it in public esteem.

When the hotel opened, its kitchen and serving staffs were the largest in the country. A hundred and fifty waiters served the needs of patrons in the three dining-rooms, and the kitchen staff was proportionately large. Five assistants, all men of long experience, carried out the orders of the chef. In addition there were three special cooks: a chief confectioner from Milan, a chief baker from Vienna, and an old Negro, Muffin Tom, whose specialty was corn bread and hot egg muffins. With this organization it was the boast of the Palace chef that any guest who wished to be served with his native foods could be accommodated, whatever his nationality. The boast was frequently made good — to the surprised delight of travelers from such varied lands as Russia, Greece, India, Korea, and the South Sea Islands.

Thanks in part to their schooling in the dining-rooms of the Palace, San Franciscans were presently enjoying the distinction of having a more subtle appreciation of food than the citizens of any other American city. Perhaps it was for this reason that the visit in 1901 of J. Pierpont Morgan, the elder, aroused so much interest. For it was not Morgan himself (he had come out for a convention of Episcopal bishops) on whom public curiosity focused, but his chef. The latter was Louis Sherry — a man as eminent in his field as the financier was in his. The fact that Morgan had come west in a six-car special train was less astonishing in the eyes of San Franciscans than his bringing Sherry to oversee the preparation of his meals. It was, the *Examiner* pointed out, equivalent to engaging the services of Madame Melba on the chance that one might feel in the mood for a bit of singing.

Morgan and his party put up at the Crocker house on Nob Hill and Sherry stopped at the Palace. This arrangement puzzled the town, and an *Examiner* man was sent to ask Sherry how he, a guest at the Palace, could supervise meals served Morgan and his party half a mile distant. He learned that distance was no handicap; Sherry had no hand in the preparation of the food; it had not been necessary for him even to enter the Crocker kitchen. All such matters were handled by his chief assistants, a chef and a steward.

Other details of this de luxe form of catering were revealed to an interested city. "Every morning the Sherry steward and the Sherry chef — the first a keen, sharp-eyed little Irishman, and the other an amiable, blond Frenchman — went marketing. Every morning the choicest ducks, the plumpest squabs, the finest capons, the tenderest poultry, went into the Morgan market basket." Their daily bills at the produce markets averaged two hundred dollars. Sherry had brought all the wines out from New York. One vintage, a rare Johannesberger, cost twenty-three dollars a bottle. The reporter made some calculations and announced the result: that wine cost Morgan four dollars a glass.

Sultan after Sultan

Once a year the full resources of the Palace's kitchen and larder were taxed to produce a Christmas dinner that for size and variety commanded respect even in an era of enormous meals. As the years passed, it became a tradition for many local families to gather each Christmas afternoon in the gaily decorated main dining-room, there to sit for hours as they happily ate their way to the very end of the long repast. It was a gastronomic feat of epic proportions — one that fortunately would not have to be repeated for a full year. These huge meals invariably ended with another Palace specialty, pudding à la Sultan, also a creation of Chef Arbogast. It was made of yellow corn flour, cooked in milk sweetened with brown sugar. Among its other ingredients were cinnamon, mint, sliced bananas, dates, and the yolks of eggs. It was served with a hot rum sauce, flavored with anise seeds, "green tea essence," mint, and sugar.

Pudding à la Sultan was regarded as a fitting climax to a Palace Christmas dinner. After so hearty a meal it was wise to finish with something light.

CHAPTER THREE

MARS AND THE MUSES

1

DURING the early years a great many Palace banquets were to honor Civil War heroes. The Rebellion had been put down a full ten years before the hotel opened, but its campaigns were still being refought about thousands of grocery-store stoves from coast to coast. By the middle '70s wartime reputations had reached their crest and scores of aging warriors had become heroes of such exalted degree that their travels about the country became a succession of triumphs.

The generals traveled a great deal, moving restlessly from city to city and pausing at each to receive the homage of the public, to ride at the heads of parades, to shake the hands of former comrades-in-arms, and to deliver modest, well-remembered speeches at complimentary dinners. During its first dozen years the Palace played host to scores of bearded men who had once led Union troops on what in retrospect seemed a glorious crusade. Invariably it was the Yankee soldiers who were thus honored. Not until years later did a few Confederate officers slip unobtrusively in and out of town.

Phil Sheridan, first of the series, had fortunately arrived in time to become the central figure of the Palace's first state banquet. Hardly a month later the grand court was again echoing with cheers for a visiting general. While an army band, brought from the Presidio for the occasion, played *Marching through Georgia,* William T. Sherman cheerfully faced the crowded tiers of galleries about the grand court. Sherman had been an esteemed local citizen nearly a quarter-century earlier, and San Franciscans regarded him as a native son. When the band swung into *John Brown's Body,* the general beat time with his hand, and new waves of applause swept through the court. Not for many minutes was it possible for him to begin his speech:

" I have seen your city grow from the little village of Yerba Buena to the present magnificent metropolis. I remember when we used to take our blankets from different taverns, and sleep out in the open air, and pay three dollars for the privilege, and now I come to this beautiful Palace Hotel, which I pronounce superior to the grand hotels of Paris and Vienna, which I have visited. . . .

" I will say a few kindly words for Billy Ralston. No matter what he has done, I hope he has gone to Heaven. He did much for your city, and you can see the many memorials of his work around you. I knew your city in '46, '47, '48 and '49. There were giants in those days, and you must be worthy of them. They laid the foundation; you are reaping the harvest. You knew Leidesdorff and you knew Folsom. They were good and noble men, and I knew and loved them. . . ."

Sherman proved a model of democracy. He had a message for all Civil War veterans: " I am perfectly willing to see any of you during my stay. If in walking

79

the streets, I should fail to recognize you, just pull me by the coat." His visit was crowded with functions. He greeted officers of the Second Brigade, all in full-dress uniforms, in one of the parlors of the Palace. He saw Edwin Booth in *King Lear* at the California Theater; he inspected the fortifications of the bay; he was entertained by D. O. Mills at the banker's house at Millbrae, and he exchanged reminiscences with dozens of pioneers of the day when Sherman's bank had been one of the financial mainstays of the town.

The climax of hospitality was Senator Sharon's grand ball at Belmont. Dancing began at ten. The " court set " consisted of the general and the Countess of Dufferin, with the Earl and Mrs. Sherman opposite. This austere company failed to dampen Sherman's enthusiasm. " He entered into the excitement . . . as heartily as if he had been dancing at a husking-bee to the music of a fiddle in the hands of a musical darky. . . ." There were twelve long dances and Sherman missed none of them.

In its role of town satirist the *News-Letter* printed a paragraph of welcome:

General Sherman is now marching through California instead of Georgia, and as the columns of our contemporaries will soon be laden with " characteristic anecdotes " . . . we herewith give a little incident of his recent stay in Chicago. One night, while ascending at a late hour in the elevator of the Palmer House, he was suddenly set upon by the only other passenger, who was subject to occasional fits of insanity. This party stunned the attendant by a furious blow with his stick, and, grappling with the general, attempted to stab him with a murderous looking knife. In the melee the lights went out and the elevator stopped between two floors. During the terrific struggle in the dark General Sherman managed to seize the maniac by the throat and force his head over the edge of the doorway. He then felt for the starting-bar with his foot, and put the machine in motion. The result was that in passing the next floor above, the head of the unhappy wretch was severed from its body, and went bounding down into the office, to the great horror of the clerks.

The general greatly enjoys recounting this incident in his own graphic style. His room at the Palace is Number 622, on the sixth floor, and all our readers are requested to go right up and hear it for themselves. Walk right in without knocking, and if the Commander-in-Chief is out, they will find some excellent four-bit cigars in the third bureau drawer. The decanter is always in the bookcase, or else under the bed with the *Chronicle* reporter.

In September 1878 the town was host to another military figure whose early career had been closely identified with California: John C. Frémont. Nearly a third of a century had passed since Frémont had played his controversial part in wresting the territory from the Mexicans, but old acquaintances observed that he retained " the quiet, well-bred suavity that had made him such a favorite when California had plenty of bears beside the one on his flag, and when the gold fever was at its height." At sixty-five, Frémont's truculent career was about to enter a new phase; he had been appointed Governor of Arizona Territory and he was on his way, with his son and his talented wife, to assume his new duties. By then survivors of the days of '46 were few, but those who remained made much of his visit. A committee from the Society of California Pioneers met his train at Martinez; later there was a reunion of veterans of the Conquest in the society's rooms on Montgomery Street. There Frémont exchanged reminiscences with Aleck Godey, who had been a guide on one of the Pathfinder's exploring trips in the remote '40s. As they talked, onlookers regarded the pair with awe; here in the flesh were two men who had known California when it was a Mexican province, remote and backward, almost completely cut off from the ambitions of a hustling and acquisitive world.

2

HARDLY HAD Frémont departed when San Francisco made ready to honor the greatest military figure of all, soon to return to native soil after a tour of the world. The nation's instinct to make heroes of its generals reached its climax as the *City of Tokio,* outward bound from Honolulu, neared the Golden Gate with General Grant on board.

San Franciscans had always loved a celebration, but the town outdid itself in its welcome to this taciturn, fifty-six-year-old ex-tanner who had miraculously become the greatest military figure of his generation. The entire city put on gala attire; bunting covered the façades of downtown buildings; triumphal arches were thrown across the cobbled wastes of Market Street; and a succession of parades, banquets, receptions, balls, and private dinners was planned. At the Palace Warren

Leland overlooked no detail that might enhance the general's comfort. For the benefit of a curious public, newspapers described the rooms he was to occupy:

The two parlors forming part of the suite are elegantly furnished with California laurel overlaid with satin. Several rare paintings adorn the walls, one of which is the well-known "November Day" by J. W. Rix. The front sleeping apartment is furnished in mahogany and black walnut covered with maroon satin. The other sleeping apartment is in California laurel. Elegant chandeliers are hung from the centers of the ceilings . . . and Carrara marble mantels with their shining grates adorn the walls. The floor is covered with genuine Turkish carpet, and the beds with Persian spreads and real Irish lavendered linen.

Not until many hours after his arrival was Grant permitted to go to his luxurious bed. Lookouts, scanning the horizon from Land's End, saw the smoke of the *City of Tokio* at three minutes after three on the afternoon of September 20, 1879. Two hours and a half later the sound of the Fort Point cannons announced that Grant was entering the Golden Gate. During the interval virtually the entire population joined in a rush to the hills overlooking the harbor. It was a mass movement, unique in the city's history. The throngs filled certain streets from edge to edge, sweeping everything before them; it was as though they were fleeing before an invading army. Within an hour twenty thousand were massed on Telegraph Hill, solidly covering its crest and seaward sides; other crowds covered every vantage point on the long slope of Russian Hill, on Black Point, and the sandy heights of the Western Addition.

Opposite the Presidio the little Pacific Mail liner hove to while dozens of welcoming boats circled about, their open whistles setting up an ear-splitting din. As they drew near, those on board caught sight of the fabulous general. Grant was seated on the hurricane deck, just below the pilot house. Grouped about were members of his party: Mrs. Grant, Colonel Fred Grant, Lieutenant Belknap, U.S.N., John Russell Young, the *New York Herald* reporter who had covered Grant's world tour. The tug *Millen Griffith* had the honor of first making fast; on board was the official welcoming committee and Ulysses Grant, Jr. The latter was first over the side; he was met at the rail by his brother Fred and hurried to greet his parents. Meantime Major-General McDowell and his staff climbed on board. McDowell and Grant had been classmates at West Point and fellow commanders during the Rebellion. The crowd stood with uncovered heads as McDowell hurried to greet his old comrade.

The meeting proved a casual one.

" How are you, Mac? " asked Grant.

" General, I'm glad to see you," said McDowell.

Others were less brief, and the welcoming ceremonies consumed hours. Not until nearly eight o'clock did the liner dock. The crowd had long since tired and gone home to supper. Thousands were back again, however, to witness the general debark. Over and over, massed bands at the dock played *Home, Sweet Home.* Through the tumult of the drive up Market Street Grant maintained his usual stolid calm. At intervals he lifted his hat in acknowledgment of salvos of applause; then again lapsed into immobility. As his carriage passed beneath the arch bearing his name at Market and New Montgomery streets he looked up with interest at some small boys who had evaded the police guard and were perched precariously on its top. At Fifth and Market, Grant entered a reviewing stand and with uncomplaining fortitude watched the progress of the longest parade in the city's history; prominent citizens, war veterans, city, state, and Federal officials, drill teams, fraternal societies, delegations from neighboring towns, early-day fire organizations, a steam calliope and bells, finally a nondescript throng: " citizens independent of organizations."

It was an exhausted hero who entered his carriage and was driven to the Palace. There yet another ovation awaited him. Although police had managed to keep the floor of the grand court cleared, the six balconies were crowded to capacity, and the cheers that greeted Grant's entrance exceeded in volume all that had gone before. The general and his party retired to their suite, the door of room 980 closed behind them — and immediately new cries began to echo through the corridors. Grant was a long time reappearing. He had had a hard day, and there was a further complication: he had lost his false teeth. Later it was learned that a steward on the *City of Tokio* had carelessly thrown them overboard that morning. Until a new set could be made, the general had trouble enunciating clearly and of course banquets were a trial. But the public knew nothing of this difficulty, and meantime guards had been removed from the entrances and thousands had filled the public rooms and hallways, their shouts all but raising the roof. At length Grant appeared on the third-floor balcony, bowed to the throng, then hurried back to his rooms. The uproar continued. In the grand court a band tried to drown the noise with fortissimo selections from *Pinafore* — and succeeded only in whipping enthusiasm to new heights. Once more the general, accompanied this time by Mayor Bryant, stepped to the balcony rail. Grant mounted a chair and the crowd roared approval. The mayor bellowed: " Fellow citizens, come to order. . . . Be still and allow me to speak. Friends, it gives me great pleasure to introduce to you General Ulysses S. Grant."

Grant delivered one of his characteristic short speeches; possibly he was even more brief than usual because of his mishap:

" Gentlemen of San Francisco: I assure you that after an absence of twenty-five years I am happy to see you again. I thank you for your cordiality and expect, during my stay here, to be more with you."

The Grant Invincibles then rendered a song, specially composed for the occasion by a local poet. It had eight stanzas; this was the first:

The hero of our nation is the gallant U. S. G.;
  He has been away in foreign lands — far, far beyond the
    sea,
But now he's coming back again to the land of the brave
    and free.
  Yes, Grant is coming home.

  Glory, glory, hallelujah: etc.
  For Grant has just got home.

The song did what all else had failed to do. Before many stanzas had been sung, the crowd began to flow outward through the hotel entrances. In fifteen minutes quiet had settled over the central part of the city. Late watchers presently saw the gaslights extinguished in the Grant suite.

During the next week an epidemic of hero-worship gripped the state, with the laconic general as its helpless victim. One could but guess what emotions lay behind the mask he wore in public. This return to San Francisco must have given him moments of quiet amazement as he contemplated the surprising turns of fortune's wheel. Today he could not venture outside his hotel without immediately being hemmed in by well-wishers who pushed and scrambled for the privilege of looking at him. Twenty-five years earlier he had tramped the same streets friendless and with empty pockets, gloomily revolving in his mind the problem of where he might find his supper and a night's lodging.

Several times during his stay there were reminders of the period when he had been less than a national hero. A delegation of former residents of Galena, Illinois, waited on him at the Palace. Their spokesman recalled with pride the years he had lived among them, tactfully omitting to mention that he had then been regarded as a moody and unenterprising young man, shiftless and discouraged, already foredoomed to failure. One day, riding in a flower-covered carriage through the streets of San Jose, he impassively acknowledged the salute of a group of workmen drawn up before a tannery, eager to cheer a distinguished fellow craftsman.

No such reminder of humbler days marred the climactic social event of Grant's stay: Senator Sharon's

masked ball at Belmont — " the most brilliant gathering that has ever taken place on the Pacific Coast." For
that event Ralston's mansion was transformed. Fifteen
hundred Chinese lanterns were hung in the grounds;
inside, potted plants, blooming trees, and festoons of
smilax " delighted the eye and ravished the senses."
Eighteen hundred guests, everyone of importance in
the northern end of the state, were present. Three
special trains brought the San Franciscans down to Belmont. The list of luxuries provided for their refresh-
ment included a hundred baskets of champagne, fifteen
thousand Eastern oysters. The ladies' dresses were " of
the most *recherché* and expensive description," and the
cost of one was specifically stated: two thousand dollars. Grant tired early and, about half past ten, sought
refuge in a quiet corner of the mansion, " near the
cloak-rooms," but dancing went on for hours longer.
The special trains left at one, three, and five o'clock.
At the station in San Francisco a hundred carriages
waited to return the guests to their homes.

Among newspaper descriptions of the event the
Call's account alone struck a slightly acid note:

In the throng of the invited were all the millionaires
on speaking terms with Sharon; all the lawyers, except
those who had been fighting his Nevada schemes and interests; all the political orators, except the one who had told
the people of Nevada how Sharon had . . . asked Meisson-
nier if he was one of the old masters, saying that he did not
intend to " patronize " any new ones and proposed to deal
with the old ones direct; all the society people who had deserved well of the rich Senator by not saying spiteful things
about his grammar, all the solid merchants who cared to

88

go, all the unidentified " prominent citizens " who had a taste for terrapin . . . and the admirers and friends — whose number was legion — of the great commander of the Union armies who had so lately been President of the United States.

The Sharon ball was the last major event of Grant's stay. Next day farewells were said at the Palace, the general and his party left for Oregon on the *St. Paul,* and citizens returned to their normal pursuits. Meantime the visitor received a final mark of esteem. Siloam Division, No. 10, Sons of Temperance, met and adopted a resolution:

Resolved, that the refusal to partake of wine when offered him at a reception tendered to General Grant at the Cliff House, was as great, noble and magnanimous a deed as was his refusal to accept the sword of General Lee . . . at Appomattox.

3

AFTER GRANT, the visits of other Civil War heroes were in the nature of an anticlimax. Yet for two decades longer the Palace continued to play host to the aging but indefatigable generals. Sherman was back in the fall of 1880, this time on the staff of President Hayes. Again he looked down from a balcony of the grand court on a sea of upturned faces. By this time speech-making had begun to pall, and Sherman enlivened his extemporaneous remarks by one drawling sentence of unusual candor: "Down where you are, there is a crowd of gentlemen, like every other crowd I ever saw in the United States, greedy to hear someone talk; good or bad talking makes no difference, they want talk."

The speech-hungry town got little satisfaction from George B. McClellan, who stopped at the hotel in September 1885. "Little Mac" had gained weight since the days when he had commanded the Army of the Potomac and opposed Lincoln for the Presidency; his mustache and imperial were snow white. But the public found him smiling and approachable, and groups of former Union officers spent hours in his suite refighting the old campaigns. To reporters McClellan announced that he was out of politics, that he had no opinion on the burning local question of Chinese immigration, and that he doubted if the French engineers who were currently trying to dig a canal across the Isthmus of Panama would succeed. A month later San Franciscans read of "Little Mac's" death in New York.

The parade continued, but at a slower pace. General West, a hero of Chickamauga, and celebrated for his escape from Libby Prison, appeared in the late '8os. He was followed by General Ely S. Parker, who had the blood of a famous Indian chief in his veins. As one of Grant's staff at Appomattox, Parker had engrossed the terms of Lee's surrender from the draft Grant had hastily scrawled in pencil — and had ever since kept the original version as his most cherished possession. In 1889 came the novelty of a Rebel general, seventy-five-year-old Wade Hampton, leader of Hampton's Legion at Bull Run and more recently Governor of South Carolina and a United States Railroad Commissioner. Although he had a few years earlier lost a leg in a hunting accident, the old warrior " strode into the Palace . . . as active and dauntless as . . . in the early '6os." There were a few others. In the summer of '96 Brigadier General Benjamin H. Grierson was in town long enough to explain to reporters how, an even third of a century before, he had led a raid from La Grange to Baton Rouge to assist Grant's operations against Vicksburg — " the most thoroughly successful cavalry raid of the entire war." When he left the Palace, Grierson announced that he was hurrying home to vote for his friend McKinley. A few months later came General Adolphus W. Greely, noted for his polar explorations. Greely, too, had served in the Rebellion, but in the ranks; he had the distinction of being the only enlisted man in the Civil War to attain the rank of general in the regular army.

Time took its toll and veterans of the '6os appeared at longer intervals. Then, as the century closed, the Spanish War providentially supplied a new crop of heroes. Two nights before Christmas 1898 the town awaited the coming of the current national idol: Lieutenant Richmond Pearson Hobson. Hobson was fresh from his exploit at Santiago, where he had sunk the *Merrimac* in an attempt to " bottle up " the Spanish fleet. He was young, handsome, and unmarried — a completely new type of war hero. Of course he overshadowed every matinee idol in the land. Not until the rise of the movie immortals, years later, did the country witness so concerted a fluttering of feminine hearts. For all that, the *Examiner's* account of the handsome lieutenant's arrival was a shade ironical:

91

Although the reception was not supposed to begin until 9:30 o'clock, the court was packed at seven with a subdued assemblage, gazing expectantly at the great glass doors through which the lieutenant was to appear in his carriage. Captain Spillane, in epaulettes, Sergeants Conboy and Brophy and a squad of police, who trod carefully on the pale marble pavement, maintained order and kept the passages clear. Detective Ben Bohen was also there, heavily disguised. He had wiped the black dye from his moustache, and few knew him. While the excitement was seething Detectives Gibson, Silvey and Eagan rounded up "Deafy" Morris, said to be a pickpocket. . . .

In the hotel lobby were many owners of naphtha launches and warriors who had fought and suffered in the Commissary Department at the Presidio, all of whom shared a fraternal interest in the lieutenant. At 9 o'clock a coupe dashed into the court.

"Here he is!" shrieked the crowd, and the band struck up "Come, Kiss Your Honey Boy."

An old man with long whiskers hopped out of the vehicle and looked as if he wanted to hop back again when he noted the demonstration. . . .

Hobson arrived an hour later. He was hustled through to the main parlor, where he shook the hands of two thousand admirers, mostly women. The police lost control of the crowd, and the room became packed to the point of suffocation. One trouble was that ladies who had already met the celebrity refused to leave. "They wanted to look at Hobson some more." One enterprising young woman climbed on the mantel and so got an unobstructed view. Sergeant Conboy relieved the situation by shouting: "Pass right down to the ice-cream parlors, ladies. There are seats for all, with va-

nilla, strawberry, and lemon ice for everybody." Mary
Dickson scored a minor triumph; not only did she
shake hands with the hero, but she also obtained his
autograph. Later Hobson talked from the balcony of
the grand court; then he hurried off to the Christmas
cotillion of the Friday Night Club at Native Sons' Hall.
There he conferred genuine, if transient, fame on a
number of daughters of the town's first families. He
danced with Mary Bell Gwin, Miss Borel, Maud Mul-
lins, Frances Currey, Alia Moffitt, and Miss Ellinwood.
He escorted Sallie Maynard to the supper room. He
sat out a dance with Mrs. Belvin. Unanimously the
ladies reported him a graceful dancer and an entertaining talker.

Next day Hobson continued his tour. Newspapers
printed daily reports of the number of girls he had
kissed.

4

IN THE late '80s a short, beetle-browed young man disembarked at the Pacific Mail dock and for a few days
surveyed scenes already familiar to him through the
writings of Bret Harte. The little Anglo-Indian journalist was unimpressed by what he saw. Even the
Palace he dismissed as " a seven-storied warren of hu-
manity." Admittedly, the hotel was big and costly, but
young Rudyard Kipling found the service lamentably
bad. The main office was illuminated at night by
incandescent electric globes — last word in modernity

— but the clerk behind its counter picked his teeth while he served the guests, and its " vast, marble-paved floor " was strewn with big, shining brass spittoons. He was critical, too, of a printed notice in his room which advised guests to keep their doors locked and to deposit valuables in the office safe. The necessity for such a warning seemed to him further evidence of the depravity of the natives. Convinced that San Francisco offered no threat to the security of the Empire — a British gunboat would make short work of Fort Point — the little colonial hurried on to New York, London, and the tremendous triumphs that lay awaiting him.

He was one of a long procession of literary lions. Eight years earlier, while the town was still recovering from its welcome to Grant, appeared another Englishman, George Augustus Sala. Short, red-faced, and garrulous, Sala immensely impressed all who came within range of his booming voice. The journalist received far more newspaper space than his considerable importance warranted. Reporters were fascinated by his physical awkwardness, his bizarre postures. " He has a way of leaning on the table in front of him, and bearing his weight on his black-gloved hands, which are held in such a position as to look like bear's claws. Then, while in this position, he slowly drags first one leg and then the other back and forth." And of course he talked all the while.

For years Sala had been England's foremost journalist. In the middle '50s Dickens had paid him a pound each for weekly essays in *Household Words,* and the two had remained friends until the novelist's death. Sala had covered the Civil War for London papers. His

sympathies had been with the South, he explained, because his mother was born in British Guiana. He
proved a mine of information about positively everything: London literary life, world politics, New York
journalism, the future of California. Interviews were
likely to be a bit breathless. " Ah! How are you? " he
greeted a reporter in his Palace rooms. " Glad to see
you. Come in and make yourself at home. Have a
cigar? Oh, Mrs. Sala doesn't mind smoking; rather
likes it. Excuse my shirt sleeves — just packing up.
Hate to go; had a splendid time." Unlike Kipling, he
had praise for the natives. " The Californians, you
may say, are to my mind the busiest, thriftiest and most
go-ahead people I have ever come in contact with.
Their ideas are immense, the consummation of their
conceptions is stupendous. . . . San Francisco is
simply magnificent — the Venice of America."

Sala was again at the Palace five years later, as energetic and loquacious as ever. The city was promptly set
to rights as to Great Britain's intentions in India and
the Sudan, and the probable consequences of General
Gordon's death. Asked his opinion of Mary Anderson,
California-born actress who had been appearing in
London, he rattled off a comprehensive answer:

" Well, for beauty I think her superb. She is in fact
too utterly lovely for anything. But as to her dramatic
genius, well, she is not much; but she is better than nothing. . . . For the past forty years I have seen all the chief
Shakesperian actresses and I cannot say that I think much
of Miss Anderson, although she is admirably schooled. . . .
I think Lord Lytton did her a great deal of harm. . . . He
is simply crazy on her, you know, and actually had the

95

impudence to say that the critics never spoke well of anyone unless they were treated to chicken and champagne.
The last time I saw Lord Lytton was at Irving's supper
when he, himself, was pegging into chicken and champagne
with a gusto that was positively alarming. . . ."

Having just arrived from New York, Sala was questioned about the newest sensation of American journalism, the *World*.

" It has made a tremendous leap since I was last here.
It was then under the editorship of my dear old friend
Hurlbert, and had a circulation of only 16,000. They say
it now has over 100,000. Well, I was invited to the Lotos
Club and I had never heard the name of the proprietor of
the *World*. Whitelaw Reid kept talking to me about
Pulitzer. Pulitzer! Pulitzer! I said: ' What is Pulitzer? Is
it a new mineral water? ' This, alas, the proprietor of the
World heard, and I'm afraid I shall always be in his bad
books."

Was it true that Pulitzer had created a disturbance
at the dinner?

" Yes, he kept interrupting Whitelaw Reid during his
speech, and made himself rather unpopular. . . .

" I saw Dana during my stay. I consider him a very
remarkable man. The best written paper in New York,
though, I think is the *Tribune*. The editorials are written
with the most consummate skill. The New York *Herald*
has probably more news than any other paper in the world,
but it wants a guiding spirit."

Sala had been tendered a banquet by the Bohemian
Club, and one of the speakers, Frank Pixley, had dwelt
on the Revolutionary War in terms so patriotic that

many feared the British guest might be offended. Sala was asked how he had liked Pixley. He laughed loudly.

" Poor old Pixley. . . . They tell me his peculiar speech was severely commented on. But it amounted to simply this: Pixley had the fag-end of an old Fourth of July speech in his mind and he tagged it on to the end of his after-dinner remarks. But he was severe on the British lion through his humble representative, Sala. And now . . . I'll stop talking. Some afternoon before I leave I'll tell you why I always wear a red necktie with a white waist-coat."

Whether that information was ever imparted is unknown, but the visitor had some entertaining gossip about London's Bohemia and its legendary figures:

". . . I remember a little tavern at Covent Garden where Thackeray, Dickens and a lot of fellows of that stamp used to meet. At 12 o'clock, midnight, Dickens invariably arose to go, and Thackeray as invariably begged him to remain. A life-long sufferer from a painful disease, Thackeray found physical relief in the bottle. ' Ah,' he used to say, ' why will you go, Dickens, just as I am beginning to feel well?' But his entreaties availed nothing. Dickens, the man of method, got into his greatcoat and slipped away. It was the same whenever we met. Nothing could induce Dickens to stay beyond the hour he had mutually agreed with himself should be the time of his departure. . . ."

Sala believed Thackeray's severe treatment of the Irish in his books was due to the fact that he had married an Irish girl whose mother he disliked. " I'm sure his mother-in-law was responsible for Costigan, Major O'Gahagan, the O'Mullegan, et al." He continued:

97

" I remember how one evening the Moot Club sat for nine hours in earnest debate whether or no George Osborne would have run away with Becky Sharp before the Battle of Waterloo if she had consented to go with him. The decision was that he would not. Think of that compliment for a novelist! The club was composed of the most famous literary men in London, and there they sat, hour after hour, discussing an incident of the Thackeray novel. . . ."

He passed on to other English writers. He believed William Black was deteriorating, although Black was but thirty-five and had an immense following.

" He is an odd fish. . . . He works not more than a couple of hours in the morning, and then eats a huge lunch, which he washes down with sherry, stout and Burgundy. The result is that he is fit for nothing but a nap for the rest of the day. His liver is beginning to resent the treatment. . . ."

For the local Bohemia he had only qualified praise:

" It is not the Bohemia of my younger days. It is a gilt-edged, swallow-tailed Bohemia. My Bohemia had its origin in Paris. We were a wild, gay lot . . . though not overburdened with money. . . . Then we transferred our Bohemia to London, and there I met my dear master in Charles Dickens. . . . What a lazy lot we were, to be sure. . . ."

5

TOWARD THE end of March 1882 an even better-known Englishman came to town. It was twenty-six-year-old Oscar Wilde on his famous tour. Wilde had already been a major sensation in a dozen cities, and his sunflower, his velvet coat, and his lectures on æsthetics — compounded of platitudes, paradoxes, and shrewd common sense — were being discussed from coast to coast. Of course San Franciscans were eager to see the odd celebrity and to learn if, as a spectacle, he lived up to advance notices. They saw a " tall, lubberly young man," with a sallow, melancholy face, light-brown hair that reached his shoulders, keen appraising eyes, and a friendly smile.

On the Palace register he inscribed: " O. Wilde and servant " in a distinguished, illegible hand, while onlookers stared hard, convinced that the hotel had never harbored a guest so startlingly groomed. Above his abundant hair was a huge, wide-brimmed white hat, suggestive of those worn by deputy sheriffs in California rural counties. But there were no Western touches about the rest of his costume: a close-fitting frock coat of black velvet, dun-brown pants, pointed shoes, velvet waistcoat, " puce-colored " tie, and yellow gloves. On the lapel of the velvet coat was a boutonniere, somewhat travel-worn. It consisted of heliotrope, a tuberose, and a daisy.

Wilde lectured that night at Platt's Hall. The audience stared at the single lily in its vase, at the speaker's knee breeches and ample, black-stockinged calves, and listened with diminishing interest to a series of truisms stated in a semi-audible monotone: " If life is noble and beautiful, art will be noble and beautiful. . . . Effect is the essence of design. . . . Art is eternal because eternally beautiful." In ten minutes the audience was yawning. Next day the papers reported that the lecture had netted $2,260. A repeat performance the following night brought in $1,600. On the third evening the poet was entertained at the Bohemian Club — and it was soon being told about town how the æsthete had matched glass for glass with the club's most accomplished drinkers, had seen them safely under the table, and had strode blithely back to the Palace.

That afternoon a girl reporter, Mary Watson, was granted an interview.

He talked, and talked well. . . . His action in throwing off his coat, the quick and well-rehearsed movement of the servant, who reached the center of the room just at the right moment to catch the outside robes of the poet, and his subsequent position on the sofa, partaking rather of an easy posture, half-reclining, half-sitting, set me quite at ease. . . .

" Is this not something new for you, Mr. Wilde? You have never met a lady reporter? "

" No," replied he. " We do not have them in our country."

I looked toward the bay-window, wherein was placed a table, and on it a vase with a large bouquet of white flowers, beautifully arranged, and, for effect, a silk handkerchief had been thrown carelessly across the two lower branches, and the air coming from the window swayed the ends in graceful movements. . . . On the table where the white flowers were placed were also strewn a confusion of scraps of paper, letters, books and newspapers. . . . On the table in the center were papers and cards from various business houses, evidently intended to convey the pleasure every merchant would have in showing him his wares. On the table near the window was a large silver fruit-dish filled with oranges, two plates, and a knife. On the sofa was carelessly thrown a dark brown rug with a pillow, over which was thrown a crepe shawl of the same color, and long fringe to match. . . .

The interview was frequently interrupted by Wilde's servant, who brought in a succession of autograph albums. The poet dutifully wrote in all, occasionally referring to one of his books to refresh his memory. " One sometimes forgets one's own lines," he remarked to reporter Mary Watson.

A more forceful speaker came to town about that time: Colonel Bob Ingersoll. Of course the local devout remained aloof and the town's preachers waged counter-warfare; none the less, a capacity crowd packed Metropolitan Temple for his lecture. Ingersoll's three-hour talk was punctuated by laughter, the clapping of hands, and the rattling of canes. The canes of the unbelievers rattled with particular vigor at the end of such passages as these: " Millions imagine they know all about, not only this world, but the next. . . . They understand all God's plans and purposes; they know that He made this world in order to raise Baptists, Methodists and Presbyterians. . . . This is a world of change; the old fights the new, but the new conquers; in time the new in turn becomes old, and goes the way of its predecessors. . . . I oppose Christianity because it wraps the cradle in gloom and the coffin in horror; because it fills asylums and makes man a cringing serf and slave. . . ."

No such dangerous heretic was tall, drawling Henry Shaw, who arrived in the summer of 1885. Shaw had entered literature in a curious way: he had first discovered his gift for amusing the public as auctioneer at Poughkeepsie, New York. He had been writing humor, under the name of Josh Billings, since 1863. Now he was a nationally famous lecturer, and his regular contributions to the *New York Weekly* brought him a princely return: " $100 for each article." Those who visited his Palace rooms found him open of countenance and unassuming in manner. His conversation was sprinkled with such salty colloquialisms as " consarn it " and " spile " — all without sign of affectation.

Shaw lectured on " The Probabilities of Life " at the Y.M.C.A. Hall, where he was introduced as " the champion orthographist of the Nineteenth Century." His platform manner proved as quaint as his speech.

Seating himself in a chair beside a small table, upon which was a volume of manuscript, Josh deliberately took a pair of glasses from his vest pocket, adjusted them upon his nose, and producing a huge white linen handkerchief, unfolded and carefully spread it upon his knees.

Listeners found his talk a curious blend of sense and nonsense; its delivery, in a broad, Yankee drawl, amusing and droll. The papers printed a few excerpts:

" I don't propose to speak of the lost arts, the rise and fall of the Roman Empire, the Chinese question or the well-recognized principle that the eight spot always takes the seven. There is no cure for laziness, but I've known a second wife to hurry it some. Mosquitoes . . . have some of the best blood of the country in their veins. I've known mules to be good for six months so as to get a chance to kick. Newfoundland dogs are good to save children from drowning, but you must have a pond of water handy and

a child, or else there will be no profit in boarding a Newfoundland. Love is like the measles, you can have it only
once, and the later in life it occurs the tougher it goes with
us. Much of the virtue in the world is merely vice tired
out. . . ."

Shaw was unwell and from San Francisco he went to
the Hotel Del Monte for a rest. Some weeks later a
doctor was summoned to the hotel. He found the
humorist seated by the fire in the lobby, apparently in
good health. Shaw said: " My doctors East ordered
complete rest from brain work, but you can see that I
don't have to work my brain for my lectures. . . ."
While he spoke he threw his hands over his head and
fell backwards. He died in a few minutes. From Mon-
terey came word that he had been a favorite at the
hotel, where his good nature and drawling, sponta-
neous humor had kept him surrounded by a circle of
admiring guests.

6

THE STREAM of lecturers, authors, editors, and publishers continued. James Gordon Bennett, athletic, sun-
burned, and prematurely gray, appeared in the fall of
1885, and walked down Montgomery Street with his
friend John W. Mackay. No one on the crowded sidewalk recognized the young man in a " Cleveland stove-
pipe hat " as the owner of the *New York Herald*.
Reporters who called at his Palace suite came away
empty-handed, and the *Alta* commented dryly:

Considerable discussion has been excited by James Gordon Bennett's refusal to be interviewed and his further statement that he has never been interviewed in his life. Mr. Bennett is the proprietor of a newspaper whose representatives have compelled about every sovereign in Europe to submit to an interview. The moral of this, evidently, is that a newspaper proprietor is greater than a king. . . .

Joseph Medill, chief owner of the *Chicago Tribune,* arrived soon after and not only allowed himself to be interviewed, but proceeded to lecture Californians on what he claimed, sensationally enough, was a want of enterprise. " I am much surprised that more energy is not directed to the development of the natural resources of the country. You have not yet recovered from the mining craze. Irrigation is what is wanted. . . ."

Medill's heresies received scant notice in the local press. More to the city's taste was the son of Charles Dickens, who came west in May 1888 to give readings from his father's works. His stay became a social event of importance. Ballenberg's Band serenaded him in the Palace grand court; later hundreds of the elite crowded the First Congregational Church and sedately applauded selections from *David Copperfield* and the trial of Bardell versus Pickwick. Mr. Dickens was admired for his beautifully modulated voice. His gestures were pronounced " graceful and appropriate without any affectation or staginess." The affair was for the benefit of the Hospital for Children.

That same month San Francisco saw another son of a famous literary figure when Oliver Wendell Holmes, Jr., registered at the Palace. He liked the city, thought the ocean beach " superb," and deplored the agitation to exclude the Chinese on economic grounds alone. " If they are excluded it should be on . . . grounds that it is desirable to keep up the standards of the race. . . ." Judge Holmes was then on the Massachusetts Supreme Court. He had been a professor at Harvard Law School, and there were those who thought he might be destined for even higher honors.

Preceding Justice Holmes by a week or two, Julia Ward Howe came to town on a lecture tour. Horatio Stebbins introduced her to a packed audience in Irving Hall and all stood entranced while Walter Campbell sang *The Battle Hymn of the Republic*. She talked of Longfellow and Emerson, both of whom she had known as young men. The youthful Longfellow had had " bright blue eyes and long locks . . . and [wore] a blue coat and gilt buttons. His voice was musical and manly. . . ." He was then a professor at Harvard. Mrs. Howe had known, too, the Mary Ashburton of *Hyperion*. She recalled that when the poem had appeared, Boston had laughed and cried: " Oh, Mr. Longfellow, we know you and your Mary Ashburton! " Emerson she remembered in the days when he had been " laughed at by many and praised by few."

She made his acquaintance accidentally and unwillingly. It was upon a railroad journey, and a friend asked her permission to introduce him, and she consented, though with the feeling, " Have I got to know this wicked man? " It was long after this first meeting before she overcame her natural prejudice and learned to admire his gentle nature. It was neither popular nor fashionable to praise him in those days. . . .

Culture-hungry San Franciscans listened with pleasure to this chit-chat of the New England immortals, and the town's non-literary beginnings seemed comfortably remote. A month later the lion-hunters overlooked another writer who, despite his lack of Boston connections, was being kindly spoken of by critics. Robert Louis Stevenson, however, gave no lecture. He stopped, not at the Palace, but at the more modest Occidental; he had, moreover, married a divorcee, and his local friends were tainted with Bohemianism — a group that would hardly have interested Julia Ward Howe. Toward the end of June the papers recorded briefly that Stevenson had sailed for the South Seas on the yacht *Casco*.

Eight years later a visiting Englishwoman, Emily Soldene, saw a crowd before the windows of one of the ground-floor shops of the Palace. The attraction was a display of Stevensoniana in Doxey's book-store: "all his works, all his editions — including the Edinburgh Edition." In the center was a facsimile of a hand-written memorandum found among the writer's papers at Vailima. Mrs. Soldene went inside and admired Doxey's collection of Stevenson portraits. She was given a copy of the memorandum:

I think now, this 5th or 6th day of April 1873, that I can see my future life. I think it will run stiller and stiller year by year, a very quiet, desultorily studious existence. If God only gives me tolerable health, I think now I shall be very happy: work and science calm the mind, and stop gnawing in the brain; and as I am glad to say that I do now recognize that I shall never be a great man, I may set myself peacefully on a smaller journey, not without hope of coming to the inn before nightfall.

The year after Stevenson sailed off in the *Casco,* yet another English writer was at the Palace: Sir Edwin Arnold, author of *The Light of Asia.* " This is my first visit to America," he confessed, " although I consider myself partly an American, having married Miss Channing, of Boston. . . ." The Boston connection established, Sir Edwin's opinion was sought on the subjects currently dear to interviewers: Gladstone, the Irish question, the comparative merits of the Harvard and Oxford methods of education, the difference between the American and English systems of government. On this last subject the visitor was admirably impartial:

" In England we have monarchy and class distinctions, and the effect of that system is to give the English people a respect for authority. In America, on the contrary, no such social distinctions prevail. All men are equal, and the result is an aspiring independence which is very good, but which is likely to be attained at the expense of some of the virtues which result from the English system."

Readers made what they could from that sage pronouncement, and the ladies of the Century Club tendered the speaker a reception. Sir Edwin and his daughter then sailed for the Orient. In due course word came back to San Francisco that the King of Siam had decorated him with the Order of the White Elephant.

By that time the town was reading of another Palace guest: Robert Bonner, owner of the *New York Ledger.*

Bonner talked fluently to interviewers — not of journalism or politics, however, but of racehorses. This was understandable, for he owned the famous Maud S. and he had come West to purchase (from Senator Stanford) the latest sensation of the racetracks, Sunol. Bonner thought Sunol capable of breaking Maud S.'s record. A few days later the deal was consummated; the publisher also carried off (for ten thousand dollars) another prize of the Stanford stables, the stallion Ansel.

While this was going on, one of the New York rivals of Bonner's *Ledger* — the *World* — was attracting wider attention by sending a girl reporter on a race around the world. Nellie Bly arrived on the *Oceanic* on January 21, 1890 and, without setting her dainty foot ashore, hurried to the Oakland Mole, where a special train waited for the final dash to New York. San Franciscans had to content themselves with descriptions of Nellie that appeared in the press. She had a pet monkey. She was slender and of medium height. She had brown hair " loosely curled in a braid," brown eyes, and a " bright and intelligent face." Her nose was retroussé and her teeth of "dazzling whiteness." Finally, she wore a long black-and-white checked ulster, and a sailor's cap on her pretty head. For the moment, Nellie Bly was unquestionably the country's most romantic figure.

The parade of literary personages continued. In December 1892 Captain Andrew C. P. Haggard, brother of H. Rider Haggard, and an author in his own right, was in town. He had recently broken his arm " while pig-sticking in Hindustan " and was on his way to Canada to recuperate. The Haggards, he told interviewers, were of old Danish stock, being descended from the Guildenstern family " mentioned by Shakespeare in his plays." Like his more famous brother, he had written novels, one of which, *Do-Do and I,* had had a " great run " in England. " I have written too a great deal of poetry and am now engaged in a volume of rather more serious effort than I have hitherto attempted in verse." Captain Haggard was decidedly not the reticent type of Englishman.

The year 1892 brought another picturesque guest: Mrs. Frank Leslie, in town for a convention of the International League of Press Clubs. She was no stranger to San Francisco; with her husband and a party of artists and writers she had paid a memorable visit in 1877. The group had crossed the continent in a private car, stopping at various places of interest — Omaha, Denver, Salt Lake City, Virginia City, finally San Francisco — to assemble pictures and text that later graced the pages of *Leslie's Weekly.*

Frank Leslie had died in 1880, leaving the *Weekly* burdened with debts, but his widow had carried on with shrewdness and good sense. By the time of her second visit she was a national figure. Everyone knew all about her — her uncanny news sense, her business acumen, her forceful personality, and her husbands. She had married four husbands; the most recent was William C. Kingsbury Wilde, brother of Oscar, whom she divorced a year later.

She was the lion of the convention. Papers described her as a striking figure, handsomely and fashionably groomed. She talked at length of her struggles to keep *Leslie's Weekly* afloat after her husband's death.

" Homeless, bankrupt in heart and purse, with nine lawsuits to fight and \$300,000 business debts to pay, who shall deny that this was a sufficiently severe entrance examination to the ' College of Journalism ' which is none other than the great school of life? " It was, she recalled, Garfield's assassination that had given her her chance: " I discovered by venturing the experiment that it was possible to produce and to lay before the public a sixteen-page newspaper, with eight pages of woodcut illustrations, in the interval between Sunday and Tuesday evening, and to follow it with two other illustrated newspapers during the same week. . . . The American public did the rest." Four months later the resourceful lady had been undisturbed by the maturing of a fifty-thousand-dollar note. " Two days previously, on the 9th of October, the total amount with the interest was returned out of the profits of journalism as a woman was learning it. . . ."

She continued to manage the *Weekly* with marked success for fifteen years. Then, in 1895, she leased the property and retired to France. But she was presently back again, claiming the title of the Baroness of Bazos. She was nearly eighty when she died, in 1914, leaving her fortune to the cause of woman suffrage.

7

MRS. FRANK LESLIE went briskly on her way and a week or two later the Palace was entertaining Charles W. Eliot, president of Harvard. Eliot had come west to deliver the Charter Day address at the University of California. Reporters hurried up to rooms 940–1 to interview the educator, whom they described, appropriately enough, as " scholarly looking." Stanford University had recently been opened and the week before Eliot's arrival its football team had defeated the California players in the first of what was to prove a long series of " big games." Eliot commented indulgently: " Sport, in a mild form, is an excellent thing for colleges. . . ." But when the questions swung to another topic the town was given a sample of Eliot's celebrated frankness. What sort of impression did young men from the state make at Cambridge? " We at Harvard are proud of the Californians who have completed their education within our walls. The great trouble with most Californians is that they are very wild, due, most likely, to the almost unlimited supply of money with which their wealthy parents provide them. It would be better if Californians had not so much cash." Many wondered if the reference might not be specifically to Senator George Hearst's son Willie, whose escapades at Cambridge were an imperfectly kept secret.

Eliot was followed by a spirited and voluble Frenchman, Paul Blouet, who, under the name Max O'Rell, had written a widely read book on America, *Jonathan and His Continent.* He was on a lecture tour. " Aha . . . you come to discuss my book. . . . You come to call me scoundr-r-el, and tell me this thing and that thing I have written is false, and then, perhaps you will invite me to choose my weapons. . . ." He rattled on; no one could get a word in. " He babbles forth . . . witty stories, small talk, profound thoughts, scholarly

ideas . . . as a mountain babbles forth water. . . ."
Blouet insisted that his book did not misrepresent
America, insisted that he liked Americans — almost as
much as he disliked Englishmen. " My vocabulary of
Americanisms is limited, and I can find only one word
to express my sentiment of the Englishmen in America
— beasts."

Far different from this yeasty Frenchman was the
Palace's next literary guest, John Fiske, historian, author of *Cosmic Philosophy,* and friend of Herbert
Spencer. Different too were Carter H. Harrison (who
in addition to editing the *Chicago Times* had found
time to write two travel books and to serve four terms
as mayor of Chicago) , and Will Carleton, whose poems
and lectures on the pleasures of rural life were then
immensely popular, particularly in the cities.

It was the heyday of the literary lecturer. James
Whitcomb Riley and Hamlin Garland were in town as
the year 1892 ended. They were followed in a few
months by Bronson Howard, thin, partly bald, with a
drooping gray mustache and thick eyeglasses. He was
America's leading dramatist, the author of such successes as *The Banker's Daughter, Shenandoah,* and
The Henrietta. His latest was *Aristocracy,* which he
thought might particularly interest Californians. It
was about an unlettered multimillionaire who " hails
from Menlo Park " and who tries to use his money to
crash the impregnable gates of New York's Four Hundred. San Franciscans tried to guess the identity of the
play's hero, but the dramatist was discreet. " I must
admit that his development is the work of my own
brain entirely. . . ."

Mars and the Muses

While Bronson Howard was at the Palace, Edgar W. (Bill) Nye and his wife were also guests; a little later came Victor F. Lawson, publisher of the *Chicago Record* and *Daily News,* full of enthusiasm for the Columbian World's Fair, then drawing thousands to his home city. Frank G. Carpenter, credited with having interviewed more great men than any other journalist of his time, arrived in April 1893. He committed the *faux pas* of driving into the grand court swathed in a fur-lined overcoat — " which proclaimed him a man unused to the glorious climate of California." Carpenter shed the offending garment with alacrity and was presently assuring reporters that his years of foreign travel had not lessened his love of his native land.

The Midwinter Fair of 1894 brought a host of journalists, among them some young men just coming into prominence. One was George Ade, currently writing the " stories " department of the *Chicago Record;* another, a young newspaper cartoonist, John T. McCutcheon, who was gaining a reputation as a black-and-white artist. Henry Watterson tarried long enough to deliver his lecture on " Money and Morals," and those who crowded Metropolitan Temple listened with respect to Marse Henry's forthright opinions on the state of the nation.

Soon after, the ornate portals of the Palace admitted a novelty in pretty Estelle Clayton, actress turned playwright. She had dramatized Rhoda Broughton's *Goodbye, Sweetheart, Goodbye,* and *The Quick and the Dead,* and she was in San Francisco to produce a comic opera, *The Gentle Savage,* for which she had written the libretto. An interviewer recalled that she was a sister of Isabelle Evesson, who was Dearest in *Little Lord Fauntleroy,* and that she closely resembled the noted beauty, Edith Kingdon, "whose face won George Gould." Miss Clayton thought little of her celebrated pulchritude. " I am glad I have passed the stage where everything depends on looks. People would not talk to me rationally once. . . . Now that I have a stack of plays, they believe there is something in my head. . . ."

After so charming a visitor it is not surprising that the town gave scant attention to Rose Hartwick Thorpe, author of *Curfew Must Not Ring Tonight,* or to Charles King, U.S.A., retired, whose published novels numbered thirty, including a great popular success, *The Colonel's Daughter.*

The spring of 1898 found a more famous novelist at the Palace. F. Marion Crawford, who had lived for years in Italy, was back in America for a lecture tour. San Franciscans were delighted to learn that he considered the local scenery not inferior to that of the Mediterranean. "The hills and the waters and the lowlands have the same sort of picturesqueness and the same indescribable charm. . . ." Crawford, tall, scholarly and heavily built, was a hard worker. He had written twenty-nine long novels in sixteen years. His latest book was about finished — " a sort of historical work about Rome." He produced the manuscript — a yellow-paged and well-thumbed notebook. " It might easily have passed for one burdened with the accounts of a corner grocery," observed a reporter.

In the nature of things it was *visiting* literary celebrities whose names are conspicuous in the annals of the Palace. To resident poets and writers and journalists the big Market Street hotel was interesting chiefly as a symbol of the town's cosmopolitanism and enterprise. Its dining-rooms, bar, lounges, and grand-court balconies were worth visiting only for the purpose of studying the wealthy and fashionable and traveled. The typical Palace guest they regarded as a material-minded fellow useful only as a character in a satirical novel, or possibly as the source of occasional loans.

Some local writers frequented the Palace from its beginning and a few put it to literary uses. Gertrude Atherton, whose star began shining in the late '80s, used it as a background in several of her early studies of the town's aristocracy, and in the latter '90s Frank Norris made occasional literary references to the big hotel. In the '90s, too, Doxey's book-store grew important. No ordinary provincial book-seller, William Doxey kept in touch with literary fashions throughout the world. The town's intelligentsia regularly visited his shop to look over the latest French novels and illustrated papers, to purchase copies of the *Yellow Book,* or to examine the attractive little volumes issued by a group of new publishers: Copeland & Day, Stone & Kimball, and an enthusiast in Augusta, Maine, named Thomas Bird Mosher.

In general, however, the local literati forgathered in less pretentious surroundings, mostly in the restaurants of the Italian quarter, where platters of spaghetti washed down with Napa Valley claret were as filling as the creations of the Palace's current chef — and far less expensive.

CHAPTER FOUR

ROSE OF SHARON

1

In the summer of 1875 the Bank of California closed sensationally and two results followed at once: William Chapman Ralston's career was tragically snuffed out and the town's immense new hotel passed into the control of William Sharon.

Sharon had little of the dead man's magnetism and none of his popularity, but he had always been Ralston's superior in shrewdness. He was a pale little man with a large head, ladylike hands and feet, and cold blue eyes. Everyone recognized that his prominence and wealth were due, in the beginning, to Ralston, for it was by Ralston's influence that he had been put in charge of the bank's agency at Virginia City and so had got his start.

What subsequently happened was, however, Sharon's own accomplishment. The agency was opened at a particularly happy time. The Comstock Lode had then been enough exploited to convince even the skeptical that it was fabulously rich. But the earlier, wildcat period was ending, the quick profits had been taken, the quick losses written off, and the whole scheme of development had bogged down. A snarl of boundary disputes clogged the courts. Dozens of mines had been shut down by injunctions. Others known to be as rich as any on the continent had never reached production at all. Their owners had exhausted capital and credit in quartz mills so hastily thrown together that they had proved unworkable. The local bankers, avid for a share of the prevailing five-per-cent-per-month interest, had vaults stuffed with paper on which they could collect neither principal nor interest. It was a bankrupt town sitting helplessly on a billion dollars' worth of treasure.

Here was an opportunity for a shrewd man with new capital, and Sharon made the most of it. His methods were simple and direct. He first decided which were the most promising mines and mills. He then got a share in them by taking over their notes from the involved local bankers, acting sometimes for the bank he represented, sometimes for himself and Ralston and D. O. Mills. To gain a controlling interest was another easy step: in some cases by foreclosure, in others by supplying new capital for equipment, for payrolls, for lawsuits, for the purchase of adjoining claims. It was a job for a man who could drive a close bargain and who could take a gambler's chance. Sharon had both qualifications, and he had, moreover, the resources of the parent bank behind him. Down at San Francisco, Ralston willingly backed his Virginia City agent's judgment, supplied promptly the thousands Sharon needed, and overcame intermittent doubts of Mills, the bank's conservative president.

With money sent up from San Francisco and judiciously expended by Sharon, the financial and legal impasse involving half a dozen of the leading properties was presently broken. Interest centered again on the neglected business of getting out the treasure lying beneath Mount Davidson. Production was resumed and speeded up. It was not long until the amount of bullion daily extracted by the mills electrified the West by its size. One result was a new rush to buy Comstock shares — almost any shares — and the real beginning of the most remarkable speculative boom in mining history. The Bank of California of course profited and so likewise did its Virginia City agent. Like everyone else in the humming town, Sharon was speculating on his own account. Moreover, his bank connection gave him opportunities denied the average operators, and again he made the most of them. With Ralston, Mills, and a few others, he organized the Union Mill & Mining Company to take over properties foreclosed by their bank. With them he built a railroad to Carson City and Reno and so gained control of traffic to and from the booming town; then he rapidly extended his activities in a dozen other directions. By 1875 a multimillionaire rejoicing in the title of King of the Comstock, Sharon topped off his career by having the Nevada legislature send him to the Senate.

Sharon was fifty-four when, in 1875, he succeeded not only to the control of the newly finished Palace but also to Ralston's country estate at Belmont. In May of that year his wife, Mary Ann, whom he had married at Sacramento in 1852, died. There were three children: Florence Emily, whose wedding a few years later to Lord Fermor-Hesketh was an international social event; Clara Adelaide, who married Francis G. Newlands and died in 1883; and a son, Fred. Thereafter the Senator shuttled between Washington and the Coast. His term as Senator ended in 1881. He kept an apartment at the Palace, entertained elaborately there and at Belmont, indulged his tastes for quoting Shakespeare and Byron, and his passion for poker.

San Franciscans knew him as a pale, chilly little man, neat to the point of old-maidishness in his person, and in his business contacts shrewd and close-fisted. He was not popular, but he was constitutionally unobtrusive. The town accepted him for what he seemed to be: an aging, dapper, sedate little figure, important only because of his millions.

On September 8, 1883 he was arrested for adultery.

2

THE COMPLAINT was filed by one William N. Neilson. It charged the ex-Senator with misconduct with a certain Gertie Deitz. Sharon was booked and released on bail; he then left on a trip east. For three weeks no word of the matter reached the public. Then on September 30 Sharon returned to San Franciso. The next morning the *Call* commented:

As the affair on its face presented a very serious aspect, the *Call* has refrained from publishing the nature of the charges until the accused could be given an opportunity to explain. . . . Mr. Sharon returned . . . last evening. To a *Call* reporter . . . he said: " The written marriage contract into which he [Neilson] claims I entered, and the other similar document bearing my name he professes to have, are simply forgeries."

The charge of adultery puzzled the town, for Sharon was thought to be a widower. But Neilson claimed to have a contract by which Sharon had, on August 26, 1880, entered into a secret marriage. Of Neilson's interest in the affair, the *Call* stated: " Mr. Neilson was neither a lawyer nor a relative of the injured woman, and the reason given by him for the persecution of Mr. Sharon was that the ex-Senator, being a man of wealth, could buy up all the lawyers in the city while Mr. Neilson, a journalist for many years . . . was incorruptible. . . ."

A day or two later there was a hearing on the adultery charge before a police-court judge. Sharon was represented by General W. H. L. Barnes, a conspicuous ornament of the local bar. Barnes denied that his client had signed a marriage contract and demanded that the document be produced. This the prosecution agreed to do provided safeguards were taken to ensure its safety. The judge interrupted a wrangle between opposing lawyers by dismissing the charge. " We certainly could not proceed. . . . As there is no law to punish adultery of the kind alleged in this state, the complaint must fail. . . ."

There the episode might have ended and have been forgotten in a month. That had been the fate of similar suits brought from time to time against others of the city's new millionaires, and of others that never reached the courts. It was easier and often more prudent for the accused to pay over a few hundreds of his abundant dollars and so avoid undesirable publicity; it was said that Sharon himself had recently adopted this reasonable course to still the clamor of another young woman. But it happened that in this instance neither principal was in a mood of reasonableness, and the case failed to follow the conventional pattern. Instead of compromising, Sharon instructed his lawyers to fight to the limit. Suit to have the purported marriage contract declared fraudulent was instituted in the Federal Court. Promptly the opposition made a counter-move. In the Superior Court, Sarah Althea Hill Sharon entered a plea for divorce, for a division of community property, and for suitable alimony.

California began to take notice, and not only California but the entire country. To bring a former United States Senator into court on an adultery charge was no everyday occurrence, even in the lax '80s. Curiosity focused on the plaintiff. Who was Sarah Althea Hill, and what of her claim that she was the ex-Senator's wife and so entitled to a share of his millions?

Not much was known of her. She was thirty-two. She had been in San Francisco ten years. Her parents, who had lived in Missouri, were dead. She had come to San Francisco with an uncle, William Sloan, and a younger brother, Morgan Hill. They had lived with her grandmother, then with her uncle's mother. Later, having quarreled with her grandaunt, she moved to a local hotel. Acquaintances stated that she gave evidence of a good education and of having been reared in a home of refinement. She was described as of medium height, fair but not a pronounced blonde, with bright, rather cold blue eyes and a notably clear complexion. All agreed that she was vivacious, quick-witted, headstrong, and uncommonly pretty.

It was not long before San Franciscans learned more

of her background. On October 4, 1883 the *Bulletin* printed a letter from Judge John L. Wilson, written from Cape Girardeau, Missouri.

The matrimonial fiasco of Miss Althea Hill and Senator William Sharon, as reported in your paper . . . caused a flutter in the social circles of this city. As this is the place of Miss Hill's nativity and where many of her relatives reside . . . I have thought that something in regard to her and her family might not be uninteresting to your readers.

Miss Hill is an orphan, both of her parents having died when she was a mere child. Her father was a lawyer, and was . . . recognized as a man of decided abilities. . . . He left to his children a handsome estate. At the time of his death he was a member of the Missouri legislature, and . . . had attracted the attention of the entire state.

On her mother's side Miss Hill has the credit of being descended from Revolutionary stock. . . . Miss Hill is a niece of the late Governor Wilson Brown, who was also eight years state auditor and held many other offices of trust and profit. She is also a cousin of Senator R. B. Oliver and a niece of the Hon. Isaac Hunter, who is a gentleman of great wealth and was also Miss Hill's guardian.

I called the other day upon a well known judge, of whose household Miss Hill was once a member. . . . He stated:

" I know Miss Hill well. . . . She is possessed of a fine mind and a handsome presence, and I was surprised to hear of her engagement with Senator Sharon. His millions would hardly compensate a handsome and accomplished young woman for his age and reputation, and certainly no one can have a higher family connection than she has. I had always expected that she would make a wiser and better alliance."

Later, on the witness stand during her divorce hearing, the plaintiff gave further details. She had come to San Francisco from Cape Girardeau in 1870. She received an income from her father's estate, which was paid by her guardian through her uncle, William Sloan. She had lived a year and a half with her grand-aunt, then had moved with her brother to the Grand Hotel. This was while the Palace, across the street, was building. There had been a number of other moves: to the Baldwin, to a house on Sutter Street not far from the Sharon residence, to the Galindo, in Oakland, back to the Baldwin. This brought her to 1880 and her first meeting with Sharon.

The examination continued. The witness testified that she had met Sharon at Redwood City. The next meeting was in the spring of 1880. Like everyone else in town she had been speculating in mining stocks, and she had had a moderate success. One day she encountered Sharon in his bank, and he had commented on her winnings in the market. He added that he was planning to boom a certain stock and invited her to call on him. She continued: " I met him again and he referred to the fact that I had not called. I said: ' You had better call on me.' I gave him my address, and that evening he called . . . at my room in the Baldwin. He made himself agreeable for an old gentleman, recited some poetry and sang ' Auld Lang Syne.' . . . He began telling me how he liked the girls and how the girls liked him, and couldn't I learn to like an old man like him? . . ."

Sharon, she stated, was presently offering a high price

for her favor — a thousand dollars a month, his daughter Flora's white horse, and " lots of other things."

Then I told him he had made a mistake in the lady.
. . . That I was an honest girl and had my own affairs to look after. Then he . . . said that he had only said that to tease me; that he had inquired about me and learned that I was a respectable girl of good family, and he wanted to marry me. I said that was a different matter, and we sat down again and talked. . . . He said that if we should be married it would have to be done secretly. I said I would not consent to that, and he said it was necessary, as he had sent a girl to Philadelphia with her mother who would create a scandal about him if he got married. The girl had no reputation to lose, and would come out and ruin his chances of election in Nevada if he got married. I told him I did not believe that story, and he took out a letter from the girl and showed it to me. He tore off part of it and gave it to me.

The witness produced the fragment from her purse, and it was admitted as evidence. Her counsel asked what poems Sharon had recited that evening at the Baldwin. His repertory, it was revealed, included Byron's *Maid of Athens:*

> Maid of Athens, ere we part —
> Give, oh give me back my heart!

For some reason the picture of the elderly ex-Senator assuming so romantic a role amused the entire town. Local papers were presently calling the plaintiff the Rose of Sharon. The phrase was repeated again and again during the years of litigation that followed.

3

THE MARRIAGE contract, cornerstone of the entire suit,
was produced and promptly published in the town's
newspapers:

In the City and County of San Francisco, State of California, on the 25th day of August, A.D. 1880, I, Sarah Althea Hill, of the City and County of San Francisco, State
of California, age 27 years, do here in the presence of Almighty God, take Senator William Sharon, of the State of
Nevada, to be my lawful and wedded husband, and do here
acknowledge and declare myself to be the wife of Senator
William Sharon of the State of Nevada.

SARAH ALTHEA HILL

August 25th, 1880, San Francisco, Cal.

I agree not to make known the contents of this paper
or its existence for two years unless Mr. Sharon himself sees
fit to make it known.

S. A. HILL

In the City and County of San Francisco, State of
California, on the 25th day of August, A.D. 1880, I, Senator
William Sharon, of the State of Nevada, age 60 years, do
here, in the presence of Almighty God, take Sarah Althea
Hill, of the City of San Francisco, Cal., to be my lawful and
wedded wife, and do here acknowledge myself to be the
husband of Sarah Althea Hill.

WM. SHARON, NEVADA

Aug. 25, 1880

The divorce complaint held that such written contracts were legal under Section 75 of the California
Civil Code. The complaint further stated that the two

125

had lived together as man and wife until November 1881, when Sharon had demanded the surrender of the contract and had threatened her with physical violence when she refused. Sharon was charged, too, with marital infidelity with the aforementioned Miss Deitz. Asking for a suitable division of property, the complaint stated that when the marriage contract was signed Sharon's fortune was not over five millions and that his monthly income did not exceed thirty thousand dollars. Since their marriage, by prudent management, his assets had increased to fifteen millions and his monthly income to above a hundred thousand. Sarah asked for an equal division of the common property.

With so much at stake, both sides were at pains to provide themselves with adequate legal advice. Sarah's staff was augmented until it numbered seven prominent attorneys of the town: Tyler & Tyler, Flournoy & Flournoy, Levy, Clement, and — presently — David S. Terry. Sharon was defended by General Barnes and O. P. Evans; later there were further additions to his staff too. With so much legal wisdom on hand, progress was slow; each step of the proceedings was subject to delay while lawyers argued points of procedure.

Sarah herself was far from awed by this array of legal talent. It early grew clear that she would not be content to play the passive role of injured and abandoned wife. Then and later she did not hesitate to take matters into her own hands if she felt her interests demanded it.

When her testimony reached the point of the signing of the marriage contract, Sarah opened her purse and produced an envelope. Presumedly it contained the contract. General Barnes demanded that he be allowed to see it. What followed reflects the bitterness already engendered between the opposing camps.

SARAH: If Your Honor will take all the responsibility upon yourself, and compel me to I will deliver the document.

COURT: I cannot take any responsibility. Is the paper inside this envelope?

SARAH: I desire that neither Mr. Sharon nor Mr. Barnes should handle it. I consider it my honor, and have regarded it as my honor for three long years. . . . Mr. Sharon knows all about it.

BARNES: I object to this lady standing there and making these statements. Mr. Sharon knows nothing about it. It is a fraud and forgery from end to end.

SARAH: He knows every word in this paper, so help me God. He dictated it to me, and knows all about it.

MR. SHARON: I tell the court it is the damnedest lie that was ever uttered on earth.

BARNES: Your Honor sees that this is what comes from permitting this kind of thing to go on.

SARAH: I say he knows all about it.

BARNES: I think she ought to be stopped.

SARAH: I do not like to offend Your Honor, but he has got his millions against me. I have been driven from my home. He has taken my money, and I have got no money to defend this with.

COURT: If you are not quiet, I shall have to ask the sheriff to remove you.

At this point, G. W. Tyler, Sarah's counsel, interposed:

Miss Hill will leave the paper in the hands of the court.

COURT: The court cannot accept it. I will hand the paper back. If she wishes to obey the order of the court she can hand the paper to the clerk. I will direct him not to part with the custody of it. That is all I can do.

SARAH: I have already had photographic copies taken and have them here with me. You can examine the paper and see that they are all right.

TYLER: The gentleman does not desire photographic copies.

BARNES: I do.

SARAH: I have apparatus in my own parlor and they can come there and photograph it.

BARNES: If this tongue can only be stopped, we can do all the talking.

TYLER (to Sarah) : You refuse to deliver it, you say?

SARAH: Unless the judge orders me to.

TYLER: He has ordered it.

SARAH: He says he refuses to order it.

TYLER: No, you are mistaken.

COURT: I will tell you. . . . If you refuse to deliver that paper to the clerk for the inspection of the opposite side, the paper cuts no figure in this case. It is so much waste paper. . . .

SARAH: As Your Honor orders it, I, in your presence, deliver it to the court and hold you, Judge, responsible for my document.

COURT: You can save yourself the trouble of making any speech like that. You understand that there is no responsibility in the matter. Now, Mr. Clerk, you will have a photographic copy of that taken today.

The paper was handed to Barnes. He glanced at it, then said to Sharon:

128

It is not your signature.

SHARON (after looking at it) : It is a forgery, the whole thing.

TYLER: I object to any such language as that on the part of General Barnes, or on the part of his client; I think it is outrageous that a man should stand here in a court of justice, after he has had the paper brought out, and before Your Honor, who is to try the case, denounce it as a forgery.

SHARON: I stand to it, and say it is a forgery.

TYLER: Don't you dare to repeat that here before the court.

COURT: The court will always protect itself. I did not hear the remark.

The wrangle between Sharon and Tyler continued, until the court broke in:

Mr. Sharon, be quiet. Mr. Tyler, another word from you and I shall certainly commit you for contempt of court. You know your duty.

TYLER: Certainly; and so do these gentlemen; and yet both repeated that remark aloud to be heard.

COURT: Mr. Sheriff, remove Mr. Sharon from the court-room.

SHARON: I won't say a word to the court.

COURT (decisively) : Remove Mr. Sharon from the court-room.

The Sheriff escorted Sharon outside.

BARNES: I want to show the paper to Mr. Sharon. Now he has been removed and I cannot show it to him.

TYLER: You shall have a chance by and by.

There was another scene before Sarah got her contract back. On the court's instructions, the clerk took the document to a photographer and had a copy made. It was then placed overnight in a safe in the judge's chambers. But when the time came to return it to the plaintiff the next day, the door of the safe could not be opened. The judge sent for a locksmith, then entered his courtroom and, in some embarrassment, explained the situation.

His story confirmed Sarah's worst suspicions. She was convinced Sharon had got possession of the contract.

Judge, this will not do. I can't go away without that paper. You promised to give it to me at twelve o'clock today.

COURT: You shall have it, just as soon as the safe can be opened.

Sarah broke into " loud lamentations." All efforts to calm her proving useless, the judge sought refuge in his chamber. She declared dramatically:

I will not stir from this place until that paper is placed in my hands. It is all that stands between me and destruction. I will not go.

The locksmith finally opened the safe. The judge returned in triumph.

COURT: I will now order this paper into the hands of your counsel, for identification.

SARAH: No, no, no! Give it to me, Judge. You said you would give it to me.

By direction of the court the paper was handed her. She gave it searching scrutiny.

COURT: Do you identify it as the paper you delivered to the clerk of this court yesterday?

SARAH: Yes.

COURT: Inspect it carefully.

SARAH (after a second examination) : Yes, sir, this is the paper.

COURT (with increasing suavity) : I very much regret the delay of twenty minutes, madam, and I beg your pardon.

Sarah folded the paper, tucked it under her cloak, and departed.

While the paper was out of her possession, the press had been permitted to examine it. It was described as soiled and folded, showing evidence of having been much handled. It was written, in Sarah's hand, on both sides of a single piece of ruled notepaper. It had a number of curious features, all of which were later the subject of prolonged arguments. For one thing, the writing started on the second page, and the last four lines were written in the unruled space at the top of the first page. Sharon's signature occupied the first ruled line on this page; beneath his signature was the date, August 25, 1880.

From these circumstances the *Call's* reporter made some deductions:

The autograph appears to be written just as a man would write it for a friend's album. It also appears to have been written in consonance with a well-established rule of businessmen and the instinct of rich men particularly, who never write their names in blank, save at the top of a sheet of paper, where it is supposed nothing can be written above it. . . .

It is understood that it is the theory . . . that he [Sharon] was asked for his autograph; that he gave it, writing his name near the top of the first page of a sheet of notepaper, and that the alleged contract was written above it, and on the other side of the half-sheet. As evidence of this they point to the fact that on the first half of the page the " contract " is written in lines much further apart than towards the bottom, when it became obvious to the writer that the space was limited, and on the side on which the signature appears, and above, four lines are crowded into the space occupied by two on the other side. . . .

But this theory, plausible as it sounded, had a serious defect. It assumed that Sharon's signature was genuine — a point both Sharon and his counsel refused to admit. By then the question of the authenticity of the contract was being debated all over the Coast. Naturally the result was inconclusive. There were numerous arguments on each side, but no really convincing evidence. The differences of opinion persisted, in and out of court, for years. In the end the issue was as much in doubt as it had been in the beginning.

4

THUS FAR the contest had hardly begun, but already it had brought on suits and counter-suits, threats and recriminations, and had divided the public into sharply opposed factions.

More was to come. Before the year 1883 was out, the

ex-newspaperman Neilson sued Sharon for slander, and a few months later Neilson was in turn sued by Sarah on an embezzlement charge. The grand jury indicted both Sarah and Neilson on charges of forgery, perjury, and conspiracy — Neilson for perjury in charging Sharon with adultery with Gertie Deitz, Sarah for swearing she was Sharon's wife.

Both sides tried hard to enlist the support of public opinion. Evidence was frequently published in the newspapers before it was presented in court. Reporters were present at the taking of depositions; witnesses gave interviews stating how they planned to testify, and Sarah's letters to Sharon and others were published in advance of their introduction as evidence.

The public read every word and became more violently partisan than ever. Groups of citizens met to discuss the progress of the trial and to support their favorites, not always with words alone. Neilson, the stormy petrel of the early days of the trial, one day addressed a crowd at the Workingman's Forum — the sandlots opposite the new City Hall — and was pelted with eggs by supporters of the capitalist. He shouted: " This is just what I wanted; those eggs were hurled at me under the direction of Sharon, and mark my words, I will make use of it to advantage. . . ." Meantime efforts to discredit the journalist, and many other figures on both sides, were under way. Rumors were published that Neilson had once been convicted of forgery in Australia. A few days later he was arrested for creating a disturbance at a meeting in Metropolitan Hall. Neilson was usually in hot water of one kind or another, a circumstance that troubled him not at all.

Everyone connected with the case presently became a newspaper notable, but Sarah was always the star of the melodrama. Her beauty (all were agreed on that if on nothing else), her suspicion of friend and foe, her sharp tongue, her occasional outbursts of rage, and her general flair for the dramatic kept her constantly in the center of the stage. Newspaper-readers early came to expect the sensational from this volcanic young woman and they were not often disappointed. She was in Tyler's office one day when General Barnes came in on business connected with the case. She rushed at the attorney shouting torrents of abuse, beside herself with anger at what she believed to be his unfair tactics while she had been on the witness stand. A little later she was quoted as having threatened to " shoot Sharon on sight " if the latter succeeded in having the marriage contract declared a forgery. Her bitterness was not lessened by the fact that detectives in Sharon's employ had been investigating her past life in the hope of uncovering something detrimental to her character. They had had but indifferent success. Finally, however, they produced a young man named Burchard who proved willing to testify that he had once been engaged to her and had, moreover, been her lover. Burchard was described as an everyday young man, of medium height, with a thin, pale face and a long, curling mustache. He had met Sarah, he stated, through friends of both at the Palace in April 1881. " She was leaning on Senator Sharon's arm . . . but accepted my invitation to stroll about the corridor." They met again in her rooms at the Grand and later at Belmont, where they had become engaged and where the alleged intimacies had occurred. In his deposition Burchard added that he presently heard reports reflecting on the young woman's character and so had broken their engagement. Subsequently he altered this story in several important respects. The result was his arrest for perjury. This added yet another to the list of criminal proceedings growing out of the main struggle.

The trial established that Sharon's infatuation with " Allie " Hill had begun in the summer of 1880, when he induced her to move from the Baldwin to the Grand, and that they had lived together, not altogether secretly, for more than a year. Long before the year was up, however, Sharon's ardor had cooled and the latter months were far from idyllic. Sharon in fact tried hard to terminate a romance that had become burdensome to one of his years and infirmities, and Sarah as stubbornly refused to be cast off.

Details of their none too tranquil romance reached the public when letters of both were read in court and made part of the record. Among Sarah's correspondents were a Mr. and Mrs. Reighart, who had been close friends of Sharon and " Allie " before the rift. A long letter to the Reigharts, written by Sarah shortly after the trial began, was introduced by Sharon's attorneys. It stated that Sharon had first tried to terminate their association following an illness, during which he feared he might die. " He at once began to importune and coax, and carried it so far as to try to buy me to give up my paper and sign a quit-claim to my rights in his estate." Sarah told him she had mislaid the paper, and he then resorted to force. She went on to relate that he had choked her until she fainted, then locked her in a closet of his bedroom, believing her dead. When she revived, Sharon, delighted to find he had not committed murder, agreed to a reconciliation. But a few days later, urged by his son-in-law, Frank Newlands, he again tried to get rid of her. The manager of the Grand Hotel, owned by the ex-Senator, ordered her to vacate her rooms. She hastened to Sharon's suite at the Palace; he refused to see her. " That afternoon I went out to my grandmother, and when I returned to my home I found every door of my rooms taken off, the bells out and the carpets ripped up. I had only my furniture and the bare floor. My maid had fled in fright and I was left alone. . . ."

Six months later there was another reconciliation, also brief. Again she blamed Sharon's relatives for the rift. She moved from the hotel and presently reached a decision to bring the matter into court. Her letter to the Reigharts ended: " You might think this case was brought wrong. Under the laws of this country it had to be brought in that way to declare and prove my claim lawful. After I am declared the wife I can ask for alimony or a divorce."

She signed herself: " Mrs. William Sharon (nee Allie Hill)."

There were a great many other letters from Sarah to Sharon and others; all were printed in the local papers. General Barnes classified them as follows:

1. Tender: from " Allie " to " Dear Sen."
2. Gossipy: from " Allie " to the Reigharts.
3. Explanatory: from " Mrs. Sharon."
4. Notes, checks, etc., signed " Miss Hill."

The attorney probably placed the following in the first group:

Senator:

I hear you are quite ill. I should like if you would let me come and read to you, or sit with you of evenings and wait on you. Perhaps I may prove entertaining enough to help drive away both your cares and your pains and you know no one would do so with a more loving heart than I. You surely have not forgotten what a nice little nurse I proved myself in your last illness, and you cannot but remember how willing I was to be with you. . . . And I assure you, you will find me as willing and agreeable now. . . . Please don't deny me the pleasure of being with you while you are sick. . . . I should like to see you today, anyway, it being the first of the month, and I would like to get some money. I don't like to have to ask for it while you are ill, but you know house bills have to be paid. . . .

With love, I am always,

A.

The letters were a source of almost endless argument. Sharon's counsel claimed that those of Sarah to the Senator were not such as a married woman, even though her marriage was secret, would write her husband. In the latter case, Barnes and his associates argued, she would have adopted a different tone — that of confidentially demanding her rights. They contended that these notes, alternately coaxing and pleading, could have been written only by a woman aware that she had no legal claim on the man to whom they were addressed and that her position in society was dependent on his whims. Sarah's attorneys countered by pointing out that she was without funds except for such sums as Sharon gave her, that she naturally desired to avoid a break with her multimillionaire husband (who was old and in bad health), and that she had hesitated to seek relief in the courts because of her promise to keep their marriage secret.

Sharon's letters to Sarah were less numerous and far shorter, but they did not arouse less controversy. They were mostly brief penciled scrawls, rather formal in tone and usually concerned with money matters. He was sending her funds, or was instructing the cashier at the hotel to advance her certain sums. He had been away longer than he had expected, but hoped to be back on a certain date. He hoped she was well. They were definitely not the letters of an ardent lover, yet their introduction seriously damaged Sharon's case. For a number of the curt and emotionless notes began: " Dear Wife."

Sharon and his attorneys met this situation by explaining that the " Dear Wife " letters were like the marriage contract; both were forgeries.

5

SARAH AND SHARON were long in the witness chair, and their testimony — some given willingly, some wrested from them during cross-examination — was avidly read all over the Coast. Flora Sharon's marriage three years earlier, to Lord Hesketh, had been one of the notable events in the social history of the state. Sharon's infatuation with " Allie " Hill had then been at its height. The two were much together, and gossip about them had reached the ears of the future Lady Hesketh. When " Allie," on the stand, was questioned about that period, the crowded courtroom listened closely.

QUESTION: Did the witness go to the wedding?

SARAH: No . . . to the reception. It was announced that only the most intimate friends of the family would attend the ceremony and as I knew that Miss Flora disliked me very much . . . I preferred to stay away and save trouble. . . . Between the time of the wedding and the departure of Mr. Sharon for the East with the Hesketh party we were together nearly all the time. . . .

QUESTION: Did Mr. Sharon write you anything from Washington about moving to the Palace?

SARAH: Yes; he wanted me to before he went away. . . . But . . . my grandmother thought I should not move until Mr. Sharon's return. . . . After his return he told me he wanted me to go down to Belmont to entertain some friends of his, and to invite my grandmother, uncle and brother. They objected to going on my invitation, and said they should be invited by him, and he invited them. Cornelius Vanderbilt, Colonel and Mrs. Stagg, Governor and Mrs. Reighart, Mr. Luxton and Mr. Burril were among those who went down. . . .

The questions swung to a later period, after Sharon's ardor had cooled and he was trying hard to rid himself of her. By what method had he ousted her from her rooms at the Grand?

SARAH: He said I should sign a paper or he would turn me out of the hotel and disgrace me. I refused. . . . It was some kind of agreement by which I was to get $100,-000 and $500 per month. I was also to give up the contract and acknowledge that I had no claim on him. . . . The next night I went to a party, and when I got back to the hotel I found that men had entered my room from a side door and torn up the hall carpet and taken the doors off from my rooms. I went over to Mr. Sharon's room and seeking Ki [Sharon's Chinese servant], asked him where Mr. Sharon was. He said he had gone to Belmont. I knew he had not gone without Ki and told him so. . . . I went back later to Mr. Sharon's room. Ki had left the outside door open, and I walked in and rapped at Mr. Sharon's room and begged him to give me a place to sleep and not to treat me in that way. He ordered me to go away, and said that if I did not he would have a servant put me out. I begged him not to treat me so and he rang the bell for a servant. I heard the man coming, and stepped into a little closet and stayed there when the servant looked for me. When he left, Ki came in and saw me in the closet. I put up my finger, like that [hand extended, index finger out], and said " Shoo "! to Ki. Ki fell down and yelled as if I had shot him. Mr. Sharon ran out and ran into the elevator. . . .

Clearly, Sharon's belated romance had not been a tranquil one. When he reached the stand, the elderly ex-Senator gave added testimony to that effect. His manner in court was cool, but he spoke in so low a tone that court stenographers had trouble hearing him. Sharon apologized for the difficulty — it was because he was not wearing his teeth. He was asked his version of the episode in which Sarah had accused him of choking her.

She climbed through the transom into my room, by
breaking the iron catch. I was very ill at the time and she
annoyed me and made me nervous by walking up and
down, and I said to her: " I wish you would break your
damned neck." I spoke calmly to her and told her to go
out of the room. She would not, and I took hold of her
and pushed her into an adjoining room. She lay on the
floor and I told her not to carry on like that or I would
send for the watchman. She still lay there and I took a
pitcher of cold water and poured it over her and told her
to get up and lie on the bed. She did so. That is the origin
of that trouble. . . .

QUESTION: Did you ever say to Miss Hill that if she
would let you live with her you would give her a thousand
dollars a month and your daughter's white horse?

SHARON: Nothing of the kind ever occurred. I offered her five hundred dollars a month to live with me,
and she accepted it. . . .

He was asked what kind of settlement he had offered.

She came into my room in November 1881 after we
had had some talk of a settlement. I told her I wanted to
settle with her, and did not want her to visit my rooms any
more, as her conduct had been offensive to me. I offered
to pay her $5,000, and she said that would not do; that she
wanted $10,000. I said I would not give her $10,000 but
would give her $7,500. I gave her $5,000 and a note for
$1,500 and another for $1,000. In return she gave me a
receipt in full for all claims and demands. . . . I gave her
a check for $5,000, payable to her order. She said she did

not want to go to the bank, and I tore that check up and gave her one payable to order, and it was paid to her Uncle Sloan. . . . The receipt I took from her I put in a pocket-book I carried in my coat. I never saw it again. . . . I was sitting in my parlor a few days later and heard Miss Hill coming. I was angry and rushed toward her and said: " You —— ——, you have stolen that receipt," for I was satisfied she had stolen it. She ran away and I sent for Mr. Thorne. . . . I told Thorne to order her out of the Grand Hotel. . . .

Such revelations gave the ex-Senator a renown far greater than his public services had ever won. A few weeks after he left the witness stand, court adjourned for the summer and Sharon went to Chicago to the national political conventions. Interest in the nominations of Cleveland and Blaine did not cause newspapermen to overlook the fact that Sharon was in town. A reporter for the *Herald* dropped in at his rooms at the Palmer House and found him " with the frankness of his kind and the training of a Pacific Coaster," entertaining a group of friends with stories of the trial.

Sharon is a character. His like was never before seen in this country. . . . He is a gentleman in manner, a keen man of business, a devoted father to his children, a prudent manager of his fortune, a warm hearted friend and a relentless foe. His weaknesses, as events have shown, are poetry, wine and women. His ardent love of the one is shown by his frequent quotations; his love of the other by frequent potations, and his experiences with the last in a limited sense by his luckless escapade with Sarah Althea. In person, Mr. Sharon's inches and avoirdupois are at strange variance with the list of his bonds or the record

142

of his loves. He is, to use a homely phrase, " a runt." . . .
But his chief charm is his Mark Tapley-like jollity in the
face of adversity that some would think even $20,000,000
could not offset. . . .

The Senator sat in his shirt-sleeves on the side of the
bed, swinging his short legs and smoking a cigar. M. C.
Budd, an old San Francisco acquaintance . . . sat in a
big arm chair. Morrow, of the Pacific Coast delegation,
sat in another big chair. . . . Senator Jones, Sharon's old-
time friend, was also there. An ebony stand, a decanter
with a plumed helmet with " C. & G." on it, a few glasses
and a box of cigars completed the outfit. Mr. Sharon was
holding open house, receiving jokes and returning jibes.
Naturally the conversation turned to the exciting court
episodes of the past ninety days. . . .

" Boys, it was a scrape and a bad one, but, thank God,
I'm getting out of it. You fellows may laugh, but what is it
the poet, Pope, says:

> Virtue she finds too painful an endeavor
> Content to dwell in decencies forever.

" I'll admit it; I've been indecent. But I'd like to
know what any of you fellows would have done under the
same circumstances."

There was a painful silence, and Mr. Budd reached
for the ebony stand.

" Yes," said Mr. Sharon, " it was pretty tough to go
on the stand and admit that I had been such a fool; but
what are you going to do — be blackmailed? Not much."

Somebody here suggested that perhaps a couple of
thousand dollars would have fixed things up.

" Oh, no; you don't know that crowd. . . . In the
first place the woman was bad and reckless. I treated her
honorably, as the world would call it. I gave her a splendid

income. But she wanted more. She invaded my rooms; she pried into my business secrets; she rummaged my papers. . . . Of course that would disgust any man. I saw I was in a box, and resolved to fly —

> Fly like a youthful hart or roe,
> Over the hills where spices grow.

" I gave her $7,500 to call it square. That was right, wasn't it Jones? "

Senator Jones nodded.

" Well," continued the " defendant," " it wasn't enough, and then she got that scoundrel Neilson, from Australia, to egg on her suit. I could have settled it any time for $20,000 — $10,000 to her and $10,000 to Neilson. But not one cent! Millions for defense — not a cent for tribute."

" But, Senator," said Mr. Budd, " — economy. You surely have spent more than that."

" To date, yes, I should say so, and twice that. But I will not be blackmailed out of a cent. I paid that woman well. I gave her a small fortune. I mean now not only to beat her blackmail suit, but I will land her in the penitentiary. I shall have both her and Neilson indicted for conspiracy and send them to state prison if I can. And I'm not so sure but I'll catch Tyler, too, her counsel."

" But, Senator," said one of the party, ". . . how did you ever get into such a snap? "

" And you ask that! " said the Senator, as he reached for the ebony stand. " What is it the poet Thompson says?

> He saw her charming, but he saw not half
> The charms her downcast modesty concealed.

Who could resist it? I read the ' Maid of Athens ' to her. She melted; then ' the kiss, snatched hasty from the side-

144

long maid,' did the business. Whatever might have been lacking, $500 a month supplied."

There was a general laugh, in the midst of which the Senator said:

" But that is past. My object now is to expose the conspiracy and get the leaders in jail. I sent two men to Australia to hunt up Neilson's record. . . . I found he had been convicted of forgery there and sentenced to seven years penal servitude. I have had detectives travelling over the country hunting up Miss Hill's earlier anteced-ents. I don't care to crush the woman more than necessary, but if it were necessary we would show her to have been an adventuress from her twentieth year. That's enough to say. Oh, I've been ready for her at every turn. What is it Pope says in ' The Wife of Bath '?

> The mouse that trusts to one poor hole
> Can never be a mouse of any soul."

And as Mr. Sharon quoted this gem his eyes shone with delight, and he invited his friends to the ebony stand.

Someone asked Mr. Sharon what Sir Thomas Hesketh of England, his son-in-law, thought of the Hill episode.

" Oh, he's a thoroughbred. He knows his father-in-law.

> 'Tis a fine thing to be a father-in-law
> To a very magnificent three-tailed bashaw.

— as the old play has it. Hesketh is a good one. I doubted him at first, and sent three men to Liverpool and London — it cost me $10,000 to hunt up his record. It was a good one. But I say (to Senator Jones) it would have been a jolly idea had he concluded at the same time to hunt up mine, eh? "

This sally was too much for some of the Senator's friends and the party broke up. . . .

6

NOT ONLY Sharon and Sarah were brought into prominence by the trial, but a dozen lesser figures: attorneys for both sides, a long list of witnesses, the presiding judge, assorted friends and hangers-on. Particular interest attached to George Washington Tyler and General W. H. L. Barnes, generalissimos of the opposing legal armies. Both were wily and resourceful, and each delighted to match wits with the other. Their exchanges could usually be counted on to enliven sessions when witnesses were prosy or lawyers of their staffs wrangled over technicalities. A writer for the *Alta* compared them to steel and flint. Barnes was the polished steel; Tyler the rugged flint. " When they meet fire is the natural result." It was said that Tyler hoped to win " half the Palace Hotel " if Sarah's contract was declared genuine, and he was accordingly extremely energetic. He personally conducted all the direct and cross-examination of witnesses, made most of the arguments, and only infrequently accepted suggestions from his five associates. This was in the early period of the trial; later he was to share authority with a new member of Sarah's staff: David S. Terry.

Tyler's handling of Sharon's witnesses was typical of his methods. His manner was mild, his questions considerate, his smile bland and affable.

But the adage of the calm preceding the storm is very applicable to this bulldog of the bar, and woe be to the opposition's witness who deludes himself with the idea that he has touched a soft spot in his heart. . . . The de-

General Grant Enters the Palace Grand Court, 1879

From a diorama in the San Francisco Building of the Golden Gate International Exposition.
Photograph by Clem Albers, courtesy the *San Francisco Chronicle*

Grant in His Suite at the Palace

lusion may be encouraged by an hour or day of quiet querying, but sooner or later a committal answer is returned to some one of Mr. Tyler's insinuating queries and then the storm breaks. It is usually of such force and violence that the unhappy wight . . . in five minutes sees a trial for perjury and all the horrors of hell fire . . . staring him in the face.

Of General Barnes it was stated that he imitated his Creator by doing all things well. Some years later the luster of his military career was dimmed when a search of the War Department files failed to disclose that he had attained a higher rank than corporal. But Barnes none the less had claim to his title. He had once been a Major General in the California National Guard. He was an important figure in local society, the cut of his clothes was admired and imitated by half the young blades of the town, and his reputation as a whist-player, billiardist, and raconteur was of the highest.

His courtroom manner was the opposite of Tyler's. So far as outward appearance went he seemed less interested in the proceedings than anyone else in the room.

When a witness is called the General gently coaxes from him the testimony desired, with as little waste of words as possible, and then resigns him to the prosecution with such an air of flattering courtesy that the unfortunate is unable to determine whether he is under obligation to the General or the General is under obligation to him. While the witness is undergoing cross-examination and is not swearing to anything objectionable Mr. Barnes employs his time in sketching his surroundings and converting innumerable sheets of paper into endless patterns of wallpaper, demonstrations of difficult shots on a fifteen-ball pool table, and fancy lettering of all sorts. [A later generation has a word for this activity.] A part of his time is taken up with teaching the press reporters a new system of forgery, which consists in simply turning the signature to be imitated upside down and sketching it. One ear, however, is always lent to Mr. Tyler's questions, and seldom does an obnoxious query secure an answer before his objection is interposed and the witness' reply checked. . . . In law and repartee the General's favorite weapon is the insidious and polished stiletto rather than the cannon or blunderbuss. . . .

Barnes did not always disdain the blunderbuss. When the "Dear Wife" letters, allegedly written by Sharon, were under discussion, an expert witness replied to a question by the remark: "Yes, it bears about such a resemblance as a jackass does to a horse."

TYLER (with a broad smile) : Your Honor, I move to strike the jackass out.
BARNES: Well take your hat and go, then.
COURT: Gentlemen! Gentlemen!

It was commented that this sort of thing was costing Sharon a thousand dollars a day.

But Sharon's troubles were not all financial. His dislike of Tyler was warmly reciprocated, and the attorney lost no opportunity to make things uncomfortable for the millionaire. He habitually referred to him, not by name, but as "that man" — to the latter's natural annoyance. At one stage in the cross-examination Tyler asked Sharon suavely if he "had other mistresses to whom you have paid $500 a month in the last five or

David S. Terry and Mammy Pleasant

Sarah Althea Hill and William Sharon

Sketched during the Trial by an Artist for *Alta California*, June 1, 1884

six years." Later Tyler launched another attack, this time on Sharon's attitude in the courtroom:

Your Honor, I will not answer for what may occur . . . if that man is permitted to remain . . . and do as he did the other day, sitting staring at my client and laughing in her face. . . .

The judge suggested that Sarah might avoid annoyance by refusing to look at the defendant. Sharon's counsel denied that his client had stared at the plaintiff.

TYLER: I don't care what anybody says. I know what I say and what I saw. . . .

COURT: Mr. Tyler, when you say you don't care what anybody says, do I understand you to include the court?

TYLER (blandly): Why, no, Your Honor. Of course I do not include the court, but I will say that that man's conduct is enough to aggravate anyone, even the devil himself. When looking at my client he seemed to gloat, and his face had upon it a look of triumph. . . .

One day Sharon and Barnes came to Tyler's office to witness the taking of a deposition. They were accompanied by two private detectives. Tyler objected to the presence of the latter and protested hotly to the general:

Say, Barnes, this is a matter of principle with me. If you can bring two men in here you can bring a regiment. What do you want these big bodyguards for? Do you think I'm going to kill your client?

BARNES: Not at all. Mr. Sharon is worth much more to you alive than he could be dead.

Tyler meantime had got himself in trouble in another of the local courts. While the county grand jury was considering the question of whether to vote an indictment against Sarah on a charge of criminal conspiracy, Tyler wrote the jurors a letter in his client's defense. The letter contained statements that the jurors deemed libelous. He was accordingly haled before Judge Toohy and ordered into custody. What happened next made entertaining reading at thousands of San Francisco breakfast tables:

The deputy sheriff approached Mr. Tyler and appeared immensely flattered when the latter took his arm, and mildly remarked: " You don't want me, you know," and dropped his arm and dropped himself into the comfortable chair. The deputy looked around with a comprehensive smile, which was frozen stiff, however, when he met Judge Toohy's stern and inquiring glance. The deputy suddenly realized that there was a duty for him to perform, and timidly advancing to Mr. Tyler, said: " Won't you walk down to the sheriff's office with me? "

Judge Tyler glared in response, but his associate, Mr. Flournoy, said pacifyingly: " Yes, walk down to the sheriff's office with him."

" Where's your order? " suddenly roared Mr. Tyler, turning fiercely upon the amazed deputy.

" I — I haven't got any," gasped he.

" Then, sir, don't you dare lay a finger on me, sir! " And with each word the roar of Tyler became mightier . . . and the deputy appeared bereft of power of thought or action as Mr. Tyler began to stalk majestically from the room.

" Your prisoner is escaping," someone yelled to the deputy, and the latter sidled up to Judge Toohy and said:

"Mr. Tyler is leaving the room, Your Honor."

"He is in your custody," laconically replied the Court.

The unhappy deputy realized that he had been bluffed and became as suddenly determined to reprieve his official dignity. . . . But Mr. Tyler had already disappeared down the stairs. The deputy started after him. . . . The crowd followed pell mell. On Kearny Street . . . the scene attracted people from blocks around. Tyler fled along with sufficient celerity to keep his lead of the deputy. The latter appeared big-eyed, breathless and greatly agitated, and the crowd pressed on excitedly. Mr. Tyler dove into the Sheriff's office, slammed the door in the face of the deputy, who turned his distracted attention to keeping out the crowd.

Tyler got off with a five-hundred-dollar fine.

7

A CURIOUS stream of witnesses presently appeared and much bizarre testimony was given.

Mammy Pleasant, elderly, coal-black Negro woman, was called to the stand. She had been in regular attendance since the trial began, a mysterious, rather sinister figure. San Franciscans knew her well — and credited her with a Machiavellian shrewdness. She was the housekeeper for Thomas Bell, eccentric local banker, and was said to rule like a despot over his gloomy wooden residence at Octavia and Bush streets. She was known to have considerable wealth and important connections, and to wield a great deal of power through the manipulation of certain obscure channels of influence. She was easily the most curious character of San Francisco's Bonanza age; many believed it was she who was financing Sarah's suit.

The faithfulness with which she attended each session of the trial bore out the theory that she had a financial stake in its outcome. Hangers-on watched for her arrival each morning a few minutes before court assembled, and stared as she was driven to the curb in a shining carriage drawn by a team of bays, descended, and stalked solemnly up the steps. She occupied a chair directly behind Sarah and Judge Terry. " Often her head is thrust between the pair as she leans forward to impart some bit of information or to get off a joke. In the case of the latter she leans back and smiles a smile that causes the observer to make an involuntary comparison with the tombstones in a graveyard on a very dark night, with a bit of red fire thrown in." She closely followed every word of the evidence, with apparently a shrewd recognition of its value. Her admiration for Sarah was boundless and she greeted with satisfaction every point that seemed favorable to her cause. General Barnes was her especial aversion — " seldom does a day pass without she accuses him of more or less disreputable doings, and always winding up by charging him with conspiring directly against her." Unlike her admired Sarah, whose daily changes of costume lent color to a drab scene, Mammy Pleasant always appeared in somber black, topped off by a huge black straw hat, its brim tied tightly down over her head so that it resembled a coal scuttle.

On the stand she proved a glib witness:

I have lived in San Francisco since 1849. I met the plaintiff in the Grand Hotel about two years ago. She wanted me to furnish a house for her. I asked to see the marriage contract to see if she had any guarantee for her money. The plaintiff showed the contract, and then I went to Mr. Sharon. I told him that I heard that he had some kind of relation with Miss Hill and owed her money, and asked him if it would be all right if I furnished the house. Mr. Sharon said all right, go ahead and furnish it and he would pay the bills. . . .

The front-row seat beside Mammy Pleasant was usually occupied by another of Sarah's friends and satellites, Nellie Brackett. She was described as a girl of about twenty, with a fresh, rather pretty face, which usually bore an expression of " complete and almost childish delight in looking at her patroness. . . ." Like Mammy Pleasant, Nellie was a faithful attendant at the trial and gave rapt attention to all that went on. " When something that particularly pleases this queerly-assorted pair occurs, their heads fly together by common impulse for a whispered comparison of impressions, and then again they resume their watchful regard of the witness."

Nellie, too, had her day on the witness stand. She stated that Sarah had shown her the marriage contract in 1882. She had often visited Sharon's rooms at the Palace with the plaintiff. Her testimony revealed that, like Sarah herself, the girl delighted in intrigue. The town was amused when she told how, in Sharon's absence, she had once inveigled Ki into a game of poker and so had distracted his attention while Sarah sprinkled " love powders " on the floor of Sharon's bedroom and put some in his whisky. Amusement heightened when the girl revealed details of another exploit: how, on Sarah's suggestion, she had concealed herself behind a bureau in Sharon's bedchamber and so had been witness to an ensuing tender scene between the elderly lover and his lady. She was with Sarah in the latter's rooms at the Grand the day Ki entered carrying Gertie Deitz's baby, allegedly on orders from Sharon. Nellie recalled the incident clearly because another of Sarah's friends, also present, had remarked that the baby resembled the senator, thereby incurring Sarah's displeasure. Miss Deitz's baby, and Sharon's liking for it, had suggested yet another plot. With Mammy Pleasant they debated the question of whether Sarah too should acquire a baby. Mammy Pleasant favored the scheme; to her eyes it presented no difficulty. She had, so the testimony ran, " often gotten babies for ladies in San Francisco."

As the trial progressed, it became evident that Sharon's attorneys planned to make much of Sarah's visits to fortune-tellers and of her belief in the efficacy of love potions. Tyler, of course, was contemptuous of the whole procedure, and so informed the court. " This matter," he stated, " of woman's belief in the power of charms to win or regain man's love runs through all history."

Unimpressed by Tyler's argument, General Barnes contended that the court should know to what lengths the plaintiff had gone to secure an " unnatural control " over the defendant in an attempt to induce him to marry her in fact. " The defense " he added, " pro-

poses to show that she did doctor his food and wine
. . . and scoured the city in search of fortune tellers,
magic, spells. . . ."

He proceeded to make good his promise. For days a
strange assortment of witnesses trooped through the
courtroom, while spectators were treated to an exposé
of the arts of black magic as it was locally practiced on
the credulous.

On the morning of March 18 Dr. Meares, county
health officer, was called. He carried a large package.
Judge Evans, one of the Sharon attorneys, opened it,
revealing a bundle of moldy clothing. He lifted one of
the articles — a man's sock — and asked Sarah:

Did you ever see this before?

SARAH: I never did.

EVANS: Did you ever see this? (He held aloft a bit
of a man's shirt.)

SARAH: I never did.

EVANS: Did you ever see this? (Exhibiting a piece of
discolored cloth that may once have been white.)

SARAH: I never did.

EVANS: Did you not, on the first of May 1883, go with
Miss Nellie Brackett and get down into a newly-made
grave and place these articles under a rough box in which
a coffin was to be placed?

SARAH: I did not.

EVANS: Did you not tell the man in charge of the
grave that you wanted to place the articles under that box?

SARAH: I did not. I never did such a thing in my life.

EVANS: Did you not tell this man, George Villard,
that if those articles could rest under that box with a body
in it, it would work a charm and draw a rich man to you?

SARAH: I did not.

EVANS: Did you not pay the man for doing so?

SARAH: I never did.

EVANS: Did he not refuse payment at first, and did you not prevail upon him to accept a silver dollar as the charm would not work unless it was paid for?

SARAH: I did not. I don't know such a man.

EVANS: Don't you know George Villard?

SARAH: No.

EVANS: Don't you know he is a friend of Nellie Brackett's?

SARAH: No.

George Villard was called and the ghoulish testimony went on. He stated that he was employed at the Masonic Cemetery in the spring of 1883; that Nellie Brackett had visited him there, with Miss Hill, and had explained that her friend wanted a charm.

I went with them to the lot of the Oriental Lodge, to a grave prepared for the remains of a man named Anson G. Olsen. I put the ladder down into the grave and went down into the rough box, in which the coffin was to be placed. The middle bottom board was loose and I took it up, and Miss Hill came down into the grave. She took a package out from under her cloak and placed it through the hole and under the board and whispered something to herself. Then she went up out of the grave and Nellie Brackett came down. . . . I got my cart and they came to me and Nellie said: " I want you to take this," giving me a silver dollar. I said I wouldn't take anything, but Nellie said that the fortune teller told them that they had to pay for everything they did about the charm or it would not work. So I took the silver dollar and took it home and gave it to my wife.

The witness was asked when he had last visited the grave.

On the 16th of last month. . . . I went in company with Mr. Smith, the superintendent, the assistant superintendent, Dr. Meares, Captain Lees, Mr. Barnes, Mr. Davis, and four grave-diggers. The grave-diggers opened the grave, the body was taken out, the water bailed out of the box; and I got down into the grave. I took up the loose board, and with my shovel took out the package. . . . I handed it up out of the grave with my shovel.

The court re-examined the contents of the package. There was a collar cut from a shirt, a sock, a portion of a shirt-tail. Counsel crowded about the table and Mammy Pleasant pushed through the group. " I just want to see how things are going on," she remarked. She lifted the sock, regarded it closely, then dropped it, saying: " That's all right; nothing the matter with that."

Sharon's investigators had done a thorough job of tracing Sarah's adventures among the town's dealers in the occult. Mrs. Laura Scott, Negro sorceress, took the stand and coolly told of Sarah's visits to her in search of a love draught.

She had been to other fortune tellers, she said, and got some stuff which she gave the senator, and it seemed to make him sick at his stomach. She was afraid it was too strong. I told her she should bring me some of it and she did so in a black bottle. It smelled awful strong. . . . When she came next time I gave her a love draught. . . . Nine drops of molasses, nine pinches of sugar, and the balance of the vial I filled with black tea. I directed her to give the senator a spoonful three times a day, or as often as she pleased, until it worked on him — the more he took the more he would love her. . . .

The witness testified that Miss Hill later returned to her, a by no means satisfied customer.

She told me my charms were no good, that they had not taken any effect at all, and that I must make her something else; that the senator had had a quarrel with her and put her out of her rooms. She brought me a pair of socks . . . and wanted me to make a charm out of them. So I took the socks and tied the toes into a very hard knot, and gave this to her with instructions to go home, and dip the toes in whisky and wear them around her left knee . . . because the left leg is nearer the heart. . . .

Mrs. Francis H. Massey, also colored, took the stand:

She [Miss Hill] told me someone had given her some stuff to charm the senator and she put it in his drink. I told her it was a mean dirty trick for any lady to do, but she wanted money, she said, and had to do it. She said Mrs. Pleasant was the lady who gave her the charm. . . .

The witness's wrinkled face aroused Tyler's curiosity and he tried to find out her age. She recalled having once seen President Harrison in Virginia. Asked if she was a grown woman then, she replied:

" Oh, no; if I had been a full grown woman then, I would now be as old as Methusalem's goat."

" I would take you to be about a hundred," hazarded Tyler.

" It may be so, sir," returned she. " I guess I am somewhere about your age."

Rose of Sharon

The courtroom shook with laughter and Tyler took up a new line of questioning.

Still another witness, Jennie Wanger, added her bit to the story of Sarah's quest for a workable love potion:

> Sometime in 1882 she showed me a charm which she carried in a little red silk bag that she kept in her bosom. She told me that she had taken a young pigeon, cut it open, took out its heart, stuck nine pins in it to dry, after which she wore it around her neck. . . .

Not all the testimony concerned these revelations of the supernatural. As the spring weeks advanced, opposing counsel wrangled over the authenticity of the " Dear Wife " letters. The defense admitted that many of the letters were in Sharon's handwriting, but contended that the word " wife " had been fraudulently inserted. Many hours were consumed while experts for both sides discoursed on erasures, paper fibers, inks, and handwriting — and of course reached opposite conclusions. Reporters tired of taking down this dull testimony and turned to describing the somnolent scene.

" If Mr. Tyler takes for his cross-examination . . . one day for each letter in the word wife, and the word wife occurs five times, how long will this thing last? "

Mr. Evans asked the question of Mr. Barnes, and Mr. Barnes, busily drawing short straight lines on a sheet of paper, figured out as his answer twenty days. The proposition not being disputed, Mr. Evans buried his head in his newspaper, Mr. Terry [Terry had recently joined Sarah's legal staff] spoke encouragingly to the plaintiff; Mr.

Cushman, witness, mopped his weeping eyes, the fringe of officers looked sleepy . . . the expert unpacked his instruments, and Judge Sullivan alone looked like a person who was even remotely interested in what was about to occupy all for another day. . . . The defendant's attorneys wrote descriptive verses . . . and read them to each other without fatal results. The plaintiff took off her hat for comfort's sake and consumed cherries and candy, shared by Mr. Terry. The reporters practised caricature drawing, and listened to a lecture by Mr. Barnes on the theory of transmitted motion for the production of certain angles, as applied to fifteen-ball pool. A lazy, sleepy hum pervaded the room, a hum over which the voices of Mr. Tyler, the witness and Judge Sullivan sounded like those of teachers and reciting scholars in a schoolroom on a warm spring day.

As always in such dull periods, what Sarah wore claimed attention. The thirty-third day of the trial found her in a dress of brocaded velvet " half concealed by the unbuttoned length of a tailor-made coat." The latter, she explained gravely, was a " Sharon ulster." Sharon had long since given up attending the trial, and even Mammy Pleasant was no longer among the regulars. Her visits, however, were always worthy of remark. " She bustles in, converses pleasantly with the young men attached to the defendant's counsel, imparts some interesting bit of news or entertaining gossip to the plaintiff, graciously inspects the court . . . and, like a wind from the south astray in northern climes, departs and leaves a chill behind."

8

WITNESSES, RECALLED to the stand, began changing
their stories. Martha Wilson, colored, who had earlier
testified that she had read the marriage contract in
1880, stated between sobs that she had not seen the
document until shortly before the suit against Sharon
was filed. Harry L. Wells returned and testified that he
had plotted with another Santa Cruz ancient to fabri-
cate a story that Sharon had been heard to introduce
Miss Hill as his wife. Both sides charged that the opposition had been buying witnesses, and threats to in-
dict the backsliders for perjury were daily made and
in some cases carried out. The whole town was interested when Sharon stated on the stand that he had recited, not sung, *Maid of Athens* to Sarah on his historic
visit to her rooms at the Baldwin. About that time
police arrested Sharon's picturesque Chinese servant
for being intoxicated and using vulgar language. The
arresting officer asked Ki if Sharon had ever recited
Maid of Athens to him.

Court recessed in June, and when the trial resumed
there was a new crop of sensations. Neilson announced
his withdrawal from the case following a quarrel
with the plaintiff. Nellie Brackett, no longer Sarah's
shadow, was recalled to the stand and changed her testimony; she had, she stated, accompanied Sarah to the
Masonic Cemetery the day the shirt was planted in the
grave. This caused further threats of prosecution for
perjury and more charges of witness-buying. Tyler
charged that Nellie Brackett had admitted to him that

her father had been offered twenty-five thousand dollars if he could induce her to abandon Miss Hill. In later testimony it was brought out that the elder Brackett had in fact received a check from Barnes for three thousand dollars. Nellie herself granted an interview: " I'm still friendly to the plaintiff but do not feel as kindly to her as I did. We had a quarrel but I don't wish to say what it was about."

At last, on August 4, after sixty-one days of testimony and argument, the doors were closed for the time against the further introduction of what counsel on both sides termed " a seething mass of perjury, corruption and conspiracy. . . ."

Closing arguments began on August 4 and continued six weeks, concluding on September 17. Practically every one of the numerous attorneys on both sides had his say, but the main burden was borne by General Barnes and Judges Tyler and Terry. The tempers of all had been worn thin by the long ordeal and each side bitterly attacked the methods and motives of the opposition.

Judge Tyler's son, W. B. Tyler, opened the argument for the plaintiff:

The suit . . . is for divorce, and the pleadings specify two causes for action, the first specifying adultery committed after the marriage, and the second, desertion. By agreement between counsel it was stipulated that if a marriage was proven, the desertion would be admitted, and for that reason the plaintiff undertook not to go into the question of adultery, an undertaking that he, as counsel, was now very sorry for, in view of the calumnies that

162

have been heaped up on his side of the case, and the filth
that has been thrown. . . .

The younger Tyler's analysis of the evidence took
three days; he was followed on August 7 by his father.
At one stage in the latter's argument he introduced a
lighter touch into the proceedings by drawing a picture
of the first meeting, when the Senator had wooed Sarah
with *The Maid of Athens.* " Why, Your Honor, did
you ever hear that passionate hymn? She says he sang
it and he says he recited it. Well, she may not have
known the difference. Whether Sharon sings or Sharon
recites it may be difficult to decide."

Tyler then read the poem with what the *Call* stated
was " great dramatic effect." That paper continued:
" When he concluded and had calmed himself, he
modestly protested that he could have recited the lines
better if, like Mr. Sharon, he was in love. ' If I had been
a young woman of twenty-seven . . . ready to throw
off the old love and take on the new, and a fifteen-
millionaire had recited those lines to me, I should have
said: " I am yours." Would not Your Honor have done
so? ' "

The judge prudently refrained from committing
himself on that point, and Tyler took up the matter of
the marriage contract:

When Mr. Sharon had exhausted on the plaintiff his
usual methods of getting a mistress, he concluded to gain
her by the marriage contract scheme. He told her to write
the document, thinking, probably, that he was not irre-
trievably committing himself. If he found after a year or

two that she was all his fancy painted, he could come out publicly and acknowledge her as his wife, but if he found that she had a temper, or was not otherwise what he wanted for a wife, he could either buy or steal the contract from her, or if he could not, kick her out and trust to his money to escape. He thought that as it was written by her and she had no witnesses, he could repudiate it and no one would believe her. That is what he thought, and so, as she has testified, she wrote as he dictated and he signed.

On the question of the authenticity of the document Tyler stated:

The writing was done while the plaintiff wore gloves, which accounted for its cramped appearance; while he dictated she hesitated, which accounts for the uneven appearance, and while she waited for his dictation she went over words or letters where the pen did not shed the ink evenly, and that accounts for the blurred words. If so clever a woman as the plaintiff had been forging a contract, she would have reversed all these peculiarities; the writing would have been even, plain, careful and all alike.

The matter of the genuineness of the contract was of course the crux of the action, and much time was spent in analyzing it. Later, when Judge Terry presented his argument, he returned to the subject with telling effect. The *Call* stated:

He [Terry] said it seemed to him that the position of counsel in regard to the contract was very strange. The appearance of the paper, its creased and dirty appearance, and the objection of counsel upon the other side that it was . . . not clean and evenly folded, was explained by

164

the extraordinary means employed by the plaintiff to preserve it as the instrument with which she would defend
her honor. . . .

Referring to the manner in which plaintiff testified
that the contract had been written, he said that counsel
and the experts had discovered a mare's nest. In what?
In the fact that the word " and " had been written over
the word " and " and the word " to " over " to," and that
there had been no alteration of an original word, save in
one instance where it had read " wedded and wedded "
when the word " lawful " had been written over the first
" wedded." Now, if she had been going to commit a forgery would any reasonable person ever conceive the idea
of presenting such a . . . document as that? . . . The
very defects in it are evidence of its genuineness.

The elder Tyler talked seventeen and a half hours,
defending the credibility of the plaintiff's witnesses and
impeaching that of those for the defense, heaping scorn
on Sharon and sarcasm on the arguments of opposing
counsel, upholding the authenticity of the marriage
contract and of the " Dear Wife " letters.

During his entire argument Tyler had a close listener in Mammy Pleasant. The old Negro woman sat
sphinx-like in her white apron and black Quaker bonnet, her eyes never leaving his face. In due course the
attorney delighted her by stating:

They utterly failed in their threats to injure Mrs.
Pleasant's character. I have known that colored woman
for thirty years, and I would ten thousand times rather
have her chance with St. Peter before the Pearly Gates
than the chance of such a moral leper and debauchee as
Mr. Sharon. If he should have his thirty millions buried

with him it would have no effect on old St. Peter and I
would not be surprised if one day I saw that good old colored lady . . . sending down a cup of cool water to the
parched lips of the men who have tried to traduce her.

When General Barnes took up the cudgels for the
defense he did not fail to go closely into Mammy Pleasant's connection with the case. After examining her
testimony regarding the marriage contract, her con-
versations with Sharon, and her claim that Sarah had
been with her at the time she was supposed to have deposited the love charms in the grave, Barnes continued:

I don't wonder he [Tyler] likes her; I don't wonder he
has canonized her. He has had her on the stand five times.
She proved the existence of the contract in 1882. She established Mr. Sharon's admission that he owed Miss Hill
money, and she actually obtained from him the confession,
after he had been arrested, that this contract of marriage
had been executed. She has . . . contradicted the defendant on every vital and important item of this case. A
very useful woman!

I don't wonder Mr. Tyler entertains the sentiments
he does towards Mrs. Pleasant. I don't know where he
would have been without her.

Barnes made much of Sarah's liking for Negroes and
her association with them. How, he asked, was one to
reconcile this with the prosecution's claim that she had
sprung from " one of the patrician families of Missouri "?

It is a most remarkable circumstance that she should
have selected Mrs. Pleasant for her confidence — quite as
remarkable as that she should have selected Martha Wil-

son, the Negro woman. Will anybody tell me why it was that during all this time this unfortunate woman never confided the secret of her marriage to one single respectable person of her own color or class in life?

Think of it. This woman with a brother, an uncle, a grandmother and an aunt, reposes her head on the bosom of Mrs. Pleasant, and goes from that kind of confidence in the hour of her trouble . . . to the frowsy habitation of this Negro on Mary Street, sleeping in a bed with the Negro woman, while the Negro husband lay on a lounge in the next room. If we find her living in such associations, and bringing from that class of people the only support of this miserable and wretched claim, there is but one conclusion to come to, and that is that there had been in her behalf deliberate, wilful and corrupt perjury.

But Judge Terry, Kentucky-born, could see nothing reprehensible in the plaintiff's liking for Negroes. She, too, he pointed out, had spent her childhood in what had been slave-holding territory. " There is nothing unnatural in it," he argued. " We who have drawn our sustenance from black breasts, we who have gone to our colored nurses for relief from every childish affliction, we who have looked upon them as second parents, know that the friendship and respect for them continues. . . . We know how staunch and true they are — faithful even to death. I am one who possesses this knowledge of the character of the colored ' mammies ' of my youth, and the plaintiff is another."

9

THE FINAL arguments continued through August and, in early September, began to draw to a close. On the 8th, General Barnes ended his summing up with this appeal to the court:

If Your Honor pleases, at the outset of my argument I ventured to declare that the facts and circumstances established, not merely by a preponderance of proof, but beyond all reasonable doubt:

FIRST: That Miss Sarah Althea Hill was never married to William Sharon, and is not and never was his wife in any form of consent, followed by solemnization or by the mutual assumption of marital rights, duties or obligations.

SECOND: That the alleged declaration of marriage, declared in the complaint to have followed the consent required by law, is utterly invalid and void, for want of compliance with the statute: and

THIRD: That the alleged declaration of marriage and the " Dear Wife " letters are established by competent proof, supported by all the surrounding circumstances, to be impudent frauds and forgeries and the basis of one of the most bold and shocking conspiracies to accomplish the most unworthy ends by means in themselves criminal which has ever been presented to any judicial tribunal.

In conclusion, I declare that the facts show the existence between Miss Hill and the defendant of a secret, meretricious relation, continuing about thirteen months, during which period Miss Hill sought to disguise the fact and escape public and private censure by groundless assertions of the existence of an agreement to marry . . . and that after the cessation of all social relations between her-

168

self and the defendant, she attempted to explain this fact by declarations equally mendacious, to the effect that the engagement of marriage had been broken by herself . . . and that concurrently with these declarations, she conceived the plan of avenging herself . . . through an action of breach of promise of marriage; that this scheme was first developed in the month of December 1881, and was considered by her until about March 1883, and was then abandoned; that concurrently with this plan was another, that had for its object the establishment of an actual marriage, forged by the plaintiff upon a piece of paper upon which the defendant had written his name, the state of his residence, and a date, and above which, in her own handwriting, she forged the contract; by admissions contained in four pencil notes written her by the defendant for the purpose of remitting her money, in which the word " wife " has been interpolated by herself, and by one letter written in ink, which is altogether a forgery; that to these instruments in writing she has added the false testimony of two young persons . . . supplemented by the testimony of a Negro woman who could not read or write, and of a white woman who lived and associated with Negroes. It is clearly in evidence that the defendant never recognized her in the relation of matrimony for a single hour, and that neither of the parties has ever, for a day, claimed from the other or assumed toward the other the discharge of the duties or obligations of matrimony. . . .

The defense concludes that in her personal narration she has been contradicted and proven to have uttered innumerable falsehoods, and that her conduct during the entire period of her alleged marriage . . . had been wholly inconsistent with wifehood; that she has borne her maiden name, lived ostensibly as a single woman, transacted business of a private nature with the defendant, received from him money in settlement of her claims for meretricious intercourse . . . and during the period over which such successive payments were extended receipted for each payment over her maiden name of Allie Hill: that her correspondence with her former friends . . . conclusively demonstrates that she had not even the expectation of ultimate marriage with the defendant, and also proves an artful and wicked attempt to suborn both of them as false witnesses in her behalf — and, in fine, that her entire case has demonstrated, in a multitude of ways, the impossibility, mental, moral and physical, of giving even the plausible guise of truth to an absolute historical lie. . . .

Judge Terry presented the final argument for the plaintiff. On the day he began, Sarah made her first reappearance in the courtroom since she had been "driven out . . . by Barnes' scorching denunciations." Spectators did not fail to observe that she wore a new outfit: pale green silk overskirt, a "modulated Mother Hubbard" waist and Dolly Varden collar, black beaded wrap, and an old-gold straw hat trimmed with brown velvet and white feathers. Add to this her straw-colored hair, blue eyes, and celebrated peach-bloom complexion, and a reporter's statement that "spectators could not keep their eyes off her" becomes credible.

Terry too had made some sartorial preparations. His appearance, in black broadcloth of fashionable cut, formed a marked contrast to his usual careless attire. Terry spoke extemporaneously. His delivery was direct and persuasive, and he avoided the purple patches highly regarded by legal lights of the time:

Rose of Sharon

This woman in 1880 was an unmarried woman. She became acquainted with Mr. Sharon and visited him at his office to get points on stock from him. They both agreed on that. After several visits Mr. Sharon became bold enough to propose to her to accept a salary and be his mistress. She declined and attempted to leave the room. . . . Mr. Sharon placed himself against the door and refused to allow her to pass. He told her he loved her and wanted to marry her. Of course he did not adopt a very delicate method of wooing, and she recovered from his insult very soon, but it must be remembered that she was not the innocent confiding young girl described by the other counsel. She was at that time twenty-seven years of age, and had just been disappointed in a love affair with another man. She was just in the position where a woman would regard with pleasure the chance of marrying a wealthy man and one high in official position like Mr. Sharon. The plaintiff made the sacrifice of secrecy for her husband's benefit, both he and she expecting his reelection, and thinking that the announcement of their nuptials would tend to defeat it by bringing upon him the wrath of a woman with whom he had had questionable relations. . . .

Once more the marriage contract was considered in detail as Terry accounted for its form and appearance and for the double writing of certain words. He continued:

When to remove the scruples of the plaintiff and to gratify his own passions, Sharon put in that silence clause to vitiate the contract, I do not believe that he ever intended to carry out that contract, but intended to perpetrate a fraud upon her. But he married himself to her as firmly as the church could have done. The relations

were amicable . . . until the middle of 1881. Then the
defendant, having tired of her, tried to obtain the contract. . . . Wishing to retain the contract she told him
that it was lost. Then he abandoned all restraint and
treated her outrageously. . . .

Terry made adroit use of the testimony of one of the
defense's handwriting experts:

Expert Hickox, in his written criticism of the contract,
says that words were printed and retouched and written
over each other, and that toward the close the writing is
smaller, and the lines closer together. I ask Your Honor to
examine this sworn statement, which Mr. Hickox submits
as his reasons for believing that the contract was forged.
Every peculiarity which he points out as a badge of fraud
is found in his own manuscript. There are words that
have been printed, words that have been written over,
there are different shades of ink in the manuscript, and
the writing is closer on the unruled portion of the paper.
This is the best answer I can make to his written criticism,
which he refutes with his own pen.

Like other of Sarah's attorneys, Terry charged that
the defense had purchased witnesses. His list included
Reighart, whom he accused of being in Sharon's pay;
Mrs. Brackett, Nellie's mother, whom he charged with
" going around the city looking for evidence to im-
peach her own daughter." He continued: " That
daughter has admitted, the day before she left the plaintiff, that she would receive $25,000 for her desertion.
It is in evidence that Mr. Brackett received a check
from Mr. Barnes for $3,000, and that according to

Nellie's statement, he deposited $2,000 of that amount in the Hibernia Bank. No attempt was made to contradict the first part of this story, but an attempt was made to prove that the $2,000 was not so deposited by introducing the testimony of an index clerk. Neither Mr. Brackett himself, though he was in court, nor the receiving teller of the bank, nor W. H. L. Barnes, who gave his check for $3,000, went to the stand to contradict the testimony."

Of another celebrated episode Judge Terry stated:

. . . It was fully proven that the plaintiff had never taken any part in that disgraceful affair of the grave, which was concocted by Mr. Sharon's Detective Davis. Mr. Olsen's grave . . . was opened without authority of law on March 16, 1884, and the shirt-tail, sock, and collar were planted there for the first time. The package, after a few moments, was then removed and brought into court. Had it been in that grave from the date of Mr. Olsen's burial, everything in it would have been completely rotted. The grave, according to the testimony, was a very wet one, and several bucketsful of water were bailed out of it before the package was discovered. When the articles were produced in court, however, the fabric was as strong as though it had never lain in a grave, and the stains showed that they had not been completely saturated. Another circumstance . . . was the fact that the grave-digger, who testified for the defense, was but an imperfect English conversationalist and had but one eye. When Nellie Brackett was recalled by the Court and told her story about being at Olsen's grave with the plaintiff, she described the man she saw there, and though carefully examined upon the subject she could not remember that this man had a strong foreign accent, or the fact that he had but one eye. . . .

Terry began his final argument on September 10. On the afternoon of the 17th it grew clear that he was nearly finished. He spoke for two hours, then closed the case. San Francisco settled back to await the outcome.

Judge Sullivan's decision was rendered the day before Christmas 1884. Meantime interest was kept alive by a number of other developments. Sarah filed suit against the *Alta,* charging libel and asking fifty-thousand-dollar damages. A few days later she swore out a warrant for Neilson's arrest on an embezzlement charge. Tyler also figured briefly in the news; he was arrested for using improper language in a public place.

On the morning of the 24th, lawyers for both sides straggled into the courtroom: Flournoy, Levy, Judge Evans, Barnes, Tyler, Terry. . . . The plaintiff slipped unobtrusively through the crowd, spoke a word or two with Tyler, and settled back calmly. Sharon was absent.

The judge entered at ten minutes past nine and began reading from a bulky manuscript. He read rapidly and without a stop until eleven forty-five. Next morning excerpts from his decision were scanned in newspapers all over the country. " The case has been disgusting beyond description and tiresome almost beyond endurance. . . ." The judge spoke of the difficulty of seeing his way through " the mass of perjury in which this case abounds " and of finding " some writing . . . whose genuineness was admitted to my satisfaction, and to subordinate the result of all oral evidence to the effect of such written testimony. . . ." He read some of Sharon's " Dear Wife " letters, finding that " the

174

preponderance of the evidence is in favor of their genuineness." He reviewed the testimony of certain key
witnesses and dismissed that of most of them — including Neilson and Reighart — as unworthy of belief.
Tyler was rebuked for intimating that the influence of
wealth might sway the court: " The honesty required
of a judge demands of him an absolute impersonality
and impartiality in awarding to rich and poor alike
what the justice of their cases may demand."

So far there had been no pointed intimation of what
way the decision might go. That was to come soon.
The judge hurried on:

> Reviewing the history of these parties, as it is estab-
> lished to my mind, it appears that on the 25th day of August
> 1880, the parties to this action, in the office of the defend-
> ant, entered into an engagement of marriage which is set
> forth in plaintiff's exhibit one; that the intercourse which
> followed between the parties was the result of that engage-
> ment; that it was the desire of the defendant that the rela-
> tions of the parties should be kept secret, and the change
> of plaintiff's residence from the Baldwin Hotel was at the
> direction and request of the defendant. . . .

As this passage was read, the eyes of spectators turned
toward Sharon's counsel. General Barnes sat " like a
statue," his eyes drooping heavily, giving no outward
sign that he recognized that his client's case was lost.
Judge Sullivan continued:

> I have reached a result favorable to the plaintiff. . . .
> I have reached the conclusion that William Sharon . . .
> by virtue of his secret contract of marriage, or written con-
> sent thereto . . . has become and now is the husband of

Sarah Althea Sharon. . . . In violation of his marriage vow, he has been guilty of wilfully abandoning his wife. . . . Under the law of this state, Sarah Althea Sharon . . . is entitled to a decree of this court dissolving the bond of marriage. . . . The plaintiff is, in my judgment, entitled to a decree of divorce on the grounds of wilful desertion, and a division of the common property.

Public Reception Room, about 1885

LEFT: *Senator William Sharon, 1875*
From the *California Spirit of the Times*

RIGHT: *Colonel John C. Kirkpatrick, Manager of the Palace
at the Time of the Fire*

This photograph shows his well-known resemblance to King Edward VII

The Shooting of Judge Terry in the Lathrop Restaurant,
August 14, 1889

From Wagstaff's *Life of David S. Terry*

Newspaper Sketch of Sarah Althea Terry, 1892

From the *San Francisco Call*, February 16, 1892

CHAPTER FIVE

THE WORLDLY HOPE

1

DECEMBER 25, 1884 was a dark, bleak day with inter-mittent cold rains, but Sarah's spirits had never been higher. The previous afternoon she had belatedly done her Christmas shopping. At the White House the proprietor himself, Raphael Weill, had piloted her from counter to counter, while hundreds of customers stopped to stare at the notorious Mrs. Sharon. Demure and gracious and triumphant, Sarah bought with a liberality that befitted her new estate: a seventeen-dollar lace collar for her Negro maid, a silk umbrella, a dozen pairs of kid gloves, a dress pattern, a pair of Mission woolen blankets. . . . Yes, they were to be charged, she smiled. Mrs. William Sharon was the name. Occasionally she paused and checked off names on her fingers, her head to one side. Not one of her friends must be forgotten.

All Christmas Day she received callers at her flat, her high spirits and a crackling wood fire combating the outer gloom. In the late afternoon an *Alta* reporter hurried through the wet streets, rang the bell, and was ushered into the bright room. Sarah was resting on a lounge, half buried in satin and plush sofa pillows. With pleasure the reporter noticed that she was reading the Christmas number of the *Alta;* that a group of champagne bottles, "some empty, others not yet opened," stood on a near-by table.

More than ever now the town wanted to know about this lady who, "by grace of Judge Sullivan, has been declared to be Mrs. William Sharon." The *Alta's* man rendered a cheerful report:

She never looked better in her life. At least she never appeared to better advantage than yesterday . . . when, smiling and serene, she welcomed the visitor. The lines of care . . . had disappeared, and a pleasing, joyous expression could be detected in her voice and manner. She evidently was one of the happiest women in San Francisco. . . .

Sarah regretted that the reporter had not called earlier. Friends had dropped in and the day had passed pleasantly. She was gracious even while she parried his persistent attempts to interview her. "I do not wish to speak on the subject. . . ." "I have nothing to say. . . ." "Please present my Christmas compliments to the proprietors of the *Alta.* . . ." The reporter gave up and talk flowed into other channels. Other visitors arrived out of the wet outdoors; a colored waiter busied himself with the champagne bottles. Christmas greetings were exchanged while cakes were passed and glasses refilled.

Back in his office, the reporter described the scene, then passed on to related matters:

The Sharon case was the principal topic of conversation yesterday. . . . All sorts of ideas and opinions were advanced, and it was a mystery how many persons knew just how the case was coming out. A gentleman popularly supposed to enjoy the confidence of Mr. Sharon said that the senator would rather throw every dollar that he had in the world into the bay than give Mrs. Sharon a cent . . . that there was no community property to be divided.

It is yet very doubtful what course will be pursued by Mr. Sharon's attorneys. That the case will be appealed there seems to be no doubt, but in the meantime alimony will be demanded, pending subsequent litigation. This alone will give the lady a large sum . . . but George W. Tyler comes to the fore with a claim for one half the spoils. . . .

Even while she was enjoying her pleasant Christmas, Sarah must have realized that she was not yet in the clear. A few hours after Judge Sullivan's decision, Judge Tyler had put on record a contract he and his client had signed more than a year earlier. In it Tyler agreed to prosecute the case and to advance the cost of litigation; in return he was to receive half of whatever might be awarded her. Tyler agreed not to dismiss the case without his client's consent or that of her agent, Neilson. This last clause aroused particular interest. Sarah had quarreled violently with Neilson, and Neilson had gone over to the opposition. She had had him arrested for embezzlement and at the police-court hearing had denied that he had ever been her agent.

It was on these points that the reporter had tried to question her on Christmas afternoon. Tyler proved less reticent. Neilson, he stated, would have a hard time collecting anything, particularly after having given testimony favorable to Sharon. Tyler professed to be unconcerned at the prospect of an appeal. He had a great deal of valuable new evidence to present. . . .

Sharon, too, granted an interview. He was happy to find the rival camp fighting among themselves. If their quarrel grew hot enough perhaps the whole truth might come out. As for the plaintiff's bad character, he had nothing to add to what had been brought out at the trial. The legal business of the case remained in the hands of General Barnes, but a motion for a new trial would be made and the battle carried to the State Supreme Court. Valuable new evidence had been found. . . .

Questioned as to how much alimony he thought Sarah might be awarded, Sharon remarked that two hundred and fifty dollars monthly had been enough when she claimed to be his wife, and that the same sum should satisfy her now. " Talk about perjury! " he concluded. " Why, she swore time and again that Neilson was not her agent; yet in her pocket and in Tyler's too, was a paper signed by both, in which he is not only styled her agent, but is given great power in the settlement of the case. . . ."

Sharon's determination to continue the fight failed to surprise old acquaintances. These recognized that unwillingness to admit defeat had long been a Sharon characteristic. Failing health had not shaken his determination, but it began to seem doubtful if he would live to see the end of the litigation. He had been ill for months and had gradually assumed the role of invalid. He seldom appeared at his office or his other haunts; even the weekly poker games in his Palace rooms had been given up. During the final phases of the trial he had appeared only when he was obliged to do so and had left as soon as his presence was no longer required. As the year 1885 advanced, his condition grew worse. On November 5, papers printed what they termed his "dying statement." The document revealed no last-minute softening of his attitude toward Sarah:

. . . I am exceedingly weak in body and suffer great physical pain, but my mind is perfectly clear. In this condition I declare that I never proposed or offered marriage to Sarah Althea Hill at any time or in any form. . . . The alleged contract of marriage . . . is a forgery. I never signed it or any other document of that nature or import. I never addressed her as my wife in any communication, and the letters produced by Miss Hill, which so address her, are, so far as the word wife is concerned, one and all willful forgeries. Her declarations under oath that I ever married her, ever signed the pretended marriage contract, or wrote her the "Dear Wife" letters . . . are all and singly willful perjuries. I have resisted her false claim to wifehood as in duty bound to myself, my family and society. . . . I have directed those upon whom representation of me or of my estate devolves to contest her pretension in every legal and proper manner. . . .

It was Sharon's last blast of defiance, for he died eight days later, on November 13. He was sixty-four. He was buried on the 16th from one of the main-floor parlors of the Palace.

The will was presently opened. A trust deed made his son, Fred, and Francis Newlands, his son-in-law, trustees of the estate. The latter was apportioned as follows: one third each to Fred Sharon and Lady

Fermor-Hesketh, and one twelfth each to Newlands and his three daughters, Edith, Janet, and Frances. The document made no reference to Sarah Hill.

Much was written about Sharon during the days following his death. He had been one of the most powerful of the Bonanza millionaires, and not the least picturesque. None of the town's reporters succeeded in obtaining an interview with Sarah, but one had the good judgment to hunt up Ki, long the dead man's servant and almost constant companion. Ki was located in Chinatown, where his pretty young wife lighted a lamp in honor of the visitor.

It was a small apartment, but as the dim rays . . . grew stronger many a familiar picture was observed upon the walls. There were . . . engravings of ex-Senator Sharon, John W. Mackay and other bonanza kings; of Washington, D.C., the Brooklyn Bridge and well-known edifices. . . . Best of all, however, was found Ki himself, who rising from a couch . . . bade the reporter welcome. . . .

The interview proceeded. Ki stated that he was born in China, that he was forty-nine, and that he had come to California in 1853. He had operated a ten-pin alley on Montgomery Street, then became a waiter at the free-lunch counter of the Bank Exchange, famous saloon of the Comstock era.

"When did you first meet Mr. Sharon?"

"In Bank Exchange Clubroom. All gentlemen go there then. Afterwards, in 1863, Mr. Sharon he asked me to go to Virginia City with him."

"What did you do there?"

182

The Worldly Hope

" I took care of the rooms in the Bank of California. He pay me always good wages. In 1875, when he was elected senator, I left the bank and went with him. Travelled all over with him. Been in Washington, three, four times; sometimes other places. Stayed with him all time afterwards till he died. . . ."

" Did he leave you any money, Ki? "

There was a merry twinkle in the little, keen eyes . . . but the careful Ki gave no other intimation as to whether he had been " fixed " or not, save that " I guess I get along nice enough in China, yes.

". . . I no have to work in China. . . . I let my queue grow again now. Goodbye. Much obliged."

At the time of Sharon's death the case had already gone through the following complicated legal phases: On September 8, 1883 Neilson had filed the original complaint charging Sharon with adultery and alleging his secret marriage to Sarah Hill. The complaint was dismissed a few weeks later, and on November 2 Sarah filed suit for divorce in the Superior Court. Meantime, on October 3, Sharon's attorneys had entered a petition in the United States Circuit Court asking that the contract be declared void on the ground of fraud. When Judge Sullivan's decision upholding the validity of the contract and granting Sarah a divorce was rendered, the action in the Federal Court was still pending. On February 16, 1885 Judge Sullivan rendered a supplementary decision fixing Sarah's alimony and ordering Sharon to pay counsel fees. Sharon's attorneys filed appeals to both Judge Sullivan's decisions, and the case went to the State Supreme Court. Sharon died on November 13, 1885. Six weeks later, on December 26,

Judge Deady of the United States Circuit Court rendered a decision declaring the marriage contract forged and fraudulent. State and federal courts thus took directly opposite views of the famous contract — the former having granted Sarah a divorce and alimony, and the latter ruling that she had never been married. As the year 1885 ended, the case was as far from settlement as ever.

2

SHARON'S DEATH and the Federal Court's rejection of the marriage contract closed two chapters in Sarah Hill's turbulent career. The first week of 1886 opened another.

On January 7, dispatches from a near-by valley town brought startling news:

Stockton. January 7: This quiet little city had a tremendous social sensation today when two of the most conspicuous residents of California were married. . . . The groom, David S. Terry, has resided here for years, and is both feared and respected throughout the entire San Joaquin Valley. His bride, Miss Sarah Althea Hill, is also pretty well known here . . . but is regarded in an entirely different light from Terry. The latter's motives in contracting an alliance with so oppositely constituted a mate have been under discussion all day yesterday and today. . . . All that is definitely settled is that Miss Hill has become Mrs. David Terry, and that she clung to the name of Sharon up to the moment of the transformation, as is shown by the name in the marriage license procured this morning. . . .

Terry was sixty-two; Sarah was thirty years his junior. He had been a conspicuous figure in California before his bride was born; while she was still in the cradle he was Chief Justice of the State Supreme Court. In 1859 he had killed Senator Broderick in a duel in the sandhills west of town and so had laid the foundation for a reputation as one willing to resort to violence in defense of his private rights or public convictions. The hot-blooded Kentuckian had time and again given proof that he feared no man — by his almost single-handed opposition to San Francisco's Vigilance Committee of 1856, by his participation in Southern plots at the beginning of the Civil War, and later by his conduct as Confederate officer in the field. But it was agreed that he had never shown more reckless courage than when he linked his fortunes with the volatile and tempestuous Sarah. Terry, a man of solid attainments in the law, on the bench, and in politics, was one of the leading citizens of the state. His bride was a notorious young woman and therefore, by the mores of the period, an outcast. Although many believed her marriage contract genuine and others felt that, contract or no contract, Sharon had treated her badly, too much was known of the young woman's unconventionalities to permit her acceptance by a society still committed to a rigid Victorian code.

Terry's marriage astonished the state, but his growing infatuation with his pretty client had been known for months. As far back as June 1884 the *Alta* had commented:

Their seats are invariably side by side. . . . All her confidences are made to him, and all her many stage-whispered sarcasms directed at the defendant, his witnesses and counsel, reach him before they do their targets. More often than not he escorts her to and from lunch, or at the theatre . . . each as oblivious to criticising spectators as a pair of freshly-betrothed lovers. . . .

Months earlier, Terry's spirited defense of his client's interests had proved one of the most dramatic episodes of the trial. Sarah had been undergoing cross-examination, and one of Sharon's attorneys had asked:

" Did you ever threaten to take Mr. Sharon's life? "

SARAH: I told Mr. Barnes that if Mr. Sharon convicted me on the criminal charge I should use every effort to end both Mr. Sharon's life and my own.

BARNES: I don't see why this witness wants to make any such statement as that; for she never said any such thing to me.

TYLER: The counsel should be sent to jail for accusing a witness on the stand of perjury.

BARNES: What does she mention my name for all the time? I don't want to be made a witness in this suit. Why doesn't she confine herself to answering questions put to her?

TERRY: The witness said that she told Mr. Barnes a certain thing. He rises in his seat and contradicts her. I believe the witness told the truth.

Mr. Barnes slowly rose, advanced to the table occupied by Mr. Terry's associates, and said: " I do not care for Mr. Terry's good opinion nor Mr. Terry's respect. I have never addressed a word to him, and thus I hope to continue to live. What he has just said was said in a very insulting manner, and was, of course, intended to be insulting. I do not propose to notice it. I shall send him no challenge, for I fight no duels."

TERRY: Mr. Barnes contradicted the witness and I had a right to retort. I said that I believed the witness told the truth. I have not altered my opinion.

At that point the attorney hastily resumed his examination of the witness, and the tension relaxed.

Curiously, this marriage of what was called the two most explosive temperaments in California gave every evidence of being a happy one. Those who expected it to be violently disrupted were disappointed. Friends reported them mutually devoted and the public observed that they were constantly together. Terry's practice made it necessary for him to travel frequently; Sarah invariably went along. The pair promptly announced that their marriage did not mean that they were to abandon their legal war with Sharon's heirs; Terry, in fact, was more determined than ever to clear his wife's name by proving the contract genuine.

It grew clear, however, that there was a variety of troubles ahead. Since their initial victory in the San Francisco court, the tide had definitely turned against them. The United States District Court had, as stated, declared the contract fraudulent and ordered that it be surrendered and canceled. Against this decision Terry had appealed to the Federal Supreme Court and another long delay followed. Meantime the State Supreme Court upheld Judge Sullivan's decision as to the legality of the marriage, but drastically reduced the amount of alimony awarded the plaintiff and reversed

187

the judgment against Sharon for counsel fees. There remained the appeal to the U. S. Supreme Court from the District Court decision ordering cancellation of the contract. Not until the fall of 1888 was the result made known. It was then customary for Supreme Court justices during recesses of the court in Washington to travel throughout the country to preside over United States circuit courts. Justice Stephen J. Field was assigned to the California district; it was he who was to render the crucial decision.

Terry got no pleasure from that prospect. Field was a former Californian; he and Terry had been acquainted for years. The men were opposites in temperament as in politics and they had long been antagonistic. As far back as the middle '50s, when Terry had been Chief Justice of the State Supreme Court and Field one of the Associate Justices, they were seldom in agreement. Field had been a protégé and friend of Senator Broderick; Terry had killed Broderick in a duel. Terry had opposed Field's appointment to the Supreme Court; Field is said to have prevented the appointment of one of Terry's friends to a Federal judgeship.

To one of Judge Terry's temperament, the fact that a question involving his wife's honor was to be decided by his enemy was galling. Never one to keep his resentments secret, he publicly expressed a conviction that his client was unlikely to get justice from Judge Field. Sarah of course shared his viewpoint; she had long since come to believe that " Sharon's millions " were responsible for the adverse decisions, and she complained bitterly of the power of money to defeat justice.

Because of all this, an atmosphere of tenseness pervaded the courtroom on the morning of September 3,
1888 when Justice Field prepared to read his decision.
Newspapers carefully explained where in the room the
various principals sat; it was as though they were describing the position of armies on the eve of battle.
Terry and his wife were at an attorney's table just below the judge's bench; U. S. Marshal Franks was a few
feet distant, standing against the west wall; deputies
were stationed about the room, alert for trouble. Justice Field and his associates, Judges Sawyer and Sabin,
filed in and took their seats. Field, bald, slight, fastidi-
ously dressed, polished his glasses slowly, adjusted them
to the proper angle on his nose, then unrolled a sheaf
of papers and began to read.

The room remained in silence as his voice droned
through pages of preliminary comment. The Terrys
listened closely; so far there was no inkling as to what
way the decision might fall. Then came an advance
warning. The court passed on to an examination of the
evidence. The listeners learned that much of the evidence on which Sarah had based her claim had been rejected, while that favorable to Sharon was upheld. A
few moments of this and the Terrys realized that the
decision was to be an adverse one.

Sarah was abruptly on her feet. Spectators heard her
demand of Judge Field:

" Judge, are you going to take the responsibility of
ordering me to deliver up that marriage contract? "

Field stopped reading, regarded the angry woman,
and ordered sharply: " Madam, sit down."

Beside herself, Sarah shouted: " You have been paid

for this decision! How much did Newlands pay you?"

The room was in an uproar. Field, losing his judicial calm, shouted: " Mr. Marshal, remove that woman from the courtroom."

Marshal Franks stepped forward. Sarah sprang to meet him, delivered a resounding blow on his face, and defied him to touch her. Terry too was on his feet. He pushed between Sarah and the officer.

" Don't touch my wife," he ordered curtly. " Get a written order."

The marshal's reply was to grasp at Sarah's arm. At once Terry's razor-edge temper flared up. " No goddamned man shall touch my wife! " he shouted, and struck the officer a " terrific blow " on the mouth. The deputies reached the spot and hurled themselves on the attorney. Despite his nearly sixty-five years, it required their combined efforts to force him into a chair and hold him there. That accomplished, the marshal and court attachés removed Sarah, " fighting and scratching and kicking," from the courtroom.

The violence was not yet over. Sarah had been taken to the marshal's office, down the corridor. Terry was released and hurried to join her, followed by the deputies. At the door officers attempted to prevent his entering. In a flash he drew a knife from an under-arm holster and ordered them to stand back. The deputies confronted him with drawn revolvers. For a moment the situation was electric, then the officers stood aside and Terry joined his wife. She, meantime, was demanding her satchel, which had fallen to the floor of the courtroom. One of the officers went for it. Before he delivered it to its owner, Marshal Franks opened and probed through its contents. He later stated that it had contained a loaded revolver, from which he removed the shells.

Back in the nearly deserted courtroom Judge Field completed the reading of the decision, adjourned court, and hurriedly left the building. While this was going on, Terry was shouting his opinion of the verdict and of the men who had reached it. He pronounced Judge Sawyer "a damned old scoundrel," and Field was worse. By then it was past noon. Terry shouted an order to one of the guards: "Tell that old bald-headed son-of-a-bitch Field that I want to go to lunch."

This time, however, Field clearly had the upper hand, for hadn't the Terrys offended the majesty of the Federal judicial system? Both were held in contempt of court and ordered to jail. Terry spent six months in the Alameda County prison, Sarah three months.

Of course this treatment failed to lessen Terry's bitterness, or that of his friends. The latter felt that the punishment had been too drastic, that the jail term had been meted out primarily to humiliate a political enemy. In any event, its result was tragic. Both Terry and his wife were quick to resent a slight, and slow to forget one. The two spent their time in prison nursing their anger and planning revenge. Neither made a secret of his intentions. To all who would listen Sarah spoke of avenging her honor by getting even with "old man Field" and Frank Newlands. It was Newlands, Sharon's son-in-law, on whom her resentment centered; with Fred Sharon, the senator's son, she remained on comparatively friendly terms. As for Terry, he seemingly had but one ambition; he looked on Justice Field as the sole author of his troubles and it was from Field alone that he wanted satisfaction.

The pair returned to Fresno and Terry resumed his law practice. Field had long since returned to Washington; no meeting between the two would be possible until his return to the circuit bench. Time brought no softening of Terry's determination. Neither his nor Sarah's temper was improved by the series of court defeats that followed. In July of 1889 the *Alta* observed that after six years the famous Sharon case seemed to be approaching its end. " The Federal Courts have decided that the alleged marriage contract . . . is a forgery . . . and yesterday the Supreme Court of this state . . . remanded the case for a new trial, holding that the contract itself, assuming it to be genuine, followed only by *secret* cohabitation, did not constitute a marriage under the laws of the state." There was a further complication. Terry announced that the contract itself had been destroyed by a fire in his Fresno residence.

Successive checks in their legal fight, combined with rancor at what they believed to be Justice Field's vindictive treatment, kept the Terrys' anger alive. In the hot summer of 1889 events moved on to another climax.

3

ON THE night of August 13 Terry and his wife boarded a Southern Pacific train at Fresno. They were bound for San Francisco, where Terry was to make a court appearance the next day. The train reached the town of Lathrop, about a hundred miles east of San Francisco, shortly after seven the next morning. Terry and his wife went to the station restaurant for breakfast. The room was already filling, and neither Terry nor Sarah observed that Justice Field (who had boarded the train at Los Angeles) was seated at another table. Field, however, had seen his enemy enter and had called his companion's attention to Terry's presence. The companion was David Neagle, deputy United States marshal and Field's bodyguard. The Justice had provided himself with a guard because Terry's threats had reached his ears and he feared personal injury at his hands.

The two men had been seated at tables about twenty-five feet apart. Field and his guard were near the center of the room, the Terrys at a table against the wall. It was Sarah who, glancing over the crowd, first saw Field. She informed Terry; the two spoke a few words; then Sarah got up and hurriedly left the room.

The feud between the two men was widely known and there were those who feared trouble. One was the proprietor of the restaurant, a man named Stackpole. He had been standing near the door and had seen Sarah hurry out. He approached Terry and asked why his wife had left.

" Judge Field is here," Stackpole stated. " Do you think your wife would be so indiscreet as to cause trouble? "

" Why do you ask? " inquired Terry.

" Because I do not wish to have any trouble here."

" I don't know," said Terry quietly. . . . " There may be trouble. . . ."

Alarmed, the restaurant man hurried back to the door, planning to intercept Sarah on her return. Terry meantime rose from his seat, walked to where Field was sitting, and stood close beside him. Exactly what happened in the next few seconds was never clearly known. This version was given by Field's bodyguard, himself a leading actor in the drama:

I passed Justice Field some sausages, and he was eating at the time. Terry turned and looked around toward Justice Field and hauled off with his right hand — that way, and that way [illustrating] — and hit him. The two blows came almost together. The first blow must have struck him here [pointing to side of face], and the other one hit him at the back of the head. I told him to stop that. Terry turned around. . . . His hand was turned around in this position — that is, he had his fist clenched at about the elevation of his shoulder and drawn back. I hollered, " Stop that! Stop that! " and jumped between him and Justice Field. I said, " I am an officer." He seemed to recognize me at that point. He looked at me. His hand came right to his breast. It went a good deal quicker than I can explain it. He continued looking at me in a desperate manner, and his hand got to his left breast — in that position [illustrating] to his left breast with his right hand. His hand got there, and I raised my six-shooter like that [illustrating], and held it to him and shot twice in rapid succession.

At the moment Terry fell, Sarah reappeared in the doorway. Stackpole grappled with her, trying to pre-

vent her from entering. Others rushed to help him,
but she broke away and rushed to Terry's side. Stackpole, however, had wrested her purse from her. Later
he opened it and found that it contained a loaded pistol.
The room was in wild confusion. Clouds of smoke
from the deputy's large-gauge shells drifted upward
and flattened against the ceiling. Terry lay face-up on
the floor; he was unconscious and died in a few moments. Sarah dropped to the floor beside him, caressing
him and sobbing. Onlookers drew about in a close circle. One of the group observed that her gray dress and
blouse had become smeared with blood.

George L. Lidgerwood, Los Angeles corset salesman,
chanced to be seated at the same table with Justice Field
and his bodyguard. He was interviewed at length:

The smoke was very dense for an instant; when it
cleared I saw a man on the floor. I said to Justice Field,
" What does this mean? " He said, " This man assaulted
me. This officer shot him." The crowd rushed in pell-
mell. Justice Field, Neagle and I stood for a moment by
the body. Neagle said to Field, " You get right out of
here." While we were walking out of the room, Neagle
seemed cool. . . .

I think I noticed Mrs. Terry as I went to the car with
Justice Field and Neagle. I went back to the room because
I feared there would be trouble. Mrs. Terry addressed me.
I saw her by the body of Terry. . . . She kneeled by him
and bent over him . . . as if heart-stricken. . . .

Mrs. Terry appealed to me for assistance, saying that
her husband had been murdered and for me to examine
him and see that he was not armed. She said she had taken
his arms from him before he left the car, as she did not

want him to have arms, but she would not have objected to a fist bout. . . .

Subsequent investigation showed that Terry had carried no weapons. But Neagle, faced by the fact that he had shot an unarmed man, continued to insist that both he and Justice Field had been in danger of their lives.

. . . When I pushed Terry aside after he had struck Justice Field [Neagle continued] he recognized me. . . . He raised his hand as if to draw a knife. . . . Then I drew my pistol with my left hand, as I am left handed, and fired the shot. Some people say I was too hasty; but look at it in another way. Suppose Justice Field had been killed or seriously injured, what would have become of me? . . .

When it became known that Terry had carried no weapon, the crowd's sympathies turned against Field and his bodyguard. Why, it began to be asked, had the Justice not fought his own battle? Bare fists were still regarded on the Coast as a proper means of settling differences, and Terry was believed to have a legitimate grievance against the Supreme Court Justice. Field, like Terry, had lived in California during the tumultuous '50s, when a man's personal safety was his own concern, not something that could honorably be delegated to a hired bodyguard.

Some recognition of this tradition must have impressed itself on the group at the Lathrop restaurant, for soon there were outcries against Field and Neagle. The latter two hurried from the room and reboarded the waiting train. Someone shouted: " Lynch them! " Sarah heard the shout and echoed it, her grief sub-

merged in anger and the hope of revenge. She turned
to the group about Terry's body, the personification
of vengeance. Would none of them help her? " Old
Field " had hired this man to murder her husband.
Was he to be allowed to go unharmed? Her father had
been a Mason; would the Masons take up her cause?
She added a crafty argument: " Had my husband killed
Judge Field this crowd would lynch him, now they will
not help me."

Her appeals began to have an effect. Someone called
for a gun with which to " get " Field and Neagle.
Others joined in the cry. Another group, favoring
Field, shouted counter-threats. The situation was becoming tense when some cooler head suggested that the
train proceed. The Lathrop constable was on board
when it left; he went forward and placed Neagle under
arrest. Anticipating trouble when the train reached
Stockton, Terry's former home, the constable and his
prisoner alighted at Tracy and drove by back roads to
the town. There Neagle was hurried to the county jail,
his handcuffed hands covered by an overcoat. He was
booked, locked up, and allowed to send for an attorney.
The jailer took away his pistol, a heavy .44-caliber Colt,
with two of its shells empty.

Terry's body reached Stockton by a later train. His
widow had insisted on riding with it in the baggage
car. Spectators looked on as the body was loaded on
an express wagon and, Sarah still accompanying it,
drawn through the streets to the morgue. A Stockton
dispatch to the *Alta* reported: " Public opinion is
largely in her favor, and many are the emphatic avow-
als that the affair was a brutal murder, and that duty

was too literally performed. . . ." Sarah continued to denounce Field and Neagle. Toward noon she left the morgue and swore out a warrant for Field's arrest. Sheriff Cunningham of San Joaquin County set off for San Francisco to serve it.

Meantime Judge Field had reached the metropolis and retired to rooms at the Palace. Friends called and offered congratulations at his escape from harm at Terry's fists. Sheriff Cunningham arrived that evening. The maneuvers incident to the serving of his warrant were described:

> In order to in no way embarrass the Sheriff . . . Justice Field, with several personal friends, waited in his apartments at the Palace Hotel until a late hour. . . . The Sheriff did not reach town until 8:45 P. M. and after registering at the Russ House, went to the police station. . . . The clerk . . . told him that Chief Crowley wished to see him at the Palace Hotel. Sheriff Cunningham, with no intention of serving the warrant last evening, thereupon went to the Palace, and meeting Marshal Franks in the corridor, the two officials went to Justice Field's apartments. . . . The hour was late and Justice Field exceedingly wearied, so the Sheriff very courteously withdrew after a few minutes' conversation in which it was arranged that he would present the warrant at the Appraisers' Building, where the Federal Courts are located. . . .

Terry was buried at Stockton on August 16. The honorary pall-bearers included many prominent Californians, most of them old-time associates of the dead man. Sarah was attended by her brother, Morgan Hill, and her cousin, Frank Rodney. The church was crowded, mostly by women. The dead man was buried in the Terry family plot, between his first wife and his second son, Samuel, who had died five years earlier. His fourth son, Clinton, was among the mourners. It was the tragic end of one of California's most tempestuous careers.

Despite popular resentment it was recognized that the charges against Field and Neagle would be dismissed. Neagle's hearing was held early in September 1889. Marshal Franks told of the outbreak in the Circuit Court a year earlier that had resulted in Terry and his wife being committed to jail. He recalled that Sarah's bag had contained a revolver, and that, when he had read the warrant committing him to jail, Terry had called the Supreme Court Justice " a bald-headed old son-of-a-bitch " and had threatened reprisals. Terry was described as a formidable opponent despite his nearly sixty-five years: " over six feet three in height, weighing about 240 or 250 pounds, and of gigantic strength."

When the two men were cleared, Field's friends wished to give him a testimonial banquet. In his letter declining that honor, the Justice defended his conduct in the affair. Californians read his statement with mixed feelings:

> Doubtless your invitation has been prompted at this time by the fact that the performance of my judicial duties during the past year . . . has been attended with circumstances of an extraordinary character. These circumstances are well calculated to arouse the thoughtful to a full consideration of the importance of protecting the Judiciary from violence at the hands of disappointed litigants. Without complete protection from personal dan-

ger the Judiciary cannot be independent, and without absolute independence there cannot be that free administration of justice on which the security of persons and property and the peace of society depend.

4

WITH BOTH Sharon and Terry dead and with Sarah's legal claims hopelessly defeated, the Sharon-Hill drama sped toward a close.

As the year 1889 passed and the new decade opened, Sarah lived in the Fresno house she and Terry had occupied most of the time since their marriage. It was a period of quiet and comparative obscurity. Friends entertained the not very sanguine hope that she might now withdraw from the stresses and tumult of her previous life and live out her days in tranquillity. Of course no such existence was possible for her. She was thirty-eight, she abhorred inactivity, and she was driven by a sense of her wrongs and a consuming desire for vindication.

During the months after the tragedy her friends observed in her no indication of a wish to settle down. She is described as nervous, impatient, moody, one moment sunk in despondency, the next bitterly assailing her enemies, planning revenge, threatening court action, or a resort to the horsewhip. Since Terry's death the feeling that she was being persecuted — always a characteristic — grew stronger. The world had turned against her; she was beset and harassed by enemies; there was no one to whom she might turn.

It was not long before the workings of this obsession again got her name in San Francisco papers. Early in 1891 she quarreled with C. G. Sayle, administrator of her husband's estate. She had gone to his office in Fresno, asking for money. Sayle told her none was to be had; he suggested that Terry's law books be sold. Infuriated, she went to the office of Sayle's attorney and created so much disturbance that the latter had her ejected. She returned and smashed a window. An acute shortage of money had by then been added to her real and imagined troubles. Terry had owned valuable farm lands near Fresno, but the title proved faulty and they could not be sold. His life insurance remained unpaid while the company asked the courts to decide if it should be paid to his widow or to his surviving son, Clinton. Terry's endorsement of the policy was held to be ambiguous.

Amid all this the harassed woman had never even considered abandoning her fight for a share of Sharon's millions. On September 28, 1891 she appeared at the county clerk's office in San Francisco to file an appeal before the Supreme Court. Next morning San Franciscans read a curious story:

On the stroke of four . . . the last moment for filing the transcript on appeal before the court expired. Sarah Althea left the county clerk's office at precisely 3:41 . . . and had exactly 19 minutes to get downtown, find the attorneys for the Sharon Estate, get their signatures of service on the transcript, and return with the document to the Supreme Court Clerk's office. Of course she failed. Any other woman would have given it up in the first place, but

Sarah Althea, borne up by her nervous energy, pushed on until the doors of the clerk's office had been closed a quarter of an hour, and then stopped only after making the best struggle possible.

She was late in getting into the county clerk's office in the first place, and did not seem to understand that it was necessary to compare the copy of the transcript in her possession with the original on file before the correctness of the copy should be certified to. . . . The desk clerks never worked so fast before. One of them read the volume that contained the transcript and compared it with the original in less than an hour — a feat unheard of. . . .

Sarah Althea seemed to think that if she failed to get the papers filed on time her last chance was gone. Some, however, think it would have simply given her a better chance before the court and make the throwing out of the case less likely.

Her conduct grew increasingly erratic. In Fresno she quarreled with Attorney N. C. Caldwell, and slapped his face in the courtroom. To the press she announced that Caldwell had wanted to marry her and had addressed her in endearing terms. Later she had Caldwell arrested, charging that he had thrown her violently out of his office and had kicked her. The attorney was acquitted. She shuttled between Fresno, Stockton, and San Francisco, often appearing unexpectedly at the houses of old friends, most of whom were shocked at the change in her appearance, her growing irresponsibility. Her interest in fortune-tellers and spiritualists was revived and intensified. There were periods when she believed herself in communication with her dead husband. One day she appeared at po-

lice headquarters in San Francisco and announced that
diamonds and laces valued at thousands of dollars had
been stolen from her room at a Sutter Street boarding-
house. Police investigated, and concluded that the
" robbery " was a hallucination.

In February 1892 the *Chronicle* stated definitely
that she was insane. The paper commented:

> This outcome of her strange career is not at all star-
> tling. In fact, many of her actions during her long legal
> contest with the late Senator Sharon and, after his death,
> with the representatives of his estate were considered by
> many as evidence that her mind was unbalanced. . . . Be
> that as it may, the long mental strain to which she was
> subjected during that scathing litigation, the subsequent
> tragic death of her husband, David S. Terry, and the de-
> feat, one by one, of her hopes and ambitions, have had
> their almost inevitable result, and it now seems probable
> that the plaintiff in the famous Sharon case will end her
> days in an asylum for the insane.

Sarah had arrived in San Francisco on the Stockton
boat a few days before, accompanied by a young man
whose identity was not learned. The two had boarded
a car at the wharf and set out for the house of one of
Sarah's friends, Robert E. Culbreth. During the ride
she kept up an animated conversation that seemed to
be addressed to no one. Fellow passengers watched the
pair descend at McAllister and Polk streets and proceed to the Culbreth residence between Polk and Van
Ness Avenue. There the young man explained her
condition; Sarah was admitted and a physician sent for.
The latter, Dr. A. A. Gilmoor, was interviewed:

She is insane. . . . There does not exist any present reason sufficient to warrant her immediate confinement . . . but in her present condition I deem her entirely exempt from moral responsibility for her actions. . . . Her mental disorder shows itself at times by a marked aversion to her known friends. In addition to this her thoughts seem concentrated upon the single idea that she is constantly attended by hosts of spirits. . . . Her conversation on subjects foreign to the imaginings of her delirium is quite coherent, but almost immediately she resumes her disordered train of thought. . . . She is not afflicted with the most dangerous form of insanity, and, under careful treatment may partially recover. . . .

Her condition became news of importance. Reporters hurried to the house on McAllister Street to interview her, members of the Culbreth household, and attending physicians. All commented on the change in her appearance since the days of the Sharon trial. Little trace remained of the former acknowledged beauty in this disheveled woman with care-lined features and unkempt hair streaked with gray. She greeted visitors with suspicion and obviously wanted to be left alone. For some time she seemed content to remain in the room provided for her; then her habitual restlessness reasserted itself and she began scheming to escape. Twice she was intercepted before she could leave the house; the third time she outwitted watchers and made her way to the street. She had come to believe that her suit against Sharon's heirs was about to come up for a hearing. Of course she must be present to " protect her interests."

For some hours her whereabouts were unknown.

Then she was located at the Thomas Bell house, under the care of Mammy Pleasant. That evening a waiting reporter joined them as they left the house for what the colored woman called "a breath of air." The three walked to a Sutter Street cable-car, rode as far as Webster Street, then alighted and sat down while Sarah rested. The reporter stated:

The front steps leading to one of the residences were selected as a resting place, and there, in the pale light of the gas lamp on the corner, sat the woman whose name at one time was familiar to the whole civilized world, and who has had more sensational experiences in the short space of about eight years than perhaps any other woman alive.

Out in the Western Addition, attended only by one lifelong friend . . . the at-one-time famous Missouri beauty, in a nervous, erratic but pleasant manner, answered readily all questions. . . .

She mentioned vague plans for becoming an actress, a musician, an artist. . . . When the little group returned to Octavia Street Mrs. Terry skipped up the front steps of Mr. Bell's residence, saying all she wanted was to be left alone, and nobody need bother about her welfare.

"That is so," said Mrs. Pleasant. "She eats three hearty meals and sleeps soundly, and is neither sick nor crazy."

Others, too, began to doubt that Sarah was insane. There was talk of reviving plans for a lecture tour, which Sarah had been considering intermittently for several years. In preparation for this venture Mammy Pleasant purchased her an elaborate wardrobe, said to fill six trunks. But soon came evidence that rendered any thought of lectures or other rational enterprises out of the question. Late in February the public's last doubt on the question of Sarah's sanity vanished when it read the following:

Pedestrians who passed the northwest corner of Kearny and Post Streets on Thursday evening had their attention attracted by the strange antics of a woman who stood unprotected against the pouring rain, on the Post Street sidewalk a few feet from the corner. The woman wore a gray ulster dripping and soggy with wet, and her hat, from which the ribbons hung limp as rags, was fastened far back on her head, exposing a broad forehead framed in damp clusters of light hair. The woman was covered with mud and presented a sorry appearance. Few who saw her recognized her as Mrs. Sarah Althea Hill Terry. . . .

Mrs. Terry stood near the corner for some time, seemingly unaware that she had attracted general attention. She approached the gutter, and, apparently fascinated by the muddy stream at her feet, stepped in boldly and walked for a distance of twenty feet in the water, which submerged her boots. Then she stepped to the sidewalk, stamped her feet impatiently, and . . . walked back in the gutter to the corner again. This performance was repeated several times. . . .

Several of the onlookers approached Mrs. Terry, who then for the first time became aware that she was being watched. The knowledge of this alarmed her, and, turning quickly, she walked up Post Street. . . .

Curious onlookers followed her. She entered a restaurant, ordered and ate a plate of soup, paid her fifteen-cent check, and left. Outside she stood for some time, staring into the rain. Then she re-entered the restaurant and approached the cashier.

" Will you loan me a dollar on this watch until I send for it tomorrow? I have no money and I must have a place to sleep tonight."

The young woman took from Mrs. Terry's hand a small gold watch bearing on one side the monogram, white and blue, " S. A. H.," and, on the other the date " 1879." Attached to the watch was a heavy gold fob chain with an egg-shaped pendant of blue, red and white agates. . . .

"I will give you the dollar," said the . . . clerk. " But I do not want your watch."

"You must take it to oblige me. . . . I do not wish you to give me money without proper security."

" Who are you? " inquired the clerk.

"I am Mrs. Terry. I will call for the watch to-morrow."

Mrs. Terry left the restaurant hastily, and went to the Alvin House upstairs and asked for a room for the night. She entered the parlor to await the arrival of Mrs. Edelman, the proprietress, and meantime played several selections on the piano. Mrs. Edelman recognized her immediately . . . and, fearing notoriety, refused to give her a room. Mrs. Terry pleaded in vain, and, although another woman in the house offered to share her room with Mrs. Terry, the obdurate landlady refused. . . . Mrs. Terry left at 9 o'clock, and it is presumed she went to the house of Mammy Pleasant. . . .

Several days later Sarah returned to the restaurant and reclaimed the watch, tendering the girl a five-dollar gold piece.

" Well, do you think I'm crazy? " she asked in curious amusement.

" No, indeed, Madam, I do not."

" I've been married twice and I ought to be able to take care of myself. . . . It's nobody's business how long I stay here or where I stay," she added with good-natured sharpness.

She resumed her wanderings, always trailed by reporters. Her every movement was recorded in the press. In his Sunday column in the *Examiner* Ambrose Bierce remarked:

The male Californian — idolater of sex and proud of abasement at the feet of his own female — has now a fine example of the results entailed by his unnatural worship. Mrs. Terry, traipsing the streets, uncommonly civic, problematically harmless but indubitably daft, is all his own work, and he ought to be proud of her. . . .

One phase of her strange odyssey had elements of pure drama. On March 1 she appeared with a woman companion at the Russ House. The proprietor refused to allow her to register.

Bidding her companion to wait her return, Mrs. Terry went down stairs and proceeded up Montgomery Street to the Palace Hotel. At the newsstand she called for ink and paper and scribbled a note to one of the clerks, which was carried in by a messenger boy, she following. . . .

As the strains of the orchestra caught her ear however, she gasped for breath, and for an instant stood with a hand upon her heart. Then she left hurriedly by a side entrance and hurried along New Montgomery Street and Market to Kearny. . . .

For several days longer the now obviously demented woman wandered about the town, stared at by the

crowds, trailed by reporters and small boys. She was
seen variously at St. Ignatius' Church, the Baldwin
Hotel (where she had lived when she first met Sharon) ,
and on a bench in Union Square. A reporter, " interviewing " her there, found her a pathetic, disheveled
figure, who talked rationally, however, on topics not
related to her obsessions. On March 7, when she was
refused permission to stay at a second-rate hotel on
Market Street, her old spirit reasserted itself, and
papers reported that she had thoroughly pommeled the
clerk.

The next day she was locked up pending a sanity
hearing. The complaint was signed by Mammy Pleasant.

5

OF THE last of Sarah's many court appearances the
Chronicle remarked:

> The poor woman, broken in spirit and mind, had her
> hearing before Judge Levy, sitting in Judge Lawler's court-
> room, his own being too small to accommodate the crowd
> that had gathered. . . . Mammy Pleasant appeared at
> once as complainant and friend, and of all the people pres-
> ent, male and female, was the only one who showed any
> sympathy for the demented creature.

Sarah was described as calm and composed during
the hearing. Observers noted that she looked neater
than she had in months; Mammy Pleasant had bought

her a complete change of clothing from " boots to bonnet."

Mammy Pleasant, the first witness called, testified that Sarah " didn't seem to have her mind. . . . Her head is all level enough save on the subject of spirits. . . . She thinks she is communicating with Judge Terry."

The familiar atmosphere of the courtroom had its effect. Once again Sarah felt under the necessity of " protecting her rights." Her interest sharpened; she leaned forward, following every action with watchful eyes. She asked for and was given permission to question witnesses.

" Is my mind all right, Mammy? "

" Yes, your mind is all right save on these subjects of spiritualism and electricity."

" Why, then, did you have me arrested? "

" For your own good; to protect you from yourself."

Sarah subsided while a reporter, Henry Bigelow, related some of her actions during the preceding fortnight. Bigelow was followed by a Doctor Windele, one of the commissioners of insanity, who stated his opinion that she was insane. As he left the stand, the old-time fire came into Sarah's eyes and she demanded his recall. The doctor courteously acquiesced. She asked curtly:

" Have you a diploma? "

" Yes."

" Where from? "

" At Edinburgh."

" Have you a certificate to practice medicine? "

" Yes."

" What is the faculty of your school? "

" I do not have a roster now."

" How long since you were there? "

" Fifteen or twenty years."

" You can't remember that far back and I can. How long have you been in San Francisco? "

" About thirteen years."

" Did you ever practice anywhere else? "

" Yes."

" Where? "

" In Ireland."

" What part? "

" In Cork."

" County Cork? "

" No, City of Cork."

" How old are you? "

" Nearly forty-three."

" And you think I ought to be sent to an asylum? "

" I do most assuredly, Mrs. Terry."

" Well, doctor . . . don't you think that if you were examined pretty closely some of these people would believe that you ought to be there? "

The doctor retired in some confusion and Sarah settled back, well satisfied with her small triumph. It was her last. Other doctors agreed on her condition and, while tears trailed down Mammy Pleasant's cheeks, Judge Levy pronounced her insane and committed her to the state asylum at Stockton.

The next day, March 11, 1892, in the custody of a deputy sheriff, Sarah left San Francisco for the last time. A crowd gathered as she was put aboard a train at Oakland and she attempted to address them. The

faithful Mammy was on hand, however, and she succeeded in quieting her. Two hours later the train
passed through the town of Lathrop. Sarah gave no
evidence that she recognized the place. The restaurant
where Judge Terry had been shot had since burned.
Before nightfall she was behind locked doors at Stockton. She remained there almost exactly forty-five years.

In July of 1936 the writers of these pages sat in a
pleasant room at the Stockton State Hospital and talked
with eighty-six-year-old Sarah Althea Hill Terry. The
neat, white-haired little figure sat in a rocking-chair.
Her shoulders were stooped and she leaned forward
slightly, regarding her visitors with bright, shrewd
eyes. She had been unwell, her heart was bad, and
some years earlier she had broken her hip, so it was
hard for her to get about. A crutch was leaning against
her chair; she kept one hand on it while she talked.

Visitors had been rare in recent years, but the old
lady showed no sign that there was anything unusual
about this call; it was as though she entertained callers every afternoon. Small talk fell nimbly from her
tongue.

We were from San Francisco? Ah, it is cool there,
the wind blows in from the sea. (The July heat made
the little room oppressive.) And we had come alone?
No ladies along?

She spoke politely, like a dutiful hostess, but she was
not much interested. She heard our questions without
surprise and answered those she chose to answer. Evidently all her infrequent visitors asked the same things.

" Judge Terry? " An ancient chuckle. " He was one

of my husbands. He was a big man." She emphasized the word " big " and looked about the room for something that might give an idea how big he was. " He could hardly get through that door. Do you know him? "

" How about Senator Sharon? "

" William Sharon? He was a rich man. He owned the Bank of California. Is he dead? Do you know my brother, Morgan Hill? Do you know Fred Sharon, my stepson? He looks like you, only he's bald-headed." Again the chuckle. " You must know *him.* He never would talk much. . . ."

" Mrs. Terry, do you recall Mammy Pleasant? "

" Of course! " There was no hesitation. " She was a black lady. . . . Took charge of my trial. She was *smart.*" Again the emphasis, on " smart." " She was a maid in Thomas Bell's home. . . . Is she dead? "

Other persons and episodes of the trial were mentioned. A few she seemed not to recall. The marriage contract? No, she knew of no marriage contract. Had she really forgotten or was she refusing to say, cannily " protecting her interests "? It was impossible to say. Belmont? She shook her head.

But of others she spoke readily enough, with a sort of good-humored patience.

" Judge Tyler? He was one of my attorneys. His son was an attorney too. General Barnes was a tall man. . . . Yes, he was William Sharon's attorney. Judge Sullivan tried the case. I won."

Of Sharon's Chinese servant, Ki: " Ki used to sit outside Mr. Sharon's door. Do you know Ki? "

" Didn't Senator Sharon like to recite poetry? "

" Yes, he did . . . and he was always joking. . . ."

" Do you remember the poem he recited the first time he called on you: *Maid of Athens?* "

The question seemed momentarily to capture her real interest. She brightened perceptibly, and she managed to recall three words more: " Maid of Athens, ere we part. . . ."

" Were you ever called the ' Rose of Sharon '? "

" The rose of Sharon is a pretty flower. . . . Are you from San Francisco? . . . Do you stay at the Palace? . . . That's my hotel, you know. It was built for me. . . . The Palace covered four blocks and there were stores and shops in front. . . . Do you know Fred Sharon? When you go back, tell him Mrs. Terry sent you. . . ."

San Francisco was mentioned. She repeated the name, adding a bit wistfully: " I'd like to go there myself. . . ."

The nurse returned, unlocked the door. Mrs. Terry was not very well that week; she must not tire herself.

She extended her small, plump hand as we left and her bright eyes followed us to the door.

Seven months later the mail brought a short note:

Your name is given as one who is interested in the case of Sarah A. Terry, and we are writing to inform you that she died on February 14, 1937, of bronchopneumonia, following influenza.

MARGARET H. SMYTH, M.D.

Medical Director and Superintendent

CHAPTER SIX

SMILAX AND LAUDANUM

1

As a symbol of the city's progress the Palace was a shining success from the day of its opening. No citizen with an out-of-town visitor on his hands whom he wished to impress with what an energetic community could accomplish was ever in doubt as to how to proceed. He loaded his guest into the nearest hack and loftily announced: " To the Palace." Magic words! The visitor might, and usually did, think well of the garden spot from which he had sprung. Not five minutes were needed to demolish that illusion and to scatter its fragments in the dust. For positively nowhere else in the land had the business of providing food and shelter to the traveling public been lifted to such a plane. The out-of-towner had but to step down from the hack and regard the black-and-white splendor of the grand court. Inevitably the realization was forced upon him that it was this hotel (and not the railroad station or opera house or waterworks of his home town) that perfectly symbolized the aspirations of late-nineteenth-century Americans.

In that respect the Palace was an incalculably valuable asset to the city. Travelers who spent a night or two under its roof were presently repeating the catalogue of its wonders to groups in the lobbies of lesser hotels from Edinburgh to Bombay. Of course it easily supplanted its local rivals. Dozens of prosperous citizens moved their families into the new suites and became permanent guests. The prestige of the name, the luxurious appointments and faultless service were regarded as well worth " Blandlord " Leland's high rates. Names well known all over the Coast sprinkled the early pages of the register. Leland Stanford, ex-Governor and multimillionaire president of the Central Pacific, occupied a suite on the Montgomery-Market corner while his forty-room mansion at Powell and California streets was building. Ralston's widow and her son and two daughters were honored early guests; the lawsuit by which she forced Sharon to pay over an additional quarter-million from her husband's estate was still in the future. Mr. and Mrs. Howard Coit were among the first names on the register — every San Franciscan knew the story of that picturesque couple — and there were scores of others.

Permanent guests were quartered on the top floor, where they constituted a separate social group, a little community within the larger one. There family groups gathered nightly on the broad gallery surrounding the grand court; the men smoked and read the *Bulletin* and the *Alta* while their wives and daughters gossiped over their embroidery, and children played among the potted shrubs or romped, not too boisterously, through the corridors. Intermittently the sound of music drifted up to their lofty shelf or the swift clatter of hoofs on macadam announced the arrival or departure of carriages far below.

Smilax and Laudanum

Beneath this genteel sphere of domesticity and quite detached from it were the vast tiers of bedrooms that sheltered a heterogeneous and shifting population: merchants and professional men from up and down the coast; Eastern tourists enjoying the unique experience of passing from ocean to ocean by rail; a trickle of foreign globe-trotters determined to conceal their astonishment at the absence of red-shirted miners and blazing six-shooters; statesmen, diplomats, politicians, promoters, noblemen, East Indian princes, actors, musicians, captains of industry, opera singers, judges, confidence men. . . .

It was not long before the town made the then novel discovery that a big hotel is in truth a city within a city. More than a thousand persons lived or worked within the walls of the Palace. Beneath its two-acre roof a student might find whatever he needed for a study of the human animal in all his complexity. Every graduation of the social scale was represented. In the public rooms, in the subterranean service quarters, and in the hundreds of upstairs apartments men and women reacted upon one another and upon their environment precisely as in the larger world outside. Whatever happened elsewhere in the way of human behavior was certain sooner or later to happen there. Within its walls men and women schemed and quarreled, gambled away fortunes and conducted profitable businesses, drank to excess and delivered lectures on temperance, lived in adultery and led exemplary lives — all according to their preferences and their opportunities.

During the thirty years of its existence the hotel provided the town's papers with innumerable human-interest stories, important and trivial, tragic and humorous, and of all stages between. Bursts of lethal gunfire echoed through its corridors and, during the same week, philanthropists announced princely gifts. Swindles were perpetrated and humanitarian movements launched. Members of the town's first families celebrated their engagements in smilax-hung chambers on the lower floor, while a few flights above empty laudanum bottles on bedside tables announced the means by which less favored guests had solved their troubles. Smilax and laudanum — both were symbols of importance in the annals of the Palace.

2

THE HOTEL had not been open three months before the town was reading of unusual happenings in a room facing one of the labyrinthian upper corridors. On the afternoon of December 3, 1875 the curiosity of ground-floor loiterers was aroused by a flurry of excitement about one of the elevators. A group of men emerged and hastened toward the carriage entrance. Bystanders recognized John Meagher of the city detective force, R. H. Jackson, the hotel's private policeman, and Charles Haley, partner of the local brokerage firm of Hopkins & Haley. With them was a young man with his head newly bandaged and a second young man with distraught expression and his hands securely manacled.

By the morning of the 4th the entire city knew the

details of the Palace's first crime. On November 28 a young man " of good appearance and address " had signed the name S. W. Harrington on the register and had been assigned to room 669. Five days later he wrote a note to Hopkins & Haley stating that he was confined to his room by illness and requesting that $3,750 in greenbacks be sent him in exchange for coin. Haley responded in person; the two arranged the terms of the exchange, and the broker left, promising to send over the currency by messenger that afternoon.

Instead of doing so, Haley, who had become suspicious, notified the police. Inquiry at the hotel revealed that Harrington had no funds on deposit in the office safe and that, far from being ill, he had been seen about the hotel in apparent good health. Accordingly, when the clerk, a young man named Ludlam, arrived with the currency, he was attended by Haley and two officers. These three remained outside the door while Ludlam knocked and entered.

> The clerk . . . announced that he had the greenbacks. Mr. Harrington said, all right, he would count them. The clerk thought that unnecessary, as the package had been put up by Mr. Haley. " I'll count them anyway," said Harrington, and the package was put into his hands. He took a seat at the table and began counting, the clerk watching his movements by the reflection through a mirror. In about ten minutes Harrington snatched up a hatchet, a new tomahawk fresh from the hardware store, and attacked Ludlam. The latter had just time to ward off the force of the blow in part, but it struck on the head, inflicting a severe cut. He hallooed " Murder! " and the officers burst open the door.

Harrington was overpowered and disarmed. A search of his room revealed that he had made thorough preparations. A coil of rope and a bottle of chloroform were found in the closet. On his person was a loaded pistol, a razor and a forged check for $3,750. In prison Harrington explained that he had been driven to his act by inability to find work. An attempt to hang himself in his cell was frustrated by another prisoner.

Unlike this dramatic arrest of the obscure Harrington was the scene in room 838 on the night of August 11, 1878. Stretched on a trestle there lay the body of thirty-four-year-old Henry J. Mann, " first of the matinee idols." Mann — his stage name was Henry Montague — had first visited San Francisco the season before, when he had played opposite Adelaide Neilson. Years later a local belle recalled that he " wore his thick brown hair parted at one side and swept back from a noble brow, with two locks brought forward to form a hook on either temple." Within a week half the girls in town were wearing " Montague curls " — and they continued to wear them for years. But the actor was ill on this second tour, and long before he reached the Coast, members of the troupe were worried about his condition. Their concern was justified. One night he collapsed on the stage of the California Theater and was carried into the wings. Now his body lay in his Palace room while members of the company sat about. Maude Granger, weeping, occupied the chair by his head — she had many times played Camille to his Armand Duval. Montague had once been secretary to Dion Boucicault; he had managed the Globe Theater in London and had had a succession of triumphs in America. The room was banked with floral pieces. One, a large cross of roses, bore the card of Flora Sharon, the senator's young daughter who later became Lady Hesketh.

Montague was born in England. With quite different emotions San Franciscans were presently reading of another Englishman's stay at the Palace. In January 1885 the *Oceanic* arrived from the Orient bearing an uncommonly large young man with a diminutive blond mustache and a strong disinclination to talk. He was Viscount Garmoyle, eldest son of Lord Cairns, former Lord Chancellor of England, and recently the defendant in a sensational breach-of-promise suit brought by a London actress.

At the Palace bar the twenty-four-year-old Englishman consumed an undetermined number of glasses of gin and sugar and reluctantly submitted to an interview. He had nothing to say about the suit brought by Miss Fortescue. If the American papers misrepresented his part in the affair, that was " too bad but he didn't care."

Would he care to tell the reporters why he had left England?

" Now, look here. I left on the 16th of lawst Feb'ry because I was badgered on all sides by you fellows. People looked at me like a pickpocket. I met Miss Fortescue and I admired her. I'd have married her if they hadn't interfered, blawst me if I wouldn't. . . ."

" Why did you break off your engagement with the lady? "

" Because my friends advised me to."

" She was perfectly respectable? "

"Yes. She came of good family, but by misfortune was driven to the stage."

"Have you received notice of the settlement of the suit?"

"Yes. My solicitors notified me yesterday that they had allowed £10,000 against the gov'nor."

"What do you think of it?"

"Don't think at all. Don't care at all. Leave the lawyers to fight it out. . . ."

The reporters carefully explained that Lord Garmoyle did not look as dissipated as expected, " — but that may have been the fault of the sea air." He was described as tall, awkward in bearing, with blue eyes, a florid face, and a retreating chin. San Francisco was of the opinion that by awarding Miss Fortescue ten thousand pounds as compensation for his loss, the London jury had been more than liberal. " The young lady may congratulate herself on having made a splendid bargain."

Compensating for that blasted romance was this curious tale, which charmed the town in the summer of 1885. Chancing to be standing near the desk one day when a group of guests checked out, an *Alta* reporter saw a personable young man make a substantial gift to one of the clerks. His curiosity aroused, he questioned the clerk, who thereupon told him a remarkable story. " The facts are known," he stated, " only to five persons: myself and the four in that carriage — mother, daughter, niece, and the young Englishman. He is the son of a wealthy manufacturer, and also has a fortune from a maiden aunt. He came here two months ago and took a room on the third floor, next to mine." Some time later an elderly lady, with her daughter and niece, arrived; the young ladies were assigned to a room next to the Englishman's; the mother across the hall.

Late one night the clerk heard a muffled scream from the Englishman's room, which adjoined his own. He went to his door and peered into the hall. Presently he saw a young woman slip out of the Englishman's room and enter another. The clerk was surprised; he had not thought the young man " that kind of a chap." Next morning the Englishman came to him and volunteered an explanation.

He had been dozing, he stated, when he was aroused by someone getting into bed with him. The room was dark but his arm encountered a tress of hair on the pillow which told him his visitor was a woman. The Englishman thought rapidly. He realized that if his visitor had made an error the consequences would be distressing unless he acted with decision. He therefore clapped his hand over the woman's mouth, partially stifling her scream. Overcoming her subsequent struggles, he addressed her with well-bred urgency: " My dear madam, it is very evident that you have made a mistake in the room. Now, if I allow you to scream you will arouse our neighbors and it will be very difficult to make a satisfactory explanation. I am a gentleman and will not do you the slightest harm if you will obey my instructions. Please don't make any noise, but get out as quickly and as quietly as possible."

Reassured by this rational monologue, she slipped out of the bed and hurried to the door. When the young man awoke in the morning he concluded that the whole episode had been a dream. Then he made a discovery. In the bed he found a small gold ring of curious design — a coiled snake with eyes of emeralds and a tongue fashioned from a sliver of ruby. Here was a means by which he might learn the identity of his visitor. Thereafter he wore the ring on his smallest finger and made a point of twirling his mustache ostentatiously while he was about the hotel. One day in the dining-room he observed a girl at a neighboring table staring at the ring in startled confusion.

The Englishman returned her property by messenger. He was asked to call. Explanations followed. She had awakened during the night and remembered that she had forgotten to give her mother some medicine. She had run across the hall and on her return had mistaken the door to her room. The young man's faultless behavior greatly impressed the girl's mother. Evidently it also impressed the girl, for the two were married the day of their departure. In appreciation of the clerk's discretion, the bridegroom had made him the gift that had caught the eye of the reporter.

Somewhat akin to that pretty tale was another happening a few years later. In December 1891 J. T. Hamilton, city official of Spokane, married one of the belles of that city and set off for San Francisco on a honeymoon. They arrived on the steamer *Oregon* and put up at the Palace. The exploit that got their names in the papers occurred a night or two later. In company with some steamer acquaintances, Hamilton had tarried overlong at the hotel bar and, when he chanced to glance at a clock, he discovered that it was after ten. He excused himself and hurried up to his room. A

224

light was burning within, but his timid knock elicited no response. The key was inside the door.

The bridegroom stood on a chair and looked through the transom. His bride was sleeping. He then took off his hat and shoes and started to climb cautiously through the transom. But the aperture proved too small and he presently found himself stuck midway. The resulting commotion aroused the bride; she regarded the red-faced man, jumped out of bed with a shriek, and pressed the call button.

A colored boy answered the bell, saw the active legs projecting from the transom and blew a blast into the speaking tube: " Everybody come up right now. There's a robbah in numbah 552! " Clerks and porters reached the scene just as Mrs. Hamilton recognized her husband and tried to help him down. But he was firmly wedged in place; not before saws and files were procured and the transom rod cut was he released.

There were a variety of picturesque adventures. In the middle '80s curiosity focused on a woman guest who for several months occupied one of the better suites on the Montgomery Street side, a personable young woman with brown eyes and chestnut hair. She had registered as the Viscountess Vera Hastings and had given her residence as Paris. However, mail clerks observed that while some of her many letters were addressed to the name under which she had registered, others were to plain Bonnie Vesta Hastings.

The slight air of mystery about her failed to detract from her popularity. She seemed well supplied with funds and gave frequent entertainments both in her Palace suite and at the Maison Riche. After such parties her Negro maid redeposited her jewels in the office safe — " a great tray of diamonds." Among her many admirers one was presently singled out for special favor: John Bradbury, aged twenty-one, the son of a Los Angeles capitalist. The two were soon reported engaged.

Meantime someone — perhaps the Bradbury family — had been investigating the young lady's antecedents. One day word reached town that she was really Bonnie Riley, daughter of the owner of a woodyard in Portland, Oregon. Other disclosures followed. Eight years earlier she had attended St. Helen's Academy in Portland, then had been sent to a school at Harrisburg, Pennsylvania. A short time later she was back in Portland, where she created a sensation by an attempt at suicide. She next tried the New York stage and became an understudy in Nat Goodwin's company, and was next heard of in Paris. Eventually she had turned up in San Francisco as the Countess Henriot. She was not quite twenty-four.

Local papers learned of the exposé and reporters hurried to the Palace. She received them graciously, dressed in her usual black, with her usual plenitude of jewels. The visitors observed that she wore from two to four rings on each finger. One finger had them " all the way down " and even her thumbs were ringed. She indignantly denied the charges. She was not Bonnie Riley and she had never lived in Portland. Her father was a French count; her mother a Russian. She was the Countess Henriot. The Henriots hailed from Charleston, South Carolina. She feared these stories might terminate her engagement with Johnny Bradbury, who was only twenty-one and small for his age, but " a nice little fellow " none the less — and with a millionaire father.

She showed the reporters one of her many rings. It had been given her by Bradbury, who, soon after meeting her, had broken off his engagement to a young lady in Los Angeles. " I think all his relatives want him to marry her," she announced. " I hope they won't make John turn against me."

But matters began to look dark for her. Newspapers, which had been checking her story, printed a telegram from Charleston:

> No such person known here. — *News and Courier.*

Meantime reporters trailed her about town. The *Chronicle* stated that she had been seen in an Ellis Street saloon shaking dice for a hundred dollars a throw and peeling bills off a thick roll. Palace bellboys reported her less generous with them. Then came word that Bradbury had broken their engagement, and she hurried to Los Angeles. No reconciliation followed, however, and she presently returned north, checked out of the Palace, and disappeared. Papers reported that she had settled her hotel account, but a number of collectors soon appeared with unpaid bills from local merchants.

Vesta Riley Hastings reappeared in local papers more than a decade later. A dispatch from New York announced her death in Paris on August 20, 1898. She had thrown herself from a window of Maxim's Restaurant because of " unrequited love." She was thirty-six. Her prosperity during her stay in San Francisco was then explained: she had been the protégé of a New York merchant who had given her a magnificent collection of diamonds and established her in a luxurious apartment on West Thirty-fifth Street. It was after that affair had terminated that she had headed west.

3

THROUGH THE years the big hotel remained a dependable source of news stories.

The whole town was amused when Baron Luttwitz, big game hunter, arrived laden down with trophies of his marksmanship and an arsenal of guns — and a night or two later threw a whole floor of the Palace into turmoil by accidentally discharging one of his biggest pistols. The ball passed between his arm and side and the marksman was undamaged.

About that time another Palace guest had his brief season of notoriety. Vicomte G. de Beughem, a young Swiss, one day received a scented note, signed only "Edith," suggesting a rendezvous on a downtown street corner. "Edith" failed to appear but the Vicomte noticed two strangers regarding him closely. Later, near the buffalo corral in Golden Gate Park, an attractive young woman "made eyes at him." When he started to follow, two men stepped from the bushes and confronted him with drawn pistols. The ardent stranger was relieved of $250; the robbers overlooked an additional $400 in his inner pocket.

Girls who used their wits to advantage were sure of

respectful notice in the local papers. One such was the Baroness de Buren, from Budapest, once plain Daisy Neuman of San Jose. She was at the Palace with her husband, renewing old acquaintances and placing sen-sationally large bets at the Emeryville racetrack. Only four years earlier Daisy, blonde and pretty, had quit her job in a local millinery shop and set off for Europe. Now she was back again, a baroness and the " hand-somest woman in the Palace." Her triumph was no surprise to former suitors, one of whom remarked: " The Baroness doesn't waste her time shooting at quail when there are plenty of fat turkeys around."

One day in 1894 pretty Zella Nicholas tripped across the marble-paved lobby and registered — under an as-sumed name. She was described as only about eight-een, with a striking expression of innocence. But a guest from the East recognized her as having recently been the plaintiff in a suit to force payment of a forty-thousand-dollar check she claimed had been given her by a famous New Yorker. It was learned that she had other names besides Nicholas: Mrs. Ruhman, Miss Graham, and Mrs. Moore; that she was born in Wa-bash, Illinois, and that her maiden name was Lytle.

A few months later guests shook their heads over the tragedy of two lovers who had carried out a suicide pact in one of the Palace rooms — and promptly forgot the matter in their welcome to " Peerless Pauline " Hall, musical-comedy star. Sixteen years earlier Pauline, then known as " the girl in the red waist," had played small parts at the Tivoli and had earned fifteen dollars a week. She was now Mrs. George B. McLellan, of New York, and a not very staunch defender of the

" new woman." The current symbol of woman's eman-
cipation was the wearing of bloomers. Pauline ap-
proved of bloomers, but with reservations. " The
French women make them with pleats and trimmings
and produce a most artistic garment, but some of our
New York girls — well, their bloomers are more like
tights than anything else, and I am not reconciled to
the idea of women wearing tights on the streets."

In March 1897 papers announced another death at
the Palace — and another strange story came to light.
The dead man was " a wealthy Pittsburgh banker and
broker," whose doctors had recently informed him
that he had only a few months to live. Long a model
citizen and the head of a family, he had none the less
decided to live out his remaining time " in his own
way." His own way included a sightseeing tour of the
country in company with a mysterious young woman
of " great beauty." She had remained with him until
he died, then had dropped from sight. The banker's
body was sent back to Pittsburgh. On its arrival an
undertaker there, through the press, complimented his
San Francisco colleague on a superior job of em-
balming.

While this was going on, a local jury was listening
with sympathy while Lillian Blair, shop-girl, told how
ex-President Barillas of Guatemala had wooed, won
and left her. " He took me to the Palace Hotel to dine
in his private parlor and meet some of his friends, and
introduced me to a number of Spanish gentlemen, kissing me before them all. . . ." How many dollars the
law granted her as compensation for such treatment is

not known, but it was pleasant to reflect that not all the town's working girls were so imposed on. A gratifying exception was Sadie Holmes, twenty-one-year-old operator of the Palace's new telephone switchboard. Guests who had admired her musical voice were astonished to learn that, by the death of an English grand-aunt, she had become Lady Bretherton, heir to a million-dollar estate. While some reflected on the odd fact that English estates inherited by Americans were practically all valued at " a million dollars," the erstwhile Sadie Holmes granted her first interview: " It is like a fairy story. . . . The property belonging to Lady Jane Bretherton passed to my father at her death, but . . . that portion of her estate that is in Wales passes to the eldest daughter of the heir. I am papa's eldest daughter. . . ." The excited girl was planning to leave soon to assume the responsibilities of her new life. Meantime guests continued to enjoy the privilege of having their calls put through by Lady Bretherton.

Shortly before the century closed a new type of celebrity came to the Palace: James J. Jeffries, world's champion heavyweight by virtue of a recent victory over Bob Fitzsimmons. All activity stopped when the ex-boilermaker, a tiny straw hat on his head and an immense diamond in his cravat, arrived, registered, and hurried to his third-floor suite. Jeff at once gave a party for his admirers, called on his friend Patsy Hogan (who was in the county jail, charged with murdering his wife), and that night visited his father at Woodward's Gardens. The elder Jeffries, an itinerant preacher, thought the champion looked thin — he weighed 240 pounds — and was scornful of his fashionable straw hat. The son's explanation that straws were " all the rage " in New York impressed him and he insisted on trying it on. Jeff accordingly put on the old man's great slouch hat and the father donned the " little fashionable wisp of straw." Onlookers reported him " a grotesque figure, but smiling. . . ."

Two days later the story of Jeff's stay at the hotel was told in retrospect by the *Examiner:*

Twenty-four hours only did Jeffries remain at the Palace, where men of the arena are not in the habit of staying. He wired for quarters from somewhere on the road, and there was no opportunity to send the usual reply. So on Thursday afternoon James made his triumphant entry in a water-front hack, led by a band of six pieces engaged for the purpose. This gorgeous pageant surged into the grand court, followed by an ardent constituency attired mostly in sweaters. . . . When the crowd dispersed the management fumigated the grand court and tried to revive the potted palms. . . .

The champion was shown to an eight dollar a day vault on the Jessie Street side, where he held a levee. He sent for four quarts of champagne and twenty-two glasses, but only one man tackled the unknown liquid. He was said to be Alex Greggains, who has kept a saloon on the south side long enough to know that there is such a beverage. . . .

When the guests departed the liquid air was turned on gradually. Jeff observed that his breath congealed while sitting in his room waiting for bellboys. That night he slept between the mattresses and could hear the liquid air crackling the walls of his eight dollar boudoir. . . . Frost settled on his hair while he was settling his bill, and it is said that the lock on his trunk contracted so much that he couldn't get the key in.

They said at the hotel yesterday that Mr. Jeffries was not coming back any more.

4

ECHOES OF General Grant's stay at the Palace in 1879 were audible for years after. It was not generally known at the time, but that famous visit had seen the blossoming of romance. During the round of entertainments the general's second son, Ulysses S. Grant, Jr. — Buck to his intimates — had been taken by the charms of Jennie Flood, daughter of the Bonanza king. Miss Flood was described as a handsome girl, intelligent and democratic, and with the prospect of four or five millions. She was one of the party that accompanied the Grants on their visit to Yosemite. There Buck Grant showed her a great deal of attention. Before the outing was over he had proposed, and the girl, following the formula of the time, blushingly suggested that he ask father.

Four years later a writer for the *Wasp* told the rest of the story. Buck duly interviewed Flood in the latter's office in the Nevada Bank. The mining man listened with sympathy, but when he questioned young Grant about his prospects Buck confessed that he had no means of supporting a wife. He made it clear, however, he was quite willing to go to work.

"Very well," said Flood. "You go back to New

York, buy the stock I tell you, and deal for six months as I suggest, and I think we can fix you up."

Young Grant followed instructions to the letter. Each point Flood gave him turned out beautifully; every transaction made money. " It was not long before young Grant had a hundred thousand dollars ahead." Meantime everyone was talking of Buck's success. Flood was delighted; now no one could say that the young man was marrying his daughter for her money.

But complications developed. " Success began to make the young man top-heavy." He began to regard himself as a financial wizard and the flattery of friends confirmed him in that opinion. More, he delayed from week to week his scheduled return to California. When he finally started west he tarried along the way, quite unlike an ardent lover. He reached San Francisco — and delayed continuing on to Menlo Park, where Miss Flood was spending the summer. Flood himself called on the young man at the Palace; he was kept waiting in a parlor of the hotel while young Grant chatted with friends. " That night Mr. Flood told his daughter that he believed they both had made a mistake." Buck finally appeared at Menlo Park, but found that Miss Flood was in San Francisco. " There she learned that he had been flirting with several young ladies, not particularly her friends." She wrote him a note offering to terminate the engagement. Young Grant continued his flirtations, and the Floods presently announced that the engagement was off.

San Francisco was thus deprived of what would assuredly have been a brilliant wedding. In the spring

234

Smilax and Laudanum

of 1898 a far from formal ceremony united Louise Lander West and Walter Sanger Pullman. Pullman was a twin son of the late palace-car magnate; his bride was the second of three West sisters. The Misses West were noted beauties of their time, blue-eyed and statuesque, with the " beautifully rounded forms " then much admired. They were daughters of Charles H. West, a pioneer of '49, who had died leaving them excellent social connections and not much else. Faced by the necessity of supporting themselves, the girls had become schoolteachers. But drilling the rudiments of the three R's into the heads of young San Franciscans did not detain them long; many proved eager to rescue them from the tedium of the classroom.

The eldest of the sisters had recently married Hugh McDonnell, a mining engineer. McDonnell spent much time in Mexico and South America, and his wife occupied one of the sixth-floor suites at the Palace. Young Pullman, who had come west to visit his sister, Mrs. Francis Carolan, also took up residence at the hotel, where he soon met Louise West. One afternoon the young couple — Pullman was twenty-three, Miss West a year younger — appeared at the home of an Oakland preacher and were married.

The elopement was a major sensation. Local papers recalled that the older Pullman had left the bulk of his fortune to his widow and two daughters; the twins, George M. and Walter Sanger, were given a mere three thousand a year.

Mrs. McDonnell gave the couple a wedding breakfast in her Palace rooms. She presented her sister with a silver loving-cup with the inscription: " Flow wine, smile women, and the universe is controlled." The cup was filled and refilled with champagne. The centerpiece of the table was " a bunch of wild oats tied and hemmed in with eschscholtzias " — California poppies.

Several years later there was another Pullman-West wedding, when Sanger's twin brother, George, married the youngest of the three sisters. It was the second marriage for both. The bridegroom died at San Mateo two months later.

Of Palace romances of the period a lamentably large percentage were to tread a thorny path. This was true of the marriage on May 10, 1900 of Dorothy Studebaker, a connection of the South Bend family of wagon-manufacturers, and Scott McKeown, wealthy young man-about-town. Again there was an elaborate wedding breakfast at the Palace. White roses, maiden-hair ferns, and the inevitable smilax made up the decorations. The table, unlike that at the Pullman breakfast, contained no wild oats, although events were to prove that they might not have been inappropriate. McKeown gave his bride a ten-thousand-dollar pearl necklace, some thoroughbred horses, and — appropriate to a Studebaker — a fine carriage. The *Examiner's* account of the wedding departed rather widely from the conventional reporting of social events:

The breakfast cost a thousand dollars exclusive of wine, and sixty-five quarts of champagne were consumed by the twenty-four guests. Mr. McKeown made the only speech of his life. It was in response to a most graceful and eloquent address of congratulation.

" Well, ladies and gentlemen," said the groom, brac-ing himself with both hands on the table, " I'm damned glad it's over! " Then he subsided. . . .

This couple proved a steady source of news. Papers reported quarrels and reconciliations. The bride made known an intention of going on the stage. A little later news services announced that she had danced the cake-walk in one of the public rooms of a Chicago hotel on a Sunday. She was asked to move to another hotel. Her desire for a stage career was gratified when she got a small part in a musical show. In July 1901 she was back in San Francisco, sipping tea at the Palace grill and telling reporters about her divorce. " It had to come sooner or later. . . . This tea tastes good. . . . Since I've been on the road there have been times when I didn't have a lone dime to buy a cup . . . too much pride to ask an advance from the box office. . . ."

Lively reading, too, were accounts of the Baxter-Tevis wedding in March 1901. Hugh Tevis was the son of a local capitalist; Miss Baxter a daughter of an ex-Governor of Wyoming, then living in Denver. A day or two before the wedding a dispatch from Denver stated that a young man there claimed to have been jilted by the bride-to-be. Of course reporters hurried to the Palace. " A charming picture the indignant girl made," they stated, " as she tossed her blonde head, while her blue eyes flashed and her cheeks reddened." " If there is blame to fall on anyone," she announced, " let it fall on me. . . ." Evidently no blame fell on her, for the marriage took place on schedule and the pair departed on a trans-Pacific honeymoon. A few weeks later a cable from Yokohama announced the bridegroom's death, following an operation for appendicitis.

The widow was back in San Francisco by the end of June — in time to hear that the rejected suitor in Denver had purchased her former home there and planned to " run the Baxters out of town socially." The elder Baxter was asked to comment, and he proved eager to oblige. His interview was sprinkled with such remarks as these: " You do not need to get very near a skunk to detect the genus. . . . It is a waste of lather to shave an ass. . . ."

Next morning San Franciscans read the above with delight; this type of breakfast-table reading-matter was exactly to their taste. A year later more of the same was provided by May Yohe.

May Yohe's background was known to every newspaper-reader in the country. Born in Bethlehem, Pennsylvania, thirty-four years before, she had attained fame in spite of severe handicaps. Critics were agreed that she had a poor stage presence and no marked ability; that her attractions were limited to a clear complexion, flashing sloe-black eyes, and a vibrant, throaty voice. " She has only four notes in her voice — but they are corkers! " On this slight equipment she had managed to make herself internationally known. The turning-point had come in 1892, while she was appearing at the Garden Theater, New York. There she was seen one evening by Lord Francis Hope, who promptly made her Lady Hope and took her off to London. There she became celebrated as " the girl with the foghorn voice " and was admired for her rendition of quaint American plantation songs. Lord Hope was said to have lost a fortune backing a show for her at the Lyric Theater. This reverse, plus other extravagances, obliged him to sell his art treasures. He was not permitted to part with the family jewels, however, including the famous Hope diamond; these came into the possession of Lady Hope, who is said to have retained them after the pair separated.

Her visit to San Francisco in 1901 was under what local papers described as " unusual circumstances." She had separated from her husband several years before, but they had not been divorced. " It seems," commented the *Examiner*, " that an absolute divorce from Hope means an absolute divorce from the Hope jewels." Meantime she was on her way to the Orient, in company with Major Putnam Bradlee Strong, known to some as " Tea and Toast " Strong. Refused admittance to the Palace, the pair went to another hotel, where they registered as " Mr. and Mrs. H. L. Hastings, Boston." That evening they dined at the Palace, where May wore an amazing display of diamonds.

Next day reporters sought out Major Strong, who displayed no great willingness to talk.

" What do you intend to publish? " he asked.

" The truth. That you, Major Strong of New York, son of ex-Mayor Strong, are registered at the California Hotel under an assumed name. . . ."

" This is an outrage. . . ."

The affair began to attract wide attention. Reporters trailed the couple wherever they went and camped outside their room. This attention proved too much for the management of the California Hotel and they were asked to move. A day or two later it was reported that the Major had sent his resignation from the army to Washington and that Secretary Root had accepted it. Toward the middle of July the couple sailed on the *Nippon Maru* for Japan.

More than a year later the Yohe-Strong visit was recalled when the Duke of Newcastle paused at the Palace on his way to the coronation of Edward VII. He was a brother of Lord Francis Hope, and thus brother-in-law of the picturesque May. Her divorce proceedings were then in progress. The Duke stated that while he was opposed to divorce on principle he was not interfering in this case. He was asked about May's jewels. " She did not have any of the Hope family jewels with her. . . . What diamonds she may have displayed . . . are none of my business. Much has been said about the Hope jewels. The collection has been much exaggerated. . . ."

May's romance with Strong was shortlived. They parted and some years later she married Captain John A. Smuts, nephew of Jan Smuts, Boer War general. In May of 1938 newspapers reported that she was working on a WPA project in Boston, at a salary of $16.50 a week — " and proud of it." She died a few months later.

After Strong and May Yohe left town the Palace's gossips had a breathing spell — a rather extended one. No guest meriting their particular attention appeared until the coming of Truly Shattuck, five months later.

Miss Shattuck, in town to do a turn in vaudeville, was another local product who had made a name far-

The Palace Looming above the Surrounding City, 1880

The Grand Entrance, Montgomery Street, 1875

From the *California Spirit of the Times*

The Barroom, after Remodeling in the 1880s

The Ballroom, about 1885

ther afield. San Franciscans recalled that the generously proportioned girl had carried a spear in the
Amazon chorus at the old Tivoli. Since then her well-
filled tights had been the sensation of two continents;
in London theater-goers had called her " Truly Shocking." She need not have been concerned by such gibes
for, as the *Examiner* pointed out, " She has money to
spend and swell attire to wear. She is a modern success." Moreover she was back in her home town as a
vaudeville headliner. Truly was no 127-pound actress
of the May Yohe type, and crowds at the Orpheum
nightly verified a critic's discovery that " her shapely
outlines are rounder than ever."

But the reminiscent mood in which she was welcomed home had a disadvantage. Not only were her
struggles as a Tivoli chorus girl recalled; an early scandal was also retold in detail: how the young woman's
mother had ordered one Harry Poole to marry her
daughter and, on the young man's refusal to go through
with an immediate ceremony, had shot him dead. A
sensational trial had followed; the mother was acquitted, and Truly went east to pursue her career.

The retelling of this episode had no adverse effect
on attendance at the Orpheum during her engagement. The *Floradora* Sextet had demonstrated that
audiences liked their beauties to have plenty of well-
distributed heft, and Truly amply met that require-
ment. This vogue was responsible, too, for the attention given Mrs. H. R. Wimsett, who came to the Palace
with her husband in the spring of 1902. Mrs. Wimsett
had recently been Marie Wilson, one of the original
Floradora six. She had been playing the stock market,

and to such good effect that she had retired from the stage.

" Don't call me an actress," she warned a reporter at Marchand's Café. " I'm nothing of the kind. I had six months on the stage and that was enough for me."

" Don't you ever long to go back and toss the feathers again and wink the little wink over the shoulder? " asked the reporter, but Marie Wilson's reply was an emphatic negative.

As the foremost hotel of the Coast, the Palace was long regarded as the city's most desirable place to stop, or to drop in for lunch or dinner or an after-theater bite. It gained an even greater distinction. To those who planned to die fashionably the hotel held an uncommon attraction. At fairly regular intervals some purposeful citizen would make his way to Market and New Montgomery streets, register, go to his room, and, in the richest surroundings the town could provide, swallow the contents of a laudanum bottle.

In a few instances these carefully planned exits failed to work out. Not long after the new century opened, the San Francisco coroner received a note signed A. L. Humiston:

> You will find my remains in a room in the Palace Hotel, if there is any virtue in a couple of ounces of laudanum. Enclosed you will find my check on the First National Bank for $75.00, with which I want you to have me cremated. . . .

A deputy coroner hurried to room 766. He found Humiston alive and evidently in good health, although he " appeared to feign illness," and a laudanum vial, half empty, stood on the mantel. Finding his services not needed, the official left and the incident seemed closed. But the next day Humiston appeared at the coroner's office and demanded the return of his seventy-five dollars. This the coroner, a stickler for form, refused to give him; he pointed out that by Humiston's own statement he was supposed to be dead. Not until the young man produced satisfactory proof of his identity did the careful official hand over the check.

Meantime the city, always interested in the picturesque diversions of the socially elect, was treated to a new sensation. In the spring of 1901 E. D. Beylard, resident of fashionable Burlingame (" Blingum " to the society reporters), inaugurated a tally-ho service for the benefit of Palace guests. Beylard borrowed his idea from the East, where the Waldorf and other smart hotels were already offering daily rides on the tops of coaches owned and driven by young men of social importance. The Beylard tally-ho rattled out of the grand court each afternoon at half past two and proceeded, via Golden Gate Park, to the Cliff House; there the four horses were changed and the return trip was made by a different route. Twelve passengers were carried and the charge was two dollars per person.

The tally-ho promptly became the most celebrated vehicle in town. In the box beside Beylard sat a footman " attired in the simple livery of the house of Perigord," who regularly sounded blasts on his horn as a warning to traffic ahead. The public's curiosity extended to the smallest details of the coach and its accouterments. The *Examiner,* always helpful in such matters, had this to say about one item of the driver's costume:

It is a mistake to suppose that the mysterious outer garment that Mr. Beylard wears when on the box is a petticoat. It is a brown, tailor-made creation, cut walking length to show Mr. Beylard's spats. He wears it only in the box, and its assumption is something of a rite. When he is about to ascend to his place of authority, the person who blows the horn produces the skirt and fastens it on the coachman. A guard takes Mr. Beylard's mufti hat and substitutes the official white tile. . . .

The public's enthusiasm for Beylard and his coach was not shared by the town's hackmen. The latter looked on the vehicle as unfair competition and they were presently complaining bitterly to the authorities. Their spokesman, " Shorty Mike " Coffey, whose stand was in front of the Mint, pointed out that the professionals were forced to pay six dollars a quarter for a license and fifteen dollars a quarter for soliciting customers; in addition they had to go before the police commission and prove their driving ability before they could get a driver's license — which cost them an additional dollar a year. Coffey made it clear that the cabmen had no quarrel with Beylard, and that they would gladly welcome him into the fold if he paid the same fees they did. " We're a companionable lot," he added. So one day Beylard's tally-ho drew up in front of the City Hall; the driver went inside, took out the necessary licenses, and so became an accredited member of the hackmen's union.

5

LATE IN 1903 the sound of gunfire echoed through the hotel's corridors and another San Francisco figure found herself the talk of the town. To have her name conspicuously in the newspapers was, however, no novelty to Lillie Hitchcock Coit; she had been enjoy, ing that distinction for more than a third of a century.

Pioneers whose memories extended back to the '50s recalled her as the liveliest of the town's limited group of children. She arrived, aged eight, in May 1851. Her father was Captain Hitchcock, former army physician; her mother later became an intimate friend of Bret Harte and a star contributor to his *Overland Monthly.* Young Lillie grew up with the town; its hustle and confusion exactly suited her excitement-loving temperament. In the early years, fires provided the most dependable excitement. Like every other San Francisco child she was charmed by the volunteer firemen in their red shirts and great patent-leather helmets, and the resplendent pumps and hosecarts. Her active figure was usually in the van of those who followed the fire-fighters on headlong dashes through the streets.

In her case the infatuation proved permanent. Long after other girls of her age had abandoned the sport, Lillie continued to chase fire engines with as much ardor as ever. When she was seventeen and an acknowledged belle, the town was delighted to learn that she had one day left a wedding rehearsal at the sound of the fire bells and raced through the streets in her bridesmaid's costume. At the fire she crowded to the front

row of the spectators and shouted encouragement to
her favorite company, Knickerbocker Engine No. 5.
In 1863 the Knickerbockers made her an honorary
member. Thereafter she used its symbol as part of her
name, always signing herself: " Lillie Hitchcock Coit
— 5." When the city organized a professional fire department, the volunteer companies continued to exist
as social organizations. For many years No. 5 celebrated its birthday, October 17, with a banquet; it was
usually held at the Palace. Lillie oversaw the arrangements of these gatherings; later she would appear in
the banquet hall and respond to a toast, wearing a black
skirt, brilliant red silk shirt, and patent-leather belt,
her helmet on her arm.

Her affections, sometimes unstable in other directions, were a model of constancy so far as the firemen
were concerned. When, an old woman, she was returning from a trip to Damascus in 1905, she suddenly
drew up her horse (the party was skirting the edge of
the Lebanon Mountains) , produced a bottle of champagne from her baggage and ordered that it be opened.
She had just remembered that the day was October
17 — " No. 5's " birthday. The party waited while
guides went higher into the mountains for snow.
When the bottle was properly chilled the party drank
a toast to the San Francisco fire company.

The exploits by which she had amused the town
were numerous. Before she was twenty she had been
engaged fifteen times. She grew tired of her nut-brown
hair and proceeded to bleach it until it was the color
of baled hay — using in the process, it was said, numerous bottles of champagne. She lived for a time near a

San Francisco medical school and once charmed a passing group of students by extending a shapely foot and calf from an upper window and chanting a line from a music-hall ballad: " Doctor, doctor, come saw off my leg! " When Gertrude Atherton in 1895 published a novel called *A Whirl Asunder* San Franciscans were convinced that Lillie Coit was the inspiration for its heroine, Helena Belmont.

Her elopement with Howard Coit, when she was eighteen, failed to subdue her. She was once discovered, dressed in men's clothes, at a cock-fight (which few of the best people attended), excitedly cheering her favorite. She invited a group of conservative friends to a party in her Palace suite; when the guests arrived they discovered that she had provided a prize-fight for their entertainment. She developed a passion for poker and played regularly, on even terms, with some of the town's plungers. Her marriage with Coit was the opposite of tranquil and the pair soon separated. She inherited a fortune and her precedent-breaking career continued. For many years " the girl who chased the fire engines " continued to be a conspicuous figure. She established a salon at her Napa Valley ranch, Larkmead, and Joaquin Miller became one of a group of semi-permanent guests. Friends fortunate enough to be invited there for a week-end returned with new tales of her unconquerable capacity for mischief. At irregular intervals she would abruptly resume her travels. The length of her absences was unpredictable; she might be gone three days or three years. Once she was abroad five years; she returned "stout and Parisian," but with her zest and energy undiminished. When she was in San Francisco she lived at the Palace and kept shrewd watch over her extensive property.

Her sixtieth birthday was almost upon her the November evening in 1903 when the report of a revolver rattled the windows of her Palace suite. The sound startled occupants of neighboring rooms; a bellboy telephoned the office and a maid hurried to the closed door, unable to summon courage to knock. Voices were audible within. After some minutes Mrs. Coit emerged and announced that there had been an accident. The maid and the bellboy scurried off in search of a physician. An elderly, disheveled man appeared in the door. He saw Mrs. Coit and shouted: " I'll spare your life! " He then tossed a pistol at her feet and raced from sight.

Two doctors arrived. Presently an ambulance was summoned and a man, evidently gravely wounded, was carried out and taken to a hospital. Meantime efforts were being made to hush up the matter. The shooting had occurred at five o'clock; not until late that night would Manager Kirkpatrick permit a statement to the reporters. He finally admitted that there had been a shooting affair. The police had been informed. He did not know the particulars. . . .

Next morning the full story came out. The victim was J. W. McClung, a former Confederate army officer and a prominent citizen. He had been calling on Mrs. Coit when Alexander Garnett, a distant relative of the lady, had forced his way into her rooms. Garnett had been manager of her local property; he was excited and " appeared to have been drinking." Mrs. Coit revealed that three nights earlier she and Garnett had played whist, and he had lost. " Much to my astonishment, he began to swear and abuse me. I ordered him out. . . ." Later he had sent her a letter of apology, which she had ignored.

The next heard of him was when he burst into her room. He opened his coat and produced a revolver, pointing it at Mrs. Coit. Major McClung jumped between them and the ball entered his chest. When the wounded man tried to reach the telephone, Garnett jerked the instrument away. He again threatened Mrs. Coit with the revolver, but while he hesitated to shoot, Major McClung grew weaker and fell into a chair. Garnett then seemed to realize what he had done. He stood aside and allowed Mrs. Coit to leave the room. A few seconds later he, too, hurried out.

McClung died on the afternoon following the shooting and that night Garnett was arrested in an Oakland rooming-house. He was tried for murder, served part of his term at San Quentin, then was sent to a mental institution in Virginia. He died there in the middle 1920s.

When Garnett's trial was over, Lillie Coit went abroad. Thereafter she returned to California only at long intervals. It was at San Francisco, however, that she died, in the summer of 1929. She was eighty-six. She made two bequests to the city: Coit Tower, a tall, fluted column on the crest of Telegraph Hill, and, in Columbus Square, her final tribute to the town's volunteer firemen. It is a statuary group, sentimental in subject and design: two firemen and a rescued child.

6

THE MURDER of McClung recalled another shooting affair that had startled the town a decade earlier.

One afternoon in the spring of 1893 a seventy-three-year-old ex-grocer with twenty cents in his pocket and a grudge against stock-market manipulators followed John W. Mackay up Sutter Street and, at the corner of Lick Place, fired a pistol-shot into his back. He then turned the gun on himself and fell on his face in the street.

A passer-by hurried to Mackay's side and inquired if he had been injured.

" No," said the millionaire in astonishment. " Why? "

" You're shot."

" I don't feel it."

" But I saw smoke coming from your coat."

Mackay put his hand under his coat and drew it out, staring at his blood-smeared fingers. He was helped into a carriage and driven round the corner to the Palace. Doctors Keeney and Morse hurried to his rooms, cut away his clothing, and probed for the bullet, the old man gruffly declining an anæsthetic. The ball was found in the muscles of his shoulder; it had narrowly missed the spinal cord. Half an hour later Mackay was dictating reassuring cables to his wife in London and his son Clarence in Paris, and telling reporters that he had never seen his assailant and couldn't account for the attack. The ex-grocer, who had wounded himself in the chest, eventually recovered and was held for trial.

To San Franciscans the most important result of this affair was that it brought Mrs. Mackay and her sons back to town for the first time in eighteen years. The family reunion took place in suite 366 of the Palace. Mrs. Mackay's private car, the *Corsair*, was met at Oakland Mole by a group of friends and newspapermen. Her social adventures in England and on the Continent had long been staple reading in California and interest was high.

Those who had feared that long residence abroad had undermined her Americanism were promptly reassured. "Wrap an American flag around me and you will see that it belongs there," she told reporters. Her two sons, John W., Jr. and Clarence, although both were described as "resplendent in English topcoats," echoed this maternal pronouncement, and the group started across the bay. On the ferry the interview continued, Mr. de Young beaming approval as one of his *Chronicle* young men framed respectful questions, while other members of the group — Miss Birdie Fair among them — listened brightly.

Meantime onlookers observed that the noted lady's hair was still black, her eyes bright, and her step "as elastic as a girl of sixteen" — all this notwithstanding the fact that her eldest son was twenty-three and safely through Oxford. Would Mrs. Mackay tell her plans for the future? She really hadn't any. Everything depended on her husband's health and his wishes. Perhaps it would be better for him to travel. For the present the united family would remain at the Palace. No, she didn't think she would establish a home in San Francisco. " Sometimes I wish I had. I have a house in Paris, and the house on Carlton House Terrace in London you know all about. . . ."

Yes, San Franciscans knew all about the Carlton House Terrace mansion; they knew too that the Mackays had been living apart for years, the old Irishman preferring his San Francisco and Virginia City cronies to the frequenters of his wife's London drawing-room. But he was proud of her social success and of his sons, who looked and spoke astonishingly like Englishmen and whose manners were so faultless. It was gratifying too to have his wife speak so respectfully of him to the reporters. Said the latter: " A happier family had never gathered beneath the Palace roof."

Their happiness was marred a few days later. Papers announced that John W., Jr. had taken an overdose of cocaine to relieve an aching tooth and had collapsed, cold and clammy, to the terror of his French valet. But mustard plasters were promptly applied and the young man was soon about again. (Two years later, in Paris, he was killed by a fall from a horse.) One evening the elder Mackay piloted his wife, her maid, and young Clarence through Chinatown; Fred Davis of the Palace staff went along too. They visited the Chinese Theater and some of the shops, and Mrs. Mackay graciously granted another interview. " This is very odd, and I have seen more peculiar things, customs and people tonight than I dreamed of; but the odor is very offensive. Mr. Davis, please take us back to the hotel."

That week the papers carried a footnote to the Mac-

kay shooting. Doctors Keeney and Morse presented
their bills and the patient bitterly protested their size.
Keeney had asked $7,500, Morse $5,000. Meantime,
W. C. Rippey, the man responsible for the costly
wound, had been sentenced to six months in jail for
assault with a deadly weapon. Rippey died in January
1896.

Mackay survived his assailant by a little over six
years. He died at London on July 20, 1902. During
his last years he had been much absent from San Francisco, for his interests had shifted from his mines to his
telegraph and cable lines. But the town remembered
him well and with affection. He was the last of the
Bonanza kings and the most colorful. The day after he
died the *Examiner* interviewed R. V. Dey, long his
secretary.

"No one ever kept books on John Mackay's charities.
There isn't a newspaper printed big enough to hold an account of the money he gave away. I sat with him in this
very office one Sunday afternoon about twenty years ago
and saw him tear up notes and IOUs amounting to $1,-
200,000. . . .

" ' That fellow's broke,' he'd say, and rip! and into the
wastebasket would go anything from $500 to $50,000.
' That fellow's dead, Dey. Can't collect from him, so here
goes.' Then he'd say of another: ' Now this fellow may get
on his feet one of these days, and if he does I guess he will
remember the amount; but in the meantime I might as
well get the evidence out of the way, so he won't be pressed
in case anything happens to me.'

" He never came to San Francisco but there was a
crowd from the entrance here to the entrance of the Palace

Hotel. He reckoned that it used to cost him $50 to walk from the Nevada Block to the Palace, and he always carried the price with him, in gold, California-like, inviting the touch, you might say. I'm speaking now only of the men who accosted him on the street. . . ."

7

IN MARCH 1905 Ashton Stevens devoted one of his brightly written columns to Hall McAllister. San Franciscans did not need to be reminded that this local figure — who at forty had abandoned the law to play small parts in Margaret Anglin's company — was the son of another Hall McAllister, leading member of the California bar through the '70s and '80s. He was therefore a nephew of still another McAllister, the formidable Ward, whose name was a household word because he was believed to be the man who decided who did and who did not belong to New York's Four Hundred.

Curiosity about the Four Hundred was then at its height; news of its leading figures was eagerly read by millions. As always, other cities did what they could to imitate the metropolis. It was not long before there were little Four Hundreds in Topeka and Cincinnati and dozens of other places, and of course scores of local Ward McAllisters contending for supremacy.

In San Francisco the brother of the authentic Ward might have had the honor without a contest. It developed, however, that Hall McAllister was busy with his law practice; besides, he had no taste for the role. The post of social arbiter therefore fell to another, a dapper little champagne salesman named Edward M. Greenway.

Greenway reached San Francisco from Baltimore in the middle '80s as agent for Mumm's champagne, but it was soon evident that his real talents lay in another direction. " He sold wine for pleasure," stated the *Examiner*, " and organized the Friday Night Cotillion Club for business." He was a bachelor, a fluent talker, and affable by nature; moreover he was well connected in the East and he had brought out letters to the right people.

The newcomer soon grew convinced that local society was in a deplorable state. In the East the lines had been sharply drawn; no one there was ever in doubt as to who was who. In San Francisco all was confusion. The town had not yet entirely outgrown its free-and-easy past, when to express curiosity about a man's antecedents was always bad form and sometimes downright dangerous. Of course there had been progress; men were no longer merchant princes one day and pushcart peddlers the next. Fortunes were reasonably stable and dozens of families had been prosperous long enough to impress themselves, and occasionally others. Out of the confusion of the earlier day society of a sort had evolved. It was still a society based almost exclusively on wealth, but San Franciscans, never having known any other, were quite content with that standard.

From this backward state the city had only partly emerged when Greenway arrived. To be sure, every newspaper-reader knew all about the New York Four Hundred, including the fact that it had been selected on the odd theory that the important thing was not the amount of money one had but how long one had had it. There had even been talk of applying the same principle locally. But little progress had been made until the time Ned Greenway arrived in town and decided to take matters into his own hands.

The opening gun of his campaign was the organization of his Friday Night Cotillion Club. Ostensibly its aim was to assemble a congenial and not too numerous group at a series of dances each winter. There were to be five dances, with refreshments, and the cost was twenty dollars per couple. In reality the club was the device by which Greenway planned to separate the authentic social leaders from the impostors. Membership was by invitation and of course Greenway issued the invitations. There was some scoffing and most of the papers poked mild fun at Greenway and his pretensions. None the less there was a scramble among the socially ambitious to secure membership. Soon an invitation to join the Greenway club had come to be looked on as indisputable proof of social consequence. Thus easily the little wine salesman made himself the social dictator of the town.

For some years the Friday Night Club held undisputed sway. Then its sponsor made a serious tactical blunder. As the foremost authority on social procedure, his opinion was frequently sought on questions pertaining to his specialty. Finally he allowed himself to be persuaded to write on these subjects for the society pages of the *Chronicle* — a bit of bad judgment that laid him open to violent attacks by the *Examiner,* the rival morning paper. Others promptly followed the *Examiner's* lead, for Greenway and his club were naturally unpopular with those who had been denied membership. It was not long before such comments as this were appearing in print:

All Americans desiring information on how to conduct dancing clubs composed of representative members of the saloon keeper, gambling house keeper, and sporty elements of society should call on Mr. E. M. Greenway, who is also prepared to give advice on how to malign all social clubs in the city whose members refuse to acknowledge him as anything more than a fake society reporter.

The writer of the above was William H. Chambliss, a young man with ambitions to challenge Greenway's supremacy. Chambliss's rise was as curious as that of his rival. He first reached San Francisco in 1887 as a subordinate officer on one of the Pacific Mail steamers. Like Greenway, he had a talent for organization and a liking for social prominence. About 1890 he abandoned the sea, took up permanent residence at the Palace, and launched active warfare on the Friday Night Club. Of course the *Examiner* welcomed the newcomer with pleasure; it gave much prominence to the activities of his new organization, the Monday Evening Club, which met in the Maple Room of the Palace.

Greenway was unconcerned by this competition. By then he had given up his champagne agency and had gone into mining as assistant to James L. Flood, owner of the Ophir mine. At the Ophir office he announced that he had grown tired of being the town's social dictator; he had about decided to "reduce the 400 to 399." Greenway wanted it understood, however, that he was not retiring because of Chambliss and his Monday Evening Club.

Meantime that young man's campaign was not working with the expected smoothness. Suspicion grew that Chambliss lacked the qualifications necessary in a social leader. As part of his campaign he launched a society weekly; its readers objected that the paper gave too much space to its owner and too little to the rest of society. "Mr. Chambliss devoted the first page of the first three issues of his publication to the printing of an excellent, if somewhat flattering, portrait of himself, accompanied by a biographical sketch which did full justice to himself as a social leader. . . ." The paper survived only a few issues.

Another business venture was also shortlived. One day while he was being shaved in the Palace barber shop it occurred to him that the ceilings of such establishments were much in the eye of reclining patrons. Why not devote the space to advertising? The result was that, with a partner, he organized the Ceiling Advertising Company. Not until they had signed enough contracts to give them a virtual monopoly on the barber-shop ceilings of northern California did the partners learn that their plan had a fatal defect: no one would buy the space. "Experienced advertisers of the commercial world did not care to invest in ceiling advertisements," Chambliss commented. The Ceiling Advertising Company also went out of business.

By that time Chambliss had become a steady source

of news and the papers made much of his activities. Thus thousands learned that he was responsible for a startling social innovation; that of wearing cotton gloves at formal functions. He had been seen " leading the german at his club with his generous hands encased in white cotton gloves such as are furnished by undertakers to impecunious pallbearers." A few days later he was in the papers again. He had charged that a group of young society men had enticed him into a poker game and relieved him of a substantial sum of money. The *Examiner* printed his exposé of the group's methods. The result was a fist-fight with one of the men accused. Both landed in jail.

By that time it had grown clear that Chambliss was not to succeed Ned Greenway as the town's social arbiter. His Monday Evening Social Club lost membership and presently disbanded. Meantime word got about that Chambliss was writing a book in which he proposed to " tell all " about local society. The announcement received immediate attention; it was conceded that there was a great deal to tell. A few weeks later the *Examiner* printed two columns of excerpts from the manuscript of *Chambliss' Diary; or, Society As It Really Is.* The samples were enough to whet public curiosity and to cause apprehension that the young man might really intend to carry out his threat to " tell all."

But when his book was ready for publication the author began to encounter obstacles. The engraver to whom he sent the illustrations refused to produce either the plates or the original drawings. Chambliss sued for the return of his property, but the matter was so long in court that he lost patience and had the artist make a duplicate set of drawings. Another difficulty soon developed. The printer who was setting the text delivered an ultimatum: he would not proceed unless references to certain local families were deleted. Chambliss took his manuscript to a group of other local printers; all made the same condition. The author-publisher refused to give up: " I took the train for New York in quest of an honest printing house."

The book eventually appeared in New York in 1894. When copies reached California, readers found that the author's promise to " name names " had been carried out to the letter. San Franciscans had the privilege of seeing in print references to scandals that had formerly been mentioned only in whispers. Of course the book had a wide reading. Notwithstanding the number sold, however, it was rarely encountered even in the early months after publication. The reason for its scarcity became known: agents for some of the persons mentioned had been quietly buying, at a substantial premium, every copy they could lay their hands on. One lady was said to have personally thrown several hundred copies into her furnace. The *Diary* remains today an uncommonly rare volume.

The burning of so many copies was no serious loss to literature. The book is a curious mixture of spite and egotism, vindictiveness and bad taste. Ironically, Chambliss's exposé of what he termed San Francisco's " Parvenucracy " revealed that its author was abundantly supplied with the very qualities against which he was railing. It was a just fate. Chambliss faded permanently from the picture. The sensation his book made in the ranks of society and its hangers-on soon died out. Ned Greenway, far from being supplanted, remained the town's undisputed social dictator.

8

As TIME passed, new figures arose to challenge his supremacy. Among them was Mrs. Monroe Salisbury, originator of the Friday Fortnightly. One of the means by which she hoped to win popularity for her organization was by making it less expensive than the Friday Night Club. Greenway charged twenty dollars per couple for five parties; Mrs. Salisbury fixed her charge at five dollars and gave nine parties. To be sure, her orchestra was not so good as Greenway's and there were no refreshments; none the less, scores joined her club.

The *Examiner,* ever a faithful chronicler of the trends of the *haut monde,* commented: " It is no longer *sine qua non* to belong to the Greenway club. You might be in society on a five dollar basis, and that suits a great many people."

When Mrs. Salisbury died and her Friday Fortnightly became inactive, another lady, Ynez Shorb White, stepped into the breach with the New Cotillion Club. Mrs. White's bid for support was made on the grounds, not of economy, but of exclusiveness. " Her sword is the pruning knife. . . . Two hundred or more of those who have been moving in the select circle are to be banished. . . ."

Recent balls had been pronounced " altogether too

promiscuous," and many thought it high time for a drastic paring of the social list. Accordingly, the New Cotillion Club was launched in January 1905, and Mrs. White seemed at the beginning of a long reign. She did, in fact, maintain her position a little more than a year. She might have done so much longer had not the city presently faced problems even more pressing than that of who did or did not belong to her dancing club.

Long before 1906, however, Ned Greenway and the other leaders had become aware of certain regrettable tendencies in the younger set. The latter had begun to manifest a spirit of revolt, a growing belief that the convention-ridden society of the day was a bore, its be-chaperoned functions stupid and dull. Members of the cotillion clubs had begun to gather at private parties where, without benefit of Greenway or Mrs. White, the staid dances of convention gave way to the far livelier steps of the public dance halls (known as " chippy balls ") , and even to imitations of the barbaric rhythms current on the Barbary Coast. It was not long before the formal cotillions began to show the effect of all this. " After dancing the dances of the tenderloin at private balls the night before " it was not likely that the young people would be as circumspect as formerly at Mr. Greenway's functions.

The result was a partial capitulation on the part of the oldsters and some liberalization of the rules. A few of the more sedate new steps were allowed. But the conservatives drew the line at one dance: the bunny hug. That was definitely taboo. Ned Greenway personally pronounced the bunny hug indecent.

Smilax and Laudanum

Soon the local journals were heralding another defeat of the conservatives in the social revolution. Women of apparent respectability were beginning to be observed smoking cigarettes in public.

The other evening in the garden of a prominent hotel, while the men were having their after-dinner smoke, all eyes were attracted to a most unusual sight. In a group sat a father, a mother and their young daughter, about nineteen years of age. Each was puffing away at a cigarette, regardless of the crowds intently watching their movements. . . .

The fad was far too sensational to make rapid progress. As late as 1903 the spectacle of two Englishwomen, a niece of the Duke of Buckingham and the wife of a British cavalry officer, smoking in a public room of the Palace was so startling as to inspire a paragraph in the next morning's *Examiner:*

These aristocratic globe-trotters are fond of cigarettes and, in the court lounging room last evening they enjoyed several of the Egyptian variety. A gentleman sat with them and, totally unconscious of the many eyes cast in their direction, they smoked leisurely and with the nonchalance of veterans. . . .

The bunny hug and women smoking in public! The world was forging onward in the booming 1900s. The older generation had suspicions as to the direction in which it was heading, but, after all, what could be done about it? One could only hope for the best and try to keep up with the parade. San Francisco society did both, and so did the Palace.

CHAPTER SEVEN

LINNETS AND NIGHTIN-GALES

1

THIS is the success story of a girl whose childhood was spent in a Nevada sagebrush town and who lived to sing before England's Queen at Osborne.

Her name was Emma Wixom; her history is as incredible as any romantic tale ever imagined by Bret Harte. Daughter of a pioneer physician who joined the eastward trek over the Sierra in the '6os, she was unremarkable in everything except her voice and her extraordinary self-assurance. The voice was a natural gift; the self-assurance was acquired. Her father, a typical product of his time and place, lived in cheerful poverty, buoyed up by the expectation of wealth tomorrow or next week. He taught his daughter a priceless lesson. Almost from the time she could walk it was impressed on her that singing to an audience was as natural a form of amusement as playing with dolls or making mud pies, and it was much more remunerative. Children were rare in the silver towns, and the '6os were a notoriously sentimental decade. Years later many retained the memory of the little girl in a gingham dress, singing in doorways along Austin's main street, the sound of her childish treble at times almost drowned by the clatter of silver coins falling about her feet.

Her mother died in the early '70s. Like more prosperous daughters of the Bonanza towns, Emma was sent to California to absorb genteel learning at Mills Seminary, " in its sheltered nest among the hills back of Fruit Vale." There she studied under the school's German music teacher, Professor Kelleher, and of course sang whenever she was asked — to the students, at faculty gatherings, to guests at Sunday evening musicales. This period, too, was remembered in later years. What former classmates particularly recalled was her unconquerable love of singing. But they also recalled that she failed to distinguish herself in the classrooms, that she was not pretty (although her up-tilted nose gave her face an attractively arch expression) , and that she fancied bright colors and wore them in extraordinary combinations. Moreover ". . . when she grew too stout for her clothes and burst them out, her style of mending was not of the best. . . . She never took kindly to stabbing drygoods with a needle. . . ."

On the " musical evenings," however, Emma came into her own.

Crowds of people from San Francisco and Oakland drove out on the lovely moonlight nights to gather in the large rooms and listen to as fine a voice as could be heard anywhere. Emma was very near-sighted, and there was a song she used to sing, " Shall I Wear a White Rose, or Shall I Wear a Red," and when she gazed at the audience with her merry eyes half closed, and her pretty mouth wearing its most coaxing smile, there was not a college boy present who did not believe she was asking his special preference.

At the school she became the special friend of one of the teachers, Dr. Adrian Ebell, a naturalist, and his wife. When the Ebells presently went to Europe they arranged to take Emma along that she might seriously begin to study for a career as a singer. Before her departure the girl paid a memorable last visit to the Nevada town and gave a final concert. In its issue of March 17, 1877 the local paper, the *Reese River Reveille,* described the event — a benefit for an injured miner, held in the Austin Methodist Church:

"The Happy Birdling" is the title of a solo sung by Miss Emma Wixom, and, judging from the brightness of the tiers of countenances . . . it seemed to impart a feeling of joyousness to all present. . . . Tremendous applause followed. On reappearing, Miss Wixom sang and played "Listen to the Mocking Bird," and Mr. House whistled as the mocking bird behind the curtain. The effect was sublime. . . .

The concert was not only an artistic success, it was a financial triumph. Receipts totaled $407, which Emma personally handed over to the miner, who had lost both feet in an accident. Next day she left Austin for New York and Europe.

In Paris she became a pupil of a noted teacher of the day, Madame Marchesi, eagerly submitting herself to the rigid discipline required of aspiring opera singers. When her patron, Dr. Ebell, died and his widow returned to America, Emma remained behind, although she had more ambition than cash and it was doubtful how long she could continue to support herself. But even in distant Paris the Comstock took care of its own.

Friends in Nevada and California learned of the girl's plight and furnished funds that permitted her to complete her training.

Three years later, in April 1880, she made her debut at Her Majesty's Theatre in London. She had dropped the name Wixom and adopted one suggestive of her background: Emma Nevada. Later, a San Francisco newspaper writer coined a still more picturesque name: the Sagebrush Linnet. Other European engagements followed — in France, Italy, and Germany — but she remained little changed by her successes. It was not Emma Nevada, noted young opera singer, but Emma Wixom, Mills Seminary, '76, who described to her first teacher her appearance before Queen Victoria: " Her Majesty asked me if I was not an American and I proudly answered ' from California ' — and I almost said ' from Mills.' "

In the spring of 1885 she started west with the Mapleson Opera Company on her first American tour. Of course the entire state made ready to welcome her, for she was the first California-born singer to attain prominence in the difficult medium of grand opera. Local papers called her " the California Patti " and reported proudly that she, the only American singer in the group, was a great favorite with the company. She was so small of stature, stated the *Alta*, that Colonel Mapleson, " the Napoleon of the managers," would call her only " Baby." Guardedly, the paper added:

Now, after eight years, she is coming back to us an acknowledged prima donna, and we are wondering how she will affect us. We have been cautioned by those who have heard her lately not to expect too much. They say that her upper notes are beautiful, that she has wonderful sustaining power which will hold a note until the audience is gasping for breath, that there is a sympathy in her voice which will make you weep; but to compare her to Patti is simply folly, such as likening a linnet to a nightingale. . . . But Nevada is our home bird, and we shall welcome her with affection, admire her voice immensely for all there is in it, and find excellencies that less loving ears have missed. . . .

But Nevada had been ill a great deal since the tour started. She had neuralgia in New Orleans; two teeth had been drawn in St. Louis; later she had caught cold and developed tonsillitis. There was doubt if she would be able to sing in San Francisco. When the company reached town in mid-March, however, the news was encouraging. So far had she recovered that it was announced she would not only keep her engagement but probably be at her best. On the morning after her arrival Colonel Mapleson had her test her voice. The *Alta* described the result: ". . . a peal of glorious, silver-toned melody rang out and filled the halls and corridors of the Montgomery Street side of the fifth floor of the Palace. . . ."

She appeared at the Grand Opera House on the evening of March 23, 1885, and the next morning's papers reported " enthusiasm bordering on lunacy." The applause was of a type and volume more frequently heard at political rallies than in an opera house.

Nothing could have been more charming than . . . when she bowed her acknowledgment to the shouts of bravo that were showered on her. At the end of the first act, when she formed a pretty background to a wealth of floral tributes, some one in the audience cried " Home, Sweet Home." With faltering voice the little lady essayed to sing the first note. . . . The attempt failed, and she retired from the stage, overcome with emotion. Responding to more applause, Mlle Nevada sang the ballad with moistened eyes.

A perfect furore was the result. Mlle Nevada reappeared and crowned Arditi [the conductor] with one of her laurel wreaths. . . . Throughout the entire performance she was as vivacious as a kitten. With the grace of a child she gathered her floral offerings and tripped lightly off the stage. . . . At the end of the second act the enthusiasm attained such a height that Colonel Mapleson himself appeared. Bouquet after bouquet, intended for Nevada, grazed his bald pate. Whenever Nevada concluded a solo she immediately became the target for floral weapons in the hands of admiring friends.

A long series of gifts were passed over the footlights and all were carefully described: a floral chair from her sister, Mrs. Bailey; a yacht made of pink roses on a sea of forget-me-nots, from Miss Hattie Crocker, a Mills Seminary classmate; a satin cushion with " Nevada " in silver letters across its top, from Mrs. Alexander Sharon. From the town of Alameda came, without unkind connotations, "a branch of a lemon tree, freighted with lemons." Mills Seminary presented an immense laurel wreath with a red streamer on which was printed an appropriate verse:

> With fragrant bloom,
> And living green
> We crown thee song's
> Victorious queen.

Emma's class at the seminary also had a gift: an orange satin basket filled with roses and marigolds, resting on a tall copper standard on the surface of which was a horseshoe entangled in a spider's web. Mrs. Mills herself sent a floral basket and a card of congratulation enclosed in a satin case. On the top of the case was painted " a view of the Golden Gate, in the foreground a branch of apple blossoms, on which was perched a linnet." Finally:

> The most substantial gift . . . was a purse of $2000 in five-dollar gold pieces, which was furnished by subscription through the efforts of the former pupils at Mills Seminary. The performance did not close until 11:15, when the green curtain hid the songstress from view, amidst endless shouts of Bravo! Bravo!

The opera? It was *La Sonnambula,* and Nevada sang the part of Amina. Her voice was described as " clear, pure, sweet and flexible . . . but never very sonorous." Local critics commented on the ease and confidence with which she essayed the most difficult passages of her role. They had praise, too, for the second-act finale, when her reed-like voice " rose over the roar of the chorus and ensemble like a skyrocket. . . ."

She appeared in two other operas during the local engagement: *Lucia di Lammermoor,* by Donizetti, and *Mireille,* by Gounod. Meantime this product of the helter-skelter life of the mining camps had become the idol of the entire Coast. Each afternoon her Palace rooms were so crowded that latecomers had trouble getting within the doors. One Sunday afternoon a re-

porter had to push through a close circle of admirers
to get near enough to interview her. Emma, a recent
convert to Catholicism, had attended mass that morning at St. Ignatius' Church, where she had remained
standing four hours. " But I didn't mind. . . . It was
penance for my sins. I feel so guilty at receiving so
much and giving so little. . . ."

All the interviewer's questions were conscientiously
answered. Yes, she hoped to sing again in Europe,
particularly in St. Petersburg. Except for Russia and
Sweden, she had appeared in all the European coun-
tries. But she disliked to leave San Francisco so soon.
She had had time to visit only the beach and the candy-
stores. San Francisco's candy was the best in the world.
Yes, candy was her weakness. " There is a dealer here
who has named some caramels after me . . . they are
called ' Nevada creams.' . . ."

Usually present at gatherings where she appeared
was her manager, Dr. Raymond Palmer. There were
rumors of a romance between the two, and a few
months later these were confirmed. They were married in Paris in October 1885.

Nevada several times returned to the Coast with
opera companies or on concert tours. In 1902 she sang
in the old theater at Nevada City, the mining town in
the Sierra foothills near which she was born. A Nevada
City paper's account of her concert stated that the
audience was sprinkled with old-time miners who had
come down from the remote ravines and flats of the
back country to hear again the Emma Wixom they had
heard as a child. On that same visit to the Coast she
sang at her old school, then Mills College. She chose

271

the songs that had been best liked during her student days: " Home, Sweet Home," " You and I," and " The Mocking Bird." Soon after, she ended her professional engagements and retired to private life, after a career unique among pioneer daughters of the West. In 1939 the Nevada Linnet was living in quiet retirement in London.

2

SAN FRANCISCO's welcome to Emma Nevada, enthusiastic as it was, did not quite equal the reception the town had given Patti a year earlier. Nevada's visit stirred local pride to heights never before equaled, but the coming of Patti touched off a city-wide excitement that was not always distinguishable from hysteria.

One of the most expertly advertised figures in history, Patti reached town on the morning of March 9, 1884. She was under Colonel Mapleson's management and this was her first visit to the Coast. Patti was then forty-one and she had of course been an international celebrity for nearly two decades. Everyone knew all about her: her marriages, her pets, her shrewd business head, her temperament, her petite personal charm, the unparalleled beauty of her voice. Colonel Mapleson was said to be paying her five thousand dollars a performance.

Her special car, the *Adelina Patti,* was almost as celebrated as the lady herself. Crowds gathered at Oakland Mole to stare at its shining exterior, and a writer

Adelina Patti, and Ella Wheeler Wilcox, Poetess

Patti photograph by Tabor, San Francisco

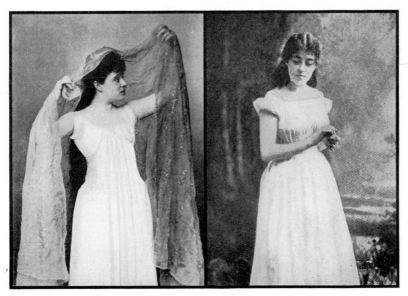

Sybil Sanderson, and Emma Nevada

Emma Nevada as Amina in *La Sonnambula*

for the *Call* was permitted to describe its wonders for the benefit of the curious all over the Coast. It was a " boudoir car "; its walls were covered with embossed leather; it had been decorated by Parisian artists; and it cost thirty thousand dollars. The description continued:

The hammered gold and silver effect of the sides and ceiling was in a design of morning glories. The parlor . . . was lighted by plate glass windows and a gold lamp which hung from above. The windows were ornamented with designs representing the four seasons. The hand-carved piano of natural wood corresponded with the rest of the woodwork in the room. There was a couch, with satin pillows ornamented with bows and lace tidies, opposite to the piano. A square table, covered with plush, stood in the center, and all around were easy chairs of luxurious depth. Mme. Patti's bed-chamber was largely pink. The paneling was of satin-wood, inlaid with ebony, gold and amaranth. Bevelled mirrors were abundant. The couch had a silk plush cover of gold, embroidered with trailing pink rosebuds, and with the monogram " A.P." in the same delicate shade. Over the velvet carpet, beside the bed, was a leopard skin. A stand was mounted with silver, and a small bathtub was concealed from view by mirrored doors. There was a closet containing the table service of solid silver, china and glass — all with the diva's monogram.

Patti crossing the uninhabited plains and deserts of the West in this ornate little box offered an interesting study in contrasts. Colonel Mapleson, however, was too busy directing the tour to reflect on the strangeness of his mission. To bring so intricate an organism as a grand-opera company out to the frontier was a large undertaking, yes, but it was all a matter of organization. There were four special cars for the singers: *La Traviata, La Sonnambula, Lycoming,* and Patti's own car. Among the artists were Madame Gerster, Madame Dotti, Galassi, Arditi, Carracciola and Lombardelli.

How had they made out? Colonel Mapleson, white-haired, red-faced, and hearty, made it all seem like a lark:

Plenty of room for everybody! The prima donnas had their different cars. We had three cooks constantly employed working for ourselves and Patti, and it was great fun stopping at places and foraging, capturing chickens and other game. You see we ran short of provisions, as we were twenty-four hours overdue. Patti and Gerster are both in excellent health and fine voice. Patti, especially, is lively as a kitten. Yesterday she seated herself at her piano in her car and while breakfast was being prepared, sang the celebrated song of the Queen of Night from " The Magic Flute," in the original key, repeatedly striking the highest notes with a bird-like brilliancy, until Nicolini rushed in, and tearing his hair, implored the diva, if she loved him, not to tax her wonderful organ, especially in a railroad car.

An Italian band greeted Patti at the ferry landing, and that evening she was serenaded in the grand court of the Palace. She then appeared on an upper balcony, waved a handkerchief to the group below, and retired to her suite. When a reporter arrived the next day to interview her he found every table and chair loaded with flowers, with still other bouquets strewn over the floor.

Linnets and Nightingales

Then his attention was caught by a beautiful parrot fluttering against the bars of its cage . . . and finally by a charming little lady who said, in a tone of assumed pique: " Will you deign to turn your eyes in this direction, monsieur? I'm a little body, to be sure, but then I am really seeable if one only tries."

The wandering eyes of the reporter from that moment ceased their wandering. A winsome lady is Madame Patti, in face, in figure, in speech and in ways of gesture. . . . The passing years have tripped so lightly by that she seems to mock the record of her birth, and to be almost as young as when she sang with Mario, twenty years ago. Sparkling eyes, piquant and mobile features, nervous, bird-like gestures, clear but rapid utterance, a small, compactly built figure, a profusion of dark, wavy hair, a costume becoming in the extreme — and behold Madame Adelina Patti, as she appeared yesterday afternoon. . . .

Patti was full of the novelty of her trip and she insisted on talking about it.

" According to every physical rule I should be very tired today, but, *au contraire,* I am so filled with the electricity of novelty and excitement that I really haven't time to grow weary. Everything possible has been arranged for my comfort in traveling, but the weather has been so very naughty that it gave me no rest at all last night. Then these washups — wash-ins — wash-outs — how do you call them? — have made such long delays that it really seemed as though we should never reach this Mecca of our hopes. Just think of it, we were stopped ten, seven, some tremendous number of hours, at one of these washing places alone. . . ."

The big opera house on Mission Street proved far too small for the thousands eager to hear her. Tickets were in such demand that the house might have been sold several times at each appearance, and the speculators reaped a harvest. Colonel Mapleson allowed so many tickets to be sold that aisles and passageways were obstructed and he was arrested for violation of a fire ordinance. After the company was back in New York, Mapleson recalled this scramble for tickets as one of the high points of the tour. The *Times* reported him as saying:

" When we reached San Francisco . . . we found the city in a ferment of excitement. It was Patti's first visit there, and everyone was crazy to hear her sing. I soon found that there was going to be trouble with the speculators. . . . The place was surrounded with them. They sprouted up out of the ground. They barricaded the entrances to the theatre, and I found that something must be done at once. I went to the mayor, and by dint of hard work succeeded in getting an ordinance passed by which the speculators were compelled to pay $100 a month for the privilege of hawking tickets in the streets. The very next day seventy-seven licenses were granted. And they kept on granting them. During our last week, when they had only four performances to sell for, they got out three licenses and paid the full amount. . . .

" People came the night before the opening and got places in line, and when the box-office opened in the morning there were so many there that many of them had not got seats when the performance had begun at night. Worse than that, half the people in the lines were not there for the purpose of buying seats at all. No . . . they came and took places in the line and stayed for seven or eight hours and then sold their places to other persons. One man came to me and said he had paid $26 for a place in the line and hadn't been able to get an admission ticket at night. Mad! I never saw people so mad! They swore at me and threatened to punch my head. . . . Then, when the performance began, I found that there had been scores of bogus tickets sold. Why, two seats, Nos. 155 and 156, were sold over six times. . . ."

With tickets at so high a premium, Mapleson had decided that the profit might better go to him than to the speculators. Accordingly, he arranged to auction the tickets for the last week of the run.

" I had a diagram of the house made the size of the drop curtain, with the numbers of the seats inscribed on it in figures four inches high. Then I put the auctioneer in Arditi's chair and I cleared out the fiddles and drums and had all my secretaries and clerks put in to do the booking. Then I wouldn't let anyone have more than six seats at a time, and we started off. At first they sold for $7 premium, making $14 per seat. As the seats became fewer the premiums became larger and finally reached $35 per seat. I got $28 in premiums, and so that was a good stroke. But they got the best of me once. They went up on the roof, took off some slate shingles, sawed a hole in the woodwork, and let 160 people into the gallery free. . . .

" When it came to the last matinee, we did have a time. . . . A line of ladies began to form at the box office the night before, and when the sale opened in the morning the line was eight blocks long. They were all elegant ladies, too, covered with diamonds and flowers. . . . Such an audience I never beheld, all dressed magnificently and fairly covered with diamonds. And then when the last act came, the Honorable Somebody leaped out of his private box upon the stage and made a speech! And there was Patti crying and the audience crying — and yes, — I cried, too. And then he gave Arditi a fiddle and Patti a great thing that high, a lovely cup of silver with gold handles. And then Patti, who was excited and shaking, sang " Home, Sweet Home," and the audience applauded and shouted and wound up with three tremendous yells — and oh! it was grand. . . ."

Patti was back again a year later, still under Mapleson's management. This time the chief event of the trip west was the death of Madame Scalchi's parrot, which so upset the lady (she was known as " the Patti of the contraltos ") that she was unable to appear in *Il Trovatore* at Salt Lake City. Her role was taken by Madame Steinbech. Scalchi was again in good spirits by the time the company reached San Francisco, and able to talk freely of her loss: " My parrot was much better than Patti's. It had been with me three years, and could talk in both French and Italian."

The artistic temperaments of the singers, and their professional jealousies, keenly interested the public. Colonel Mapleson let it be known that Patti was above such nonsense. " With a naturally kind heart and generous impulses, she is without the slightest jealousy toward contemporary artists, whom she treats with consideration and appreciation, it being her habit always to kiss Scalchi after the performance of ' Semiramide.' " Moreover Patti was so seldom ill that Mapleson called her, not altogether gallantly, his " old reliable."

Further details of the temperament of opera stars were supplied by Mapleson's assistant, Frederick Rullman, an old-time manager and an encyclopedia of opera lore. He was interviewed by the *Alta:*

" Have I been in the operatic line very long? Well, I knew Patti when, at seven years of age, she sang in concerts in Niblo's thirty years ago. There, now, that gives her age away, doesn't it? [Patti was forty-two] and I really didn't mean to do it. Well, she needn't be ashamed of her age, for she has achieved wondrous successes. No singer that ever lived has approached in any degree her surpassingly marvelous qualities as a singer, and it is scarce probable that the world will ever see her equal. . . . I have heard them all. But there was one fine singer that I shall never forget. That was Anna De La Grange. Ah, she was the girl. . . . It was in 1854 that I took a company out of New York and she was my leading lady. She wasn't like the singers of today. Why, she sang eighty opera nights without once getting sick or playing sick. There were no capers about her, and if the managers of today had such singers they wouldn't find themselves in hot water so often. A singer gets sick, and instead of the manager being sympathized with, the public seems to regard him as responsible for the affliction. . . ."

Rullman was asked about Patti and Gerster, whose relations on their tour the year before had been far from tranquil. Gerster was not in the company this year.

" Do I think Gerster will ever attain Patti's degree of perfection? Emphatically no! You nor no one else will ever hear Gerster sing again. She has sung her last note. She is now at her farm in Italy, where she lies seriously ill with throat troubles, and has had to have her tonsils out. That ruins her as a singer."

San Franciscans had already heard something of the Patti-Gerster rivalry from Madame Eugenie Pappenheim, Viennese prima donna, who was in town in the summer of 1884. A *Call* reporter, interviewing her at the Palace, asked if quarrels between Italian and German singers were frequent.

" There is a little irritation sometimes. It is useless to deny it. . . . The feeling goes beyond mere artistic rivalry, and has a national prejudice, I think, as a basis. I found it so in my case, at least."

" You left Mapleson on that account, I have understood."

" Not altogether. I came from England with Mapleson in October last year, and after traveling with Patti and Gerster for some time, found there was a studied purpose to withhold my best roles. I thought too much of my reputation to submit to such treatment, and therefore told Mapleson, by the advice of my friends, I would cease to travel with him. . . ."

" Mapleson must have had his hands full with such exacting prima donnas as Etelka and Adelina? "

The Madame smiled. " You know the old proverb, ' Where two ride on one horse, one must ride behind.' One prima donna is quite enough for a manager to handle. Two, of course, doubles the trouble. Three means distraction. One or the other must always dictate. Patti was the dictatress in this case, and the consequence was constant fighting. Gerster thought she was quite as good as Patti, and wanted the same extravagant attention paid her — and same salary, a private traveling palace car, and in every particular, so far as the manager's pocket was concerned, to be on the same level with Adelina. It was wrong in Gerster to demand this, because the artistic conditions were different. These bickerings assisted in making up my mind to quit the company. Between the two I had a most unpleasant time."

" Do you concede, then, Adelina Patti to be at the head of the lyric stage? "

" Unquestionably. There is only one Patti. Her voice is almost flawless in certain roles; comparing it with a gem, you may call it a diamond of the first water. Its delightful natural quality in the first place, and the thorough schooling by which it is enabled to resist in a great degree the effect of advancing years, combine to give her the first place in our art. You must," said the Madame, " credit me with being free from all envy when I am thus candid."

3

INTEREST IN Patti and all that pertained to her was intense and sustained. The public never tired of reading about her; no detail of her life or habits, her dress, mannerisms, opinions, or eccentricities was too trivial to be set down in type. On her first visit in 1884 columns of newspaper space were required to satisfy public curiosity. Patti was fond of pets. Patti was girlish and vivacious. Her disposition was amiable. She had a naturally kind heart and generous impulses. She was quick at repartee and could converse intelligently on any subject. She could speak with fluency Italian, English, French, German, and Spanish. Continued the *Alta:*

Patti keeps informed of the current news events, but only occasionally reads the papers herself, preferring to be the listener. Frequently she will take a box at the theatre for the purpose of seeing a star actor or actress. By midnight she generally retires, but on nights after she has been singing, will return to her hotel, and when she has been made comfortable . . . will sit down to a late supper. It is against her practise to eat dinner before singing, but after the late supper she will sit and chat for an hour or two . . . on the opera, the audience, etc. When at home and upon all ordinary occasions, the queen of song dresses with much simplicity. With the exception of a pair of diamond ear-rings and a solitary finger ring, Patti does not wear any jewelry. Her shoes are high heeled, button kids, number $2\frac{1}{2}$, of which she has an assorted stock, purchased in Paris. . . .

Even in the advertising columns Patti's visit was not ignored. During her local engagement the public learned that the same style of corsets and paniers worn by the great diva were to be had at Freud's corset house, Nos. 742 and 744 Market Street.

Patti was back again two years later, this time under the management of Henry E. Abbey. She put up at a nine-room suite on the second floor of the Palace, spoke graciously of the " handsome girls and women " one saw in Golden Gate Park on sunny afternoons, and announced that this was her last professional visit to San Francisco. But another of her many farewell tours brought her again to the Coast in the spring of 1890. One incident of that stay makes curious reading now:

A well dressed young man, who carried a large box, walked into the Palace Hotel yesterday and asked to see Madame Patti. His card bore the name of G. F. Thompson and he wrote on it " important business." Patti's curiosity was evidently excited, for she sent for the young man to come up to her room. He went up in the elevator looking very happy. In a few minutes he came down red in the face and muttering to himself. He unbosomed himself to the clerk . . . :

" Patti's no good. I made her a square business proposition and she laughed at me."

" What was it? "

" Well, you see, this is Patti's farewell tour, and I thought the people of San Francisco would want something to remember her by. So I hustled around and got a phonograph. I asked her to sing into it and offered to pay her $10 for each song. She commenced laughing at me, and a little dark man took me by the arm and led me to the door. . . . If she had accepted my offer I could have made a mint of money by letting people hear her sing after she had gone."

The young man sadly picked up his big box and walked out. . . .

During that visit the singer celebrated her forty-seventh birthday by a dinner in her Palace suite. The menus were small banners of white satin suspended from gold bars, with hand-painted flowers on the back. Patti wore pink satin and " fairly dripped with diamonds."

The last and most eventful of her farewell tours took place in 1904. By that time a note of flippancy had crept into the newspaper accounts. Patti was still tremendously interesting to the whole country, but she was then regarded less as an artist than as an indomitable survival of an earlier age. On her arrival at Oakland Mole she boarded a ferry crowded with men returning from the racetrack at Emeryville. The *Examiner* described the scene:

Patti was in a hack, the same kind of a hack anybody can hire for a dollar and a half. . . . On the boat besides Patti and the hack were a few thousand persons who like horse racing, and the Baron, too [Baron Rolf Cederstrom, Patti's third husband]. He was on the boat, sitting in the hack with Patti.

The word was quickly buzzed around that the hack was not coming from a funeral. The men stopped talking about the tickets they had torn up and commenced to talk about Patti.

When men who go to the races stop talking about the track to talk about Patti it means that Patti is a power. . . .

There was an interesting argument on the boat. It was about how old is Patti. Some said she did not appear to be forty, but they had heard folks telling of the triumphs she had scored many years ago, and knew she must be at least sixty. They even went further and wanted to bet " she was seventy, if she was a day. . . ."

Patti was born in 1843; she was therefore sixty-one at the time. At the Palace she granted an interview:

" Here I find myself once more on the border of the Western Hemisphere and looking forward to singing perhaps to sons and daughters of fathers and mothers to whom I sang before. Here I am seeing the same sights — with improvements here and there — that I saw when both California and myself were — well, a trifle younger.

" I do not attempt now to use my voice every night. That would be too much. . . . You tell me that San Francisco is waiting with arms wide open to welcome me. My arms, too, are widely stretched. . . ."

Linnets and Nightingales

Patti's face at a glance shows the beauty that once was in it and which helped to make her famous. She wears her years lightly. . . .

She sang in the Grand Opera House on the night of January 7. Among her songs were the " Jewel Song " from *Faust,* " Home, Sweet Home," and " Comin' through the Rye." The applause was hearty and she responded generously with encores. Ashton Stevens, a young man who was making a reputation as the *Examiner's* critic, wrote:

As many men and women as the police would permit paid the price of curiosity, or of sentiment, and went chattering to their seats and cheerfully listened to one of the oldest women on any stage exploiting the most perishable of all the great gifts.

Sincerity was written all over that audience. Fashion was not the lure. Nobody seemed to be gowned for anybody else. Most of the oldsters leaned back comfortably in their chairs, as to say: " I shan't be disappointed if she does no more than make signs. I heard Patti when she was Patti — the greatest the world ever knew! " To the youngsters the woman who had sung their fathers to their feet, causing them to clasp hands with strangers across these same Grand Opera House aisles . . . to dance on the upholstery of their chairs — to the youngsters, that Patti was a superstition, a purely legendary personage. . . . They saw only a fine little old lady, with the manner of a queen; they heard only the spook of a great voice — as in a phonograph. . . .

While Patti was at the Palace another world-famous woman — Lily Langtry — came to town. The Jersey Lily was on tour in *Mrs. Deering's Divorce,* soon to

285

open at the Columbia. There had been difficulty over bookings in Los Angeles a week earlier, and relations between the two ladies were not cordial. Local papers willingly supplied the details. Langtry had originally been booked to appear at the Mason Opera House for three nights, Thursday, Friday, and Saturday. Marcus Mayer, Patti's manager, wanted the Opera House for his star on Saturday night, and he succeeded in having the management cancel Langtry and substitute Patti. Langtry had been forced to play a one-night stand at Santa Barbara, and the house had been half empty. She had arrived in San Francisco in a " wrathy state."

Representatives of both celebrities issued statements. Said Victor E. de Kiraly, spokesman for the Jersey Lily:

" Mrs. Langtry does not desire to get into any newspaper controversy with Madame Patti, nor does she blame the latter for the substitution of dates at Los Angeles. It would appear that Marcus Mayer, the manager for Patti, went out of his way to crowd Patti into a date at the Mason Opera House that Mrs. Langtry was entitled to. . . ."

Mayer hastened to make public his version of what had happened:

" There should be no hard feeling over Patti appearing in Los Angeles last Saturday night in place of Mrs. Langtry. Mr. Wyatt (manager of the Mason Opera House) agreed to the substitution and I have every reason to think that Mrs. Langtry and her party were also, at one time, satisfied to have Patti appear. . . . Patti played to over $9000 on that night, and if she had not gotten the Mason Opera House she would have drawn as large a crowd at the Simpson Auditorium, which place had been first engaged for her."

The presence of the two women provided opportunities for comparisons that local journalists did not neglect. Langtry arrived with thirty-two trunks and twenty-eight leather hat-boxes and valises; Patti overshadowed her with thirty-six trunks and " any number of valises." In one of the Langtry valises, however, was a souvenir not to be matched in all Patti's baggage: a foot-long revolver, once the property of Roy Bean, who had founded a town in Texas and named it Langtry, presumably after the actress. On the way west her train had stopped in Langtry long enough for the presentation to take place and for citizens to give her what was described as " a pistol and whisky reception." The Jersey Lily Saloon, leading drinking-place of the town, had been gaily decorated in honor of the event.

Not only the Texas six-shooter but the Langtry jewels were objects of interest.

When Mrs. Langtry registered at the Palace last night one of her two maids handed to the clerk a small leather case to put in the hotel safe. It contains $250,000 worth of her diamonds, on which she has an insurance policy of $100,000. Off the stage she never displays much jewelry. She has with her one of her famous ropes of pearls and a large number of diamond rings, many of which were given her by titled persons both in Great Britain and on the Continent.

Like Patti, the Jersey Lily did not escape a frank discussion of her age.

If it is true that a woman is as old as she looks, Mrs. Langtry is still very young. . . . Her eyes still sparkle with the old-time fire, and her hair is doubtless the envy of many women much her junior. She still possesses a girl's skin, with its clear and velvety softness, and yet Mrs. Langtry . . . to state a fact in all its baldness was born in 1852. . . . Mrs. Langtry is eight years older than Lillian Russell and ten years the senior of May Irwin. On the other hand, she is nine years younger than Patti and eight years younger than Modjeska. . . . In spite of the lateness of her arrival and the fact that she had traveled all day, the actress stepped from her hack into the Palace faultless in dress from her hat to her gloves. . . .

San Franciscans found their newspapers dull reading after Patti and Langtry left town.

4

THE PUBLIC's interest in opera singers and all that pertained to them did not grow less with the passage of the years. One day in the fall of 1901 Ashton Stevens interviewed Maurice Grau in the latter's suite at the Palace. Homer Davenport, *Examiner* cartoonist, went along to sketch the opera manager. He proved a frank and willing talker:

" I understand that management in this go-ahead country is personal rather than impersonal as it is in Europe. In Europe very few people knew as much as the name of the opera manager, which never appears in the bill. European artists, when they first come over, are surprised to see my name there. Indeed, they have often asked me: ' What part do you sing, Mr. Grau? ' "

He doubted the feasibility of municipal opera houses in America, and went on to state that prima donnas earned from $50,000 to $75,000 a season in this country.

" How much do the same singers receive in Europe? "

Mr. Grau side-stepped the question a little. " A good orchestra musician over there is worth $15 a week. I pay my orchestra musicians from $50 to $100."

" And the same ratio would apply to the salaries of the artists? "

" I suppose so; but you are treading on delicate ground. . . . Did you ever hear the story of the manager who wanted to cut the salary of Adelina Patti? This manager said to Patti: ' Why, you are getting more money than the President of the United States.' And she said: ' Why, then, don't you get the President to sing for you? ' "

One of the members of Grau's company — Sybil Sanderson — held a particular interest to Californians, for she, like Emma Nevada, was a native daughter. It was her first visit to the Coast in sixteen years, and she returned bearing lightly the honors she had won abroad. Californians were familiar with her career. Daughter of S. W. Sanderson, early-day attorney who became Chief Justice of the California Supreme Court, she was born at Sacramento in 1865. The family moved to San Francisco, where the quality of her soprano voice was admired, and at nineteen she was sent to Paris for an operatic career. A few years later she attracted the attention of Jules Massenet, then at the height of his fame. The sponsorship of the composer assured her success. She made her debut in the title role of Massenet's *Manon* in 1888, at The Hague. Massenet later wrote two operas for her: *Esclarmonde* and *Thaïs.* Her first Paris appearance was in *Esclarmonde,* at the Opéra-Comique in 1889, when she scored remarkable success. She later sang in Brussels, St. Petersburg, London, and New York, but she always had her largest following in Paris, particularly in Massenet's operas. The composer pronounced her an " ideal Manon " and an " unforgettable Thaïs."

When Sybil Sanderson came to San Francisco with the Grau company, Ashton Stevens, the *Examiner's* indefatigable critic, hastened Palace-ward.

I was on hand with the milkman yesterday morning to see just how a California girl who had become a great prima donna and all but burned Paris would look and talk when she came back home for the first time in sixteen years. But she had got there first. There it was on the register in a clean, compact little hand: " Madame Sanderson Terry and maid. . . ."

" Well? " said Sybil Sanderson; and the eyes repeated the interrogation, " I do none of those crazy things the newspapers credit singers with doing. On the morning of the day I am to sing I sleep good and late and eat the biggest breakfast I can and trust to luck. . . . But some singers do train — that is no joke — and some are superstitious. Now, Calvé, for instance . . . she's frightfully superstitious — never goes on the stage without a necklace with all sorts of funny charms on it. My superstitions are just one. I simply won't go through a funeral. . . .

" There is nothing I love better than a good ' coon

song.' I've promised Emma Eames a night at the minstrels at the Bush Street Theatre. How are Billy Emerson and Charlie Reed — as good as ever? "

I explained that the old minstrel days were no more these last dozen years. . . .

Stevens started to ask her opinion of society, but she brushed the question aside.

" Don't talk society to me. When I married and was out of opera I tried society. It was awful. I had to stand in line and wait my turn at the shops; dressmakers said they could arrange to fit me next week. Now I'm back in harness, and there is no waiting in line and the dressmaker comes when I want her.

" Well! if here isn't my old friend, Henry Redington, the first man that ever took me out alone at night! My! but didn't I feel grown up that night. . . ."

She sang in *Manon* and, surprisingly enough, the applause was only moderate. Local audiences liked her better a few nights later as Juliette.

Sybil Sanderson died in Paris in 1903; she was only thirty-eight. It was by her influence, in 1900, that a young American singer, Mary Garden, made her debut at the Opéra-Comique.

The Grau company of 1901 was studded with stars: Gadski, Homer, Sembrich, Calvé, Scotti, Journet, Fritzi Scheff, Bispham, de Reszke and others, including Sanderson. Walter Damrosch was the conductor. The *Examiner's* team of Stevens and Davenport interviewed and sketched them all. Their meeting with Damrosch at the Palace deserves to be preserved. Stevens reported that Davenport was late for their appointment — he had been visiting Paul Dresser and Dick José, and José had sung " about everything Dresser had ever composed." As they went up in the elevator, Stevens tried to restrain the cartoonist's enthusiasm. He reminded Davenport that they were going to talk to a noted conductor about the music dramas of Richard Wagner; José and Dresser represented an entirely different sort of music. " A single bar of ' The Wabash ' or ' The Blue and the Gray ' would be profane." Stevens continued:

But music was too strong for the soul of the artist. " I was just saying that I would have been here sooner if José and Dresser hadn't hypnotized me," said Davenport as he and Damrosch shook hands. " Being a musician yourself, of course you know Paul Dresser, the man who wrote ' The Wabash '? "

Mr. Damrosch was polite but he did not know the composer of " The Wabash," nor the song. Davenport went on genially.

" Oh, Dresser has written other things that are even better. . . . I wish you had been there to hear José sing ' A Mother's Grave.' Now there's a song. . . ."

" Envying mother her grave," Stevens interrupted with:

" Mr. Davenport was just telling me that even the popular ballad composers are not beyond the influence of Wagner. He was saying that the snatches of ' Dixie,' ' Marching Through Georgia,' and ' Yankee Doodle ' employed contrapuntally in the accompaniment of Dresser's ' Blue and the Gray ' are substantially the same as Wagner's use of the *leitmotif* in the music dramas of the Ring."

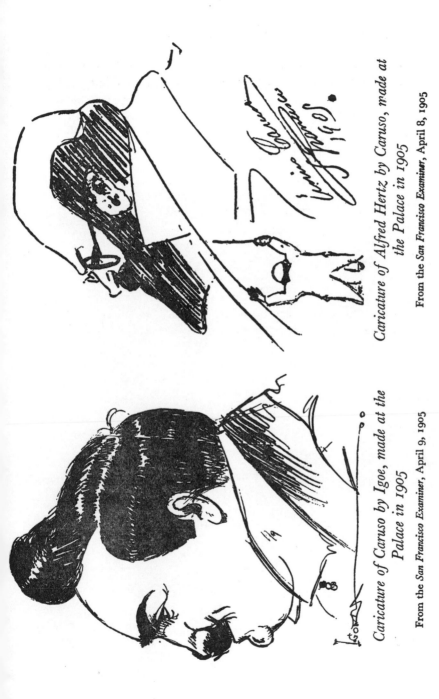

Caricature of Alfred Hertz by Caruso, made at the Palace in 1905

From the *San Francisco Examiner*, April 8, 1905

Caricature of Caruso by Igoe, made at the Palace in 1905

From the *San Francisco Examiner*, April 9, 1905

Linnets and Nightingales

It was a wild thing to say, but it silenced Davenport for a bit and started Damrosch right at the heart of the Wagnerian wisdom we were looking for. . . .

Most picturesque of the male stars in the Grau company was Scotti, whose progress through the corridors of the Palace, in clothes that would " have made Beau Brummell look like a suburban relation," always caused the suspension of other activities. Of course Stevens made a point of calling on him:

My card had just gone up from the Palace office when it struck me that this was Scotti's night to sing Dr. Mala-testa in " Don Pasquale " and there in the hall, waiting with a smile and a handshake, was Scotti himself.

He was unruffled; the windows of his room were wide open; in his lips was a cigarette . . .

I looked twice. . . . " Don't you sing tonight? "

Scotti laughed until the tips of his black mustachios almost tickled his ears . . . as he explained the open windows, the unoccupied bed, the unswathed throat. . . . As for the cigarette, it was a mild Russian brand, and Scotti smoked ever so few. How many? Oh, say twenty-five a day. He is a man of moderation . . . always puts mineral water in his Scotch, and even dilutes his white wine. . . . " What do you say we have a little drink? " . . .

He turned to the piano and hummed a few passionate bars. A rattle and bump as of bucket and mop came from without the door and Scotti woke up. " Men! Clumsy men! This is a beautiful hotel, particularly on the sixth floor, with the palms and flowers. But everybody who works for the hotel seems to be a man. It is a pity; really it is a pity, with everything else so beautiful."

I asked him what kind of music he sang when — well,

when he was not working; and he swung around to the piano again and sang " Hello, Ma Baby," pounding out a syncopated accompaniment. . . . " But the songs I love, the real boudoir songs, are those of my own Naples. Listen to this, ' Carmeli ' is its name."

And he sang dreamily, with half closed lids. . . .

" I can refuse the ladies nothing. . . . They make the theatre look like a beautiful garden and me forget that I am paid to sing. . . . I like them and I like to please them — but not as a Don Juan. Don Juan, he was, you know, a pretty bad fellow. I am — well, I am not so bad. . . ."

A handsome girl got out of the elevator as we reached the turn in the hall. Scotti's hat was low at his side in a flash, his head bowed a shade in mute politeness. When she had passed he poked me under the arm with his thumb.

" Très jolie! "

Four years later, in April 1905, Stevens wrote of a countryman of Scotti, and a greater artist, Caruso. The two interviews had more than a shade of similarity. Said Caruso:

" The first time I came to America, I did not speak English as now. I was invited to supper at the house of a great Madame, and everyone shout: ' Speech, Mr. Caruso! Speech, Mr. Caruso! ' And I take my glass and say: ' Ladies and gentlemen — how are *you*? I love you very much. Thank you. Good-by. One Forty-four East Thirty-Seventh street! ' Eh? "

" But why the One Forty-four East Thirty-Seventh street? "

" That was my address," laughed Caruso.

Caruso was only thirty-three, but he was already, as Stevens remarked, more widely known than many monarchs. The Palace had never had a guest more explosively energetic. Stevens and his cartoonist (not Davenport this time, but Hype Igoe) were entranced, as was Ettore Patrizi, editor of *L'Italia,* who was also present. The critic wrote:

Never again shall I call a tenor haughty or arrogant. . . . At 4:40 of the afternoon of his arrival . . . we met in the Caruso suite at the Palace. It was after six before I could wring myself away. . . .

The room was full of talk, talk, talk — Italian, English, now and then an exclamation in French. We sat around a mahogany table, and Caruso said with a great laugh . . . " A cocktail, an American cocktail — eh? "

He turned to Igoe and said, " Have a drink? "

" Temperance! " cried the caricaturist.

Caruso shook his head. " I like temperance, but I like too the little thing to drink, and the macaroni, and — oh yes! — the roastbeef. I love the roastbeef. I love it too much."

Tenderly he rubbed his palm over the place where the good roast beef belongs, and sighed. " I sing on roastbeef. I am a roastbeef singer — only I must eat it at one o'clock. . . ." He placed two palms where one had been before. Fortunately his frock coat swings from a generous chest hung high and even magnifies his five feet eight inches. He is a thick man from cheek to calf, but as active as his eyes. The very hair of him — black as doom — is active. He is a thick-set specimen of what mothers call " the dark and dangerous " type. . . . He has been a mechanic, the son of a mechanic. . . .

" As water flows from a faucet, so does the music from Caruso when he opens his mouth," said the editor of the Italian paper.

295

" Was it so when he was a mechanic? " I asked.

Caruso heard the signal word. . . . Then in Italian he rapidly spoke to Patrizi and I got the interpretations in splashes.

" I sang always. As a boy I sang in the choir at Naples. As a mechanic I sang as I worked. I serenaded the ladies. One day when I was at work I sang the Litany one hundred times and was given two lire — forty cents. I make a little more money now by not singing so much. . . . I was a boy soprano and my voice failed me at fifteen. But at seventeen I was a tenor. . . . I couldn't go on the stage. I went into the artillery, and my major wanted to know who was that fellow who was singing all the time. . . . One great day he took me to a friend, a wealthy amateur musician, who listened to me and taught me the tenor roles in ' Cavalleria Rusticana ' and ' Carmen.' One day I did not sing at all. The major sent for me.

" ' Why do you not sing today, Caruso? '

" ' I cannot sing, sir, on greasy soup.'

" Next day my soup was strong and there was no grease on it. But the other soldiers called me the son of the major. Six months later I was making my debut in Naples. . . ."

Caruso seized paper and made swift cartoons of Stevens and Igoe, which the *Examiner* printed the next day. The talk turned to a familiar theme: the tenor's popularity with the ladies.

Caruso laughed in amber scale. " You should hear the American girls say ' Mr. Car-r-uso! Mr. Car-r-uso! You sing very fine. How love-*ly*! How love-*ly*! And your voice, Mr. Car-r-uso! Oh! Oh! ' "

We wandered into other rooms. In one he had forty pairs of boots and as many caricatures of himself. . . .

He took my arm on the march to the elevator and we passed a beautiful woman.

" Phew! " said Caruso, and " Phew! " And then with a hand on his heart:

" Oh, Mr. Car-r-uso! Mr. Car-r-uso! How love-*ly*! " — and laughter like that of Rupert of Hentzau.

A year later, in April 1906, Caruso was back in town, but that time the citizens had to cope with a force even more formidable than the volcanic tenor. For once in his career Caruso was shoved into the background. But it took a major earthquake to accomplish the miracle.

5

NOT ALONE singers, but an impressive array of dramatic stars thronged the Palace during the three decades of its existence. Their names constitute a roll call of the artists who made the late nineteenth century a high point in the development of the English-speaking stage. The San Francisco that had known Booth and McCullough in the '50s and dozens of the great and near great during the following decade was, by the time the Palace opened, as theater-wise as any city in the country. The citizens knew what they liked, and why, and they habitually passed judgments without much regard to the visiting actor's reputation or lack of it. The consequence was that even established stars faced local audiences with trepidation, aware that mediocre performances would be recognized as such and their reception gauged accordingly.

In the summer of 1884 Lawrence Barrett, well remembered for his dramatic dash across the continent
on the Lightning Express eight years earlier, was again
in town. He had recently concluded a season in London, and he brought news of other San Francisco favorites: Irving, Booth, Mary Anderson, California's
own Lotta Crabtree. Lotta had made her London debut the previous winter and Barrett brought encouraging reports of her. This favorite child actress of the
mining towns had, twenty years later, scored a genuine
success in the British capital. Her play *Vitouche* was
particularly liked. Barrett added: " I must say they
were disposed to pooh-pooh her at first, but indomitable pluck gained her popularity, and now she has a
warm place in the London heart."

One of the high points in the annals of the San Francisco stage was of course Sarah Bernhardt's first visit in
the spring of 1887. Not for years did the town forget
how Sarah had arrived at her eight-room Palace suite,
surrounded by a mountain of baggage, groups of reporters, delegations of French citizens, throngs of *hoi
polloi,* and her two pets — a parrot and a baby tiger.
The next day she delighted the *Alta's* man by inform-
ing him — in English he described as " limp " — that
she had seen many if not all of the crowned heads of Europe, but that this was the first time she had set eyes on
a California reporter. To the standard question of how
she liked America, she returned the standard answer;
then she qualified the statement: she did *not* like
Chicago. She denied, too, newspaper stories that
she had kicked a tray out of a waiter's hands in the
East.

Linnets and Nightingales

She opened in Sardou's *Fédora,* and the critics were enchanted.

Everything she does seems so natural that the feeling is unavoidable that one is looking at a chapter in real life. . . . It is in the scenes where her passions are aroused that she is at her best, and then it is that her quick, fierce cry, her lightning-like movement and her blazing eyes remind one strongly of the traits of the tiger. . . .

Her later appearances — in *Frou-Frou,* in *Adrienne Lecouvreur, Le Maître des Forges,* and *Théodora* — were all greeted with deafening applause by capacity houses. San Franciscans liked her even in *Camille,* for she endowed that " chestnut of the dramatic stage " with qualities that made them agree " they had never seen it really played until last night." Her portrayal of Marguerite Gautier was compared with Clara Morris's rendition of the role. One critic observed that " it is undeniable that the French woman is the more attractive in her love-making. . . ."

In February 1901 Sarah was back, fourteen years older, but to all appearances as young as ever. " Time writes no wrinkles in her marble brow." For the benefit of doubting reporters she " gaily pulled her tangled mass of touzled hair in proof that it was all her own," then inquired after a local fur dealer whom she had patronized on her last visit. Bystanders informed her that he was dead; she appeared heartbroken.

The papers reported a slight contretemps in the courtyard of the Palace:

Mme. Bernhardt was going out for a drive. Marcus Mayer stood by the carriage door, visibly and bodily apologizing. . . . It seems that Bernhardt carries around with her on her travels her private coachman by whom she insists on being driven. That is all right in the tame and trampled East, but in San Francisco it is different. No San Francisco hackman is going to sit on his coach box and play second fiddle to a foreigner. . . .

No international incident resulted and Sarah appeared a night or two later in *L'Aiglon.* Ashton Stevens refused to be impressed. " If a woman must assume a role beneath her years, let her keep to her own sex." But the audience failed to agree with him. San Franciscans applauded wildly; she was still the divine Sarah.

This was to have been her farewell visit, and so it proved, but for one. The exception was the ancient lady's vaudeville tour, nearly twenty years later, when a curious crowd a full generation removed from her own crowded the old Orpheum and stared at the strange seated figure as though at an exhibit in a museum. Sarah had recently had one of her legs amputated. The local papers retold a story of the showman who had cabled asking what she would charge to allow her leg to be exhibited in the United States. The indomitable lady had cabled back: " Which leg? "

In the fall of 1893 a nine-car special train brought the London Lyceum Company to town and local playgoers packed the Grand Opera House to hear Henry Irving and Ellen Terry. Irving, tall, commanding, his black hair streaked with gray, received as much attention as visiting royalty. Crowds followed with awe his passage through the public rooms of the Palace; his great head bent forward, his shoulders raised, walking with a curious sidelong gait. " One can hardly call him graceful, but none can resist the fascination of a face and the charm of an individual which has made Irving the first of actors and one of the foremost scholars in the eyes of the world." At the Chinese Theater he sat through the long performance with absorbed interest; he told questioners that he would no longer play Hamlet because there had been criticism of his interpretation of the role; he went for long tramps through San Francisco streets followed by his black and white dog.

Ellen Terry drove daily about the city, in company with her daughter, Ailsa Craig, who played small parts in several of the plays. Both Irving and Terry were entertained by the city's elite. So were other members of the company, including a young actor named Bram Stoker, who later wrote *Dracula*. Another actor, William Terris, told reporters: "We passed through Benicia this morning and it quite interested me. I saw the great prize-fight between Sayers and the Benicia Boy, the greatest, I think, that was ever fought."

Their plays were *Nance Oldfield, Becket, The Bells, The Lyons Mail,* and *The Merchant of Venice.* The series opened with *Nance Oldfield,* a comedy by Charles Reade — and the audience responded with an ovation. Ellen Terry received six curtain calls. Irving's rendition of Mathias in *The Bells* aroused equal enthusiasm. "The verdict . . . must unequivocally record him the most important actor of the era. . . ."

In March of 1898 appeared Anna Held, "alluring, seductive and elusive," the Anna of the celebrated kissing contests (156 kisses without stopping), of the no less celebrated milk baths, of *La Poupée* and "Won't

You Come and Play Wiz Me? " She appeared at the
Baldwin in *The Gay Deceiver*. Between times, in company with Managers William A. Brady and Florenz
Ziegfeld, Jr., she saw the town, improved her marksmanship at shooting galleries, took the standard tour
through the opium dens of Chinatown, and at its end
informed waiting reporters: " It is the most curieuse
and surprise evening that I have ever know. C'est
ignoble, c'est extraordinaire, c'est droll and, phew! it
smell 'oreeble! "

The *Examiner's* critic called her " a rare bit of
feminine bric-a-brac " who had been brought across
the continent for San Francisco's inspection and grati-
fication.

Such a tiny little woman to make such a fuss over! She
stands for a restful moment against the ruby background,
then trips down with the lightness of a sprite and sings her
little song in a fine, clear little voice that penetrates to
every part of the house. . . .

The little Parisienne has all that has been claimed for
her — chic, beauty, fascination, diablerie. She is as dainty
and exquisite . . . in face and form, from the aureole of
brown-gold hair to the toe of her little slipper as anything
that has ever been let out from under a glass case. . . .
There are only some five and fifty inches of her, and every
inch is vivid with life. . . .

One of San Francisco's periodical earthquakes occurred during Anna's stay; there were those who
thought she might have been in some way responsible.

6

THERE WAS no lack of great names in the '90s. One morning toward the middle of the decade crowds took the ferry to Oakland Mole in the hope of seeing thirty-five-year-old Ignace Jan Paderewski leave the train and cross the bay to his Palace suite. They were disappointed; the pianist remained in seclusion and for four hours a nondescript group pressed about the sides of his car while torrents of music flowed from his piano. It was an odd setting for a concert: the dim, barnlike terminal where trains pulled in and out, switch-engines shunted cars from track to track, and baggage carts rattled past the drawn windows. Scores of railroad workers joined the listening group. One said to another: " This is what they pay five dollars for."

Paderewski left the car at last and was escorted to the ferry. There the crowd, pushed forward by pressure from the rear, formed a tight circle about him and his party. The pianist, annoyed by their curious stares, remarked to a friend: " That man must be a tailor. He has done nothing but look at my clothes." Reporters must also have looked closely, for their descriptions of his person were models of detail:

Paderewski's hand is very white and the blue veins are distinctly traced, like the lines in leaves in the early spring. . . . It is a short hand, small, not very wide . . . with fingers lightly flattened at their ends, but withal a beautiful hand, full of individuality. . . .

His leonine mane is blonde, with red lights. . . . It is longer than in his photographs and sets out three inches or more beyond his silk hat and overcoat collar. It does not blow in the wind. . . .

Paderewski refused to read what American journalists wrote about him (perhaps the sample above will explain why) and his secretary clipped out all personal references before the papers reached him. Nor would he often read what critics thought of his performances.

" Why should I? If they say I do not play well, I shall not play any better, and if they say I play well, I shall not play any worse. . . .

" But you Californians have not the very good manners. In Los Angeles they called me Paddy on the street. Boys whistled that tune, ' Paddy, Get Your Hair Cut,' and one day a little newsboy brought me a paper with my picture. I was dining, and he climbed into a chair and began to drum on the cloth while I read. That I did not mind. The others I disliked. . . ."

His concert at the California Theater was not without incident, for Paderewski had his share of artistic temperament. He came on the stage " with a brisk little walk, his arms hanging limp and jointless, his hands dangling," played his first selection, acknowledged the applause with " a queer, stiff little nod of the head " — and began his second.

A peculiar thing happened. Paderewski played the opening bars, rose and hurriedly left the stage. He groped along the scene, as though the light blinded him, missed the door, found it, and disappeared through it, while the audience sat quietly, too astonished to giggle. . . .

Some maladroit stage person had walked across the stage with heavy shoes. In an instant an avenging angel with a shock of bronzed, wavy hair was behind him, swearing volubly in a strange tongue and gesticulating wildly. The super was hurried to the lower regions and Paderewski reappeared.

The pianist's tour made his name a household word. But he was no better known than another middle-European celebrity: Sandow, the Strong Man. Sandow, in fact, surpassed Paderewski in one particular; his fame inspired impostors to tour the country, borrowing his name and copying his act. In March 1894 San Francisco billboards heralded the coming of one " Sandowe." Close on his arrival at the Palace came a wire from New York to the hotel manager:

Notify papers that Sandowe, who is advertised to appear in San Francisco, is an impostor. His right name is Montgomery.

F. Ziegfeld, Jr.

A few weeks later the real Sandow — without the " e " — was in town. He was twenty-seven; his weight was two hundred pounds; and it was said that his decision to make himself a " perfect physical specimen " had dated from a visit to Florence and a study of Cellini's David. The devices by which he got public attention make it clear that the arts of ballyhoo were in full flower in the '90s. He offered ten thousand dollars to anyone who would equal his weight-lifting feats; he staged a wrestling bout with a lion; he held a reception at the Palace and invited the city's elite to inspect his muscles at close range.

The contest with the lion was held at Central Park;

305

a throng of three thousand bought admittance in the happy expectation of seeing the strong man clawed to ribbons. But Commodore, the lion, proved small and without ambition, a sorry specimen of the king of beasts. Moreover, Commodore was muzzled and leather pads had been laced over his paws. The strong man tossed the docile beast about while the crowd hooted its derision.

More successful was Sandow's reception in the Maple Room of the Palace, where he appeared in pink silk tights, displayed his muscles, expanded his chest, and permitted spectators to punch him in the stomach. " My greatest feat in all probability," he told reporters, " is to turn a somersault, blinded, with fifty-six pounds in each hand."

The California Midwinter Fair was then in progress and Sandow shared with the dancer, Little Egypt, the distinction of being its greatest card. He appeared nightly at the Vienna Prater, where he turned back-springs with dumbbells in his hands and hung suspended from a pole holding one 150-pound and two 56-pound weights, with two men clinging to them. As a finale he lifted and balanced three horses on a platform.

Every evening after the regular performance Sandow holds a private reception in the banquet hall of the Vienna Prater. Parties of society ladies have been present on each occasion and have satisfied their curiosity by minutely examining the phenomenal muscles of the strong man.

Not only were society ladies fascinated, but small boys as well. For weeks after the strong man had gone on to new triumphs back lots all over town were filled with urchins attempting feats of lifting and balancing. The parade of actors and actresses was continual through the '90s and all the important ones stopped at the Palace; that was one of their ways of proving that they *were* important.

In 1894 young lady guests admired the wavy dark hair and handsome mustache of Wilton Lackaye, currently appearing at the Baldwin in *Lady Windermere's Fan,* by the fashionable Dublin dramatist. Papers announced that the actor's wardrobe included sixty-five pairs of trousers, forty-three vests, and " enough neckties to circle the Midwinter Fair site." Lackaye indignantly denied the story. " I am directly opposed to that sort of thing. . . . Of course I require an extensive wardrobe in my business, but I think no man should dress in a manner to attract attention in the street."

John Drew arrived that same summer and, in *The Butterfly* and *The Masked Ball,* justified his right to be called " the prince of light comedy." The town was not so sure about his feminine lead, who was billed as " the youngest leading lady on the American stage." One critic stated: " She has acquired a little affectation since she became so well known. . . ." Her name was Maude Adams.

Nat Goodwin was an almost yearly visitor and no one bothered to inquire whether or not *he* was affected. When he arrived from an Australian tour in the fall of 1896, Goodwin was already well started on his famous series of marriages and divorces. Maxine and Gertrude Elliott were in his company, and a romance was reported between Goodwin and the ample but charming Maxine. The latter had just obtained a divorce; Goodwin's mate was suing for one. " Miss Elliott," observed the *Chronicle,* " is free from her encumbrance but Mr. Goodwin still wears his millstone." But he wore it lightly, and reporters found him " the same gay, irresponsible carrot-topped fellow he was when he went away."

He was asked if he was in love with Miss Elliott.

" Everyone is in love with her, but I can't tell which sister I admire the more. Both are talented and both are lovely. I have never seen sisters so devoted. They are inseparable. . . ."

The papers had been printing disturbing news from the East, where two young ladies were threatening to file suits for breach of promise should the actor marry Miss Elliott. Goodwin commented:

" Why I didn't even know that Miss Elliott was suing for a divorce. . . . She never told me, because she knew, I suppose, that I can't keep a secret. I have had all the matrimony I want. . . . As for Dorothy Unser and Blanche Walsh, both of 'em were disgruntled. The former was only a little understudy who took to calling me pet names."

Maxine Elliott was present at the interview and deprecated the whole affair. Her divorce had no connection with any rumored romance with Goodwin. It was hardly fair to start such stories while she was in far-off Australia and had no means of refuting them. She continued:

" We knew nothing about all this . . . until we were almost ready to return. It made me feel very bad. . . . I

308

accepted this engagement because it was very advantageous to me. . . . The divorces were mere coincidences. Just say that I have no immediate intention of becoming a bride and that there is neither veil nor orange blossom in my wardrobe."

She and Goodwin were married a few months later, and were divorced in 1908.

La Loie Fuller was at the Palace in November 1896 and moved packed houses at the California Theater to cheers by her sensational " Danse du Nuit." La Loie was no sylph: " She is built like a column — round and firm and compact." But her head was full of " uncommon American sense " and reporters admired her curly blond hair (which she wore loose) her retroussé nose, blue eyes, and bubbling good humor. Nature had been over-generous with her in another direction, but she was undisturbed. " My feet? Well, I told you I was born in Chicago. They are made to stand on."

After the beginning of the new century Ashton Stevens's work for the *Examiner* set the town's playgoers to reading that paper's theater news with sharpened interest. The following excerpts from his interview with Frederick Warde may explain why:

The archives of the stage do not record another tragedian who has fought so long for recognition without attaining it. Others have fought, but have fallen. Warde has received knocks as hard as any, but the road still knows him, year in, year out. He is perhaps the most successful failure in the history of the theatre. . . . The name Frederick Warde is as familiar as the name of any other actor on the stage in every place except the big places like New York. . . .

Talk with Warde ten minutes and you will see what bars him from great actorhood.

The explanation is in the nature of a paradox. Warde has the actor temperament to an excess that precludes credibility. Every visible muscle is at play as he talks; every word is chiseled and rounded with a precision that is too perfect. Every gesture is Romanesque. . . .

Warde's stay in 1901 was not without romantic interest. One evening the tragedian's son and manager, Arthur F. Warde, dropped into a theater on Powell Street to see the play. " He saw his fate as well. He fell in love with the little girl on sight and sought an introduction." The " little girl " was Polly Stockwell, stepdaughter of L. R. Stockwell, a locally celebrated comedian, and manager of the Powell Street house. The romance developed in best story-book fashion and when the company returned to San Francisco a year later the two were married in the elder Warde's apartments at the Palace. They were divorced, however, in 1904.

7

DAVID WARFIELD arrived toward the close of 1902 and Stevens was on hand to interview this local boy who had so decidedly made good. Warfield was full of reminiscences of his stage-struck youth, when he had been an usher at the Bush Street Theater and fate had checkmated his every effort to get behind the footlights.

Stevens asked: " Is it right, then — about the stage

manager ringing down the curtain in the middle of your debut at the old Wigwam? "

" The story is right — but mild. It was really worse. I'm glad you mentioned it because I am glad it happened. If I had succeeded that night, twelve, thirteen years ago, I might have stayed here and worked myself up. I might now be the stage manager at the Bella Union at a salary of $25 and with a head as big as — " He made a gesture. " But that failure hurt. . . . Everybody believed in it so sincerely. My friends said: ' Just as I told you, Dave, you won't do for the stage.' But it takes more than one failure to kill the truly stage-struck. In three weeks I was on my way to New York, as hopeful as ever. Fifteen dollars a week was my first salary. . . .''

Warfield was appearing as Simon Levi in *The Auctioneer*. On the opening night an old friend, Rabbi Nieto, met him in front of the house.

" He asked if I intended to sprinkle the clothes and smoke them up for the fire sale. I said ' Yes ' and he said ' Don't do that '; and then I said, ' Rabbi, we are going to play the Jew as he is, sprinkling pot and all, and if you wait through the whole performance you will see that in the long run he's about as white as any other fellow. . . .' "

Not only was Rabbi Nieto convinced, but the whole town as well, for *The Auctioneer* scored a triumph.

Another noted success, *David Harum*, came to town the following spring with the veteran William H. Crane in the title role. In Crane's rooms, Stevens remarked that the actor looked as young as ever — and was rewarded by some tales of the early days of the Palace.

" Why, I lived in this very hotel the first year it was open. Good gracious, yes! I lived here in 1875, when I came out with the Hooley Comedy Company, and stayed exactly one year. I'll never forget! — one day I had been particularly fortunate at the common diversion of those days, and came home with a sack containing seven hundred dollars. . . ."

" Poker? "

" Good gracious, no! Stocks. That was the time when Consolidated Virginny was jumping around like forked lightning. Well, I gave the money to the hotel clerk . . . asked him to put it away in the safe for me. A couple of days later I went to the hotel office for my money, and the clerk said, ' You'd better call for that tomorrow, Mr. Crane; we had to make a cash payment today of five hundred dollars in gold, and being a bit short, we took it out of your sack.' Talk about actors! Here's an actor that trusted a hotel! "

Crane was prolific of stories. He recalled one about Maurice Barrymore, which had also happened at the Palace:

" Maurice was playing a game of billiards here one day, and was nearing the end of his string. One more point would give him the game, and there was quite a crowd gathered around the table. Barry banged away on his last shot — and missed the first ball. But his stroke was heavy and his cue ball went clean around the table and scored by hitting both the others on the way home. One of the spectators cried, ' Holy God! ' ' Not wholly God,' said Maurice in a flash. ' *I'm* partly responsible.' "

Trixie Friganza arrived in the fall of 1903 — and did *not* stop at the Palace. This was so contrary to

custom that the comedienne — she was playing the
widow in *The Prince of Pilsen* — felt under the necessity of explaining why:

" I did try the Palace, but Mr. Palace was so proud and
indifferent. He didn't seem to think it would make any
great difference whether I put up at his hotel or some
other; so I came over where I thought I could make an
impression. And I'd hardly registered when the hotel management sent up a bouquet. I was tickled to death — till I
found that they send flowers to everybody. I think they
have prop bouquets. . . ."

On her tour the actress had scored a hit in each town
by composing a final verse to one of her songs, filled
with local references. But in San Francisco she had encountered difficulties:

" I wanted to sing the real Frisco verse, but they
wouldn't let me. They thought it might offend the first
nighters. The idea! I'll hum it for you." And this is what
she said. Miss Friganza, like most of the others in " The
Prince of Pilsen," says, rather than sings, her songs:

> Here's a girl from a town that's won renown
>   As the home of the golden nugget.
> Each girl out there is so wondrous fair
>   It's proper and right to hug it.
> There the girls are brave, but not too bold —
>   Still, an armful's all that a man can hold.
> There's no danger of anyone catching cold
>   From a girl in San Francisco.

" Now just imagine that with the ' Hot Time ' swell-
ing in for the chorus! . . . Do you know why I talk my
songs instead of singing them? Because I can't sing, that's

all. . . . Ah, here comes Mercury with the nectar. Mercury, please notify the Coroner that we are about to taste these things, and here's a quarter for floral tributes. . . ."

A lively, refreshing, unpredictable trouper was Trixie Friganza. Critic Stevens was delighted with her, and so was the rest of the town.

Lively, too, and just as outspoken, was honey-haired Lillian Russell, who early in 1904 appeared at the Grand Opera House with Weber and Fields. At the Palace, Ashton Stevens found " Airy, Fairy Lillian " surrounded by enough flowers to stock a florist's shop. He wanted to know the name of the song she had been singing when he knocked.

" It's the ' Evening Star ' . . . the song by Stromberg, our old leader at Weber and Fields. It may be trash, but there's . . . something that touches — especially for those who knew the composer. You know they found the manuscript in his pocket after he died. He killed himself. . . .

We discuss popular songs, the tunes that come and go like hats. " How do you like singing them? "

" This is not necessarily for publication, but singing cheap music is hell." Lillian Russell finds the fit word in the first sentence.

Her admiration for Weber and Fields was immense but she had found that singing in their company had drawbacks. She explained:

" The chorus — I can't sing without the chorus — it isn't permitted. And every member of the chorus is working all the time — that's what it's there for. And sitting out in front is a large delegation of johnnies, following every movement and glance of the girls — that's what they

314

are there for. And," Miss Russell sums up with a comprehensive gesture, " if you think it's an easy job to get the attention of the audience in a situation like that, you should
try it, not for five years, but just one."

Palace guests were almost as interested in Miss Russell's pet dog as in the actress herself. The animal was
a Japanese terrier, said to be valued at ten thousand
dollars. Weber and Fields were of course as popular as
ever; within a few hours half the town was repeating
such exchanges as these:

WEBER: You say you will make me a magnate. What
is a magnate?

FIELDS: There are two kinds of magnates. The first
kind eats holes in a cheese, and the other kind eats holes
in pockets.

WEBER: A true friend. Never have I met it. What
is it?

FIELDS: A true friend is one who knows you are no
good and is able to forget it.

WEBER: Are we gentlemen?

FIELDS: Yes, but one of us ain't.

When Mrs. Patrick Campbell arrived in April 1903,
Stevens, waiting at the doorway of one of the large public rooms at the Palace, saw the actress emerge from
an elevator and ask to be directed to the rendezvous.

She is addressing not me, but a stranger. I am a
stranger, too, for that matter, but I have an appointment;
she is asking the way to the meeting place, and I know how
much easier it is for a camel to go through the eye of a
needle than for us to enter the kingdom of propinquity
after the great length and stretches of the Palace Hotel

315

parlor have once come between us. I have been here before. Therefore, I am waiting in the hallway. And, hearing her voice from afar . . . I follow and save her from entering that labyrinth alone, where she might be lost for hours, years, forever.

Mrs. Campbell does not smile when I tell her of the dangers that menace the stranger who adventures unguided across these treacherous acres of plush. She is very tranquil, very serious, as we take the long walk from the nearest door to the nearest window. I have been told that she has complained of other hotels, and wonder that she does not remark the absence of trolley-service in the mammoth parlor of this one. . . .

The British actress was appearing in *The Second Mrs. Tanqueray* and in Sudermann's *The Joy of Living*. Her stay was enlivened by a visit from the American poetess Ella Wheeler Wilcox. The latter was then at the height of her fame; her *Poems of Passion* were on tens of thousands of parlor tables, and a half-dozen other small volumes, bound in limp leather, were to be found on every book-store counter. In 1901 William Randolph Hearst had sent her to the coronation of Edward VII, and her series of commemorative odes written from the very firing-line of the ceremonies had been featured in the Hearst papers. She was in San Francisco on a lecture tour, and stopping at the Palace. Local papers commented on the fact that " a star of the first dramatic magnitude should come into immediate juxtaposition with a star of first literary magnitude " — and an interested city awaited their meeting.

Miss Wilcox graciously made the first move. " We are under the same roof," she wrote, " and may never

have another opportunity to meet. I leave tomorrow.
If you have a few moments to spare, may I see you
today? "

The *Examiner* tells what happened next:

Mrs. Campbell's maid brought a verbal response.
Mrs. Campbell would see Mrs. — Mrs. — was it Wilcox?
— just five minutes, but no more.

" Very well," replied Mrs. Wilcox. " I can spare five
minutes."

On the threshold of the actress' apartment, she paused,
expecting the welcoming smile to which she is accustomed.
It was not in evidence. Mrs. Campbell stood, regarding
her with that especial sort of politeness in look and attitude
which plainly says, " Well, who are you, and what do you
want? "

Mrs. Wilcox advanced and extended her hand . . .

" I believe you did not make out my name," she said.
" I do not write very plainly — I am Mrs. Wilcox."

Mrs. Campbell bowed uncomprehendingly.

" I am Ella Wheeler Wilcox," particularized the
poetess.

Then Mrs. Campbell, searching her memory, found
a clew. . . .

" Ah, I believe you are the lady who said nice things
of me in the morning paper? Is this a call, or an interview? "

" I chanced to speak of your play in print," Mrs. Wilcox replied, " as it was interesting to me, but of course you
know that my work is — "

" I only know you through the kind of criticism you
gave me in the paper — you see, I am so busy. What is
your work? "

" Why — I — have written some seventeen books, for
one thing . . ."

" But you see I am seldom in this country," apologized the actress. " I am English."

" Truly," responded the author, " — the same nationality as King Edward, who had one of my poems sung at his mother's funeral anniversary, and Queen Alexandra, who selected another of my poems to send with flowers to Mr. Gladstone's obsequies."

" Really! " said the actress, interested for the first time. " I must get your poems right away."

Then, with a woman's tact, she looked her visitor over. " How sweet your gown is, and how much you resemble Ellen Terry! "

The two great ladies then sat down for a friendly chat.

The new century advanced and the Palace, now thirty years old, continued within its big lofty rooms to shelter the transiently great of the theatrical profession. To be sure there were a few who, after 1904, deserted the old hotel and took to stopping at the new St. Francis up on Union Square. But these were mostly newcomers; actors and actresses who had only recently come to the fore and who were too young to realize or perhaps to care how many of the great names of their profession had been identified with the Market Street hostelry, and over how long a period.

CHAPTER EIGHT

THIS BATTER'D CARAVAN–SARY

1

In the winter of 1904, any San Franciscan with two thousand dollars to spare might have made himself a public benefactor by presenting the city with an Omori seismograph and thus writing — to quote the *Examiner* — " an assurance policy . . . against earthquakes."

An only mildly interested city learned that Omori was a Japanese scientist who had perfected an instrument by which earthquakes could be forecast and their character analyzed. No philanthropist stepped forward, but the seismograph provided a welcome new conversational topic across bars and dinner tables and most citizens agreed it would be nice to have one. Alexander G. McAdie, San Francisco's " weather man," was particularly intrigued. With a municipal seismograph on the Farallones Islands, it would be possible, he stated, to advise architects how to plan earthquakeproof buildings; more, he could send out advance bulletins telling of the approach of temblors. Again it was agreed that this would be a desirable extension of Mr. McAdie's services. With a weather man who told citizens not only when to wear their rubbers but how to avoid having their crockery jarred off the pantry shelves, San Francisco might advance another notch up the scale of well-governed cities. To be sure, in the past there had sometimes been a more serious side to earthquakes, but on that point, too, Mr. McAdie was reassuring. " We have," he stated, " lost only thirty killed in the past sixty years." He added a mild joke: " We could lose half a man for a long time each year without noticeable effect on the population."

The seismograph remained unpurchased and the next quake hit the city with no more advance warning than had its predecessors. It chose New Year's Day, 1905, for its visit; cups and glasses and plates again rained down from their shelves, bric-a-brac bounced off mantels, and here and there a window was broken. Newspapers ran their accustomed editorials:

> It may be comforting . . . to note the classification applied to our local disturbances. College professors call them geotectonic. A geotectonic earthquake is a sort of tame variety which may chafe against its chains now and then, but never really does any harm. . . .

Geotectonic quakes were felt several times during 1905 and were sensibly ignored by the citizens. There were those, however, who felt that one chose a bad time to demonstrate its harmlessness. On a Sunday in December the congregation of St. Dominic's Church listened placidly to Father F. P. Driscoll's sermon on the Last Judgment. Well along in his discourse and fully warmed to his subject the good father shouted: " He shall not come unannounced! Signs shall precede His coming, signs great and fearful! " At precisely that instant an earthquake hit the town with the suddenness of an exploding firecracker. The big stone building rocked from crypt to steeple. The preacher stopped in mid-course. Some worshippers dropped to their knees; others, more material-minded, bolted through the nearest doors; several women swooned. The shock ended as abruptly as it had begun and Father Driscoll completed his sermon before an alert but diminished congregation. Next morning the *Call* commented: ". . . one of San Francisco's most violent earthquakes of recent years went its way after one of the most remarkable coincidences in the city's history."

The following spring, during the first week of April, San Franciscans were distressed to learn that Vesuvius had again become active. " Naples Fears the Fate of Pompeii," stated the headlines, and the accompanying stories announced that thousands were homeless. A relief committee was organized and arrangements were made for a benefit baseball game at Recreation Park. San Franciscans were eager to help these unfortunate Italians, but they couldn't help wondering what prompted people to live practically on top of an active volcano. Really, the thing was hardly sensible.

2

IN THAT same month of April 1906 there was talk of adding another two floors to the Palace. This would increase the number of rooms from 800 to 1,200 and would maintain the hotel's place as the largest in the West, a distinction it had then held more than thirty years. The cost would be close to three hundred thousand dollars. But competition had to be met and the owners were determined that the Palace must concede nothing in the way of luxury and service to the new houses.

The latest competitor, the Fairmont, was nearing completion on the old Fair property on Nob Hill, one of the most magnificent sites in the city. For several weeks Mrs. Herman Oelrichs, formerly Theresa Fair, had been in town with her decorator, planning the furnishings of the new hotel. She stayed at the Palace. Rumors were heard that the Fairmont was to be leased to the Palace owners and that the two hotels would be operated under one management. Instead, the Fair heirs announced the sale of the property to Herbert E. and Hartland Law, San Francisco brothers who had recently made a fortune in patent medicine. The town was curious to learn who would operate the hotel for the Laws.

No announcement was forthcoming, and public interest focused on a more important matter. The Metropolitan Opera Company was making a spring tour of the provinces and San Francisco's fashionables prepared for the biggest musical and social event of the year. It was the golden era of the Metropolitan; its roster sparkled with great names: Sembrich, Eames, Walker, Alten, Van Rooy, Plançon, Rossi, Alfred Hertz, the conductor, and — Caruso. All these arrived in special cars from Kansas City, along with Ernest Goerlitz, manager of the Conried company. Still

322

others followed: Fremstad, Abbott, Ralph, Jacoby, Poehlmann, Rappold, Homer, Weed, Journet, Begue, Parvis, Dufriche, Reiss, Scotti, Campanari, Paroli, Burgstaller, Goritz, Blass, and Muhlmann. Not in years had San Francisco seen such an array of songsters.

Dressmakers struggled to have gowns ready for the opening night, April 16, and social columns were extended beyond their usual length with lists of guests at pre-opera dinner parties or post-opera suppers. The barnlike Grand Opera House was only a block or two from the Palace. Many of the artists stopped there and of course the public rooms were thronged before and after each performance. " The Ladies' Grill and the Palm Garden were beautifully decorated with flowers and ferns to please the first night patronage."

Despite all this, San Francisco pronounced the opening performance a disappointment. The opera was *The Queen of Sheba* with Edyth Walker as the Queen and Rappold, Alten, Van Rooy, Dippel, Blass and Muhlmann in the cast. The *Call's* society reporter, Laura Bride Powers, confessed: " I prophesied a brilliant house for the opening . . . and it really didn't make good." Everyone knew the reason. Not until the second night, the 17th, did the season really begin — with Olive Fremstad and Caruso in *Carmen*. This time the *Call's* critic, scribbling rapidly to catch the early editions of the 18th, found nothing wrong with the spectacle.

The thrill, the throb, the quiver — without which opera becomes a mere recital — was in the air last night. It was sublime! The house was a terraced garden of or-

chids and narcissus and nodding roses, with fruit blossoms
scattered between. And the odor of roses from the pit as-
sailed the senses like the breath that blows from the flowery
orchards of Santa Clara.

Getting down to particulars, Miss Powers stated that
not all the fashionable ladies appeared to best advantage in lavish displays of jewels. More to her taste was
the comparative simplicity of such costumes as that of
Mrs. James Flood, whose jewelry was limited to " a
tiara, a dog collar, shoulder straps, a stomacher and
corsage decorations of diamonds and pearls "; and of
Mrs. Frederick Kohl, who wore a jeweled headgear, a
two-inch-wide dog collar of pearls and diamonds, with
an " assorted lot of shimmering things on the corsage
line, and outshining them all, a brilliant American
beauty rose." Dozens of other ladies in the boxes and
pit had their presence recorded and their beauty,
dresses, and jewelry described.

It was a busy night in the offices of the morning
papers. While society reporters ground out stories of
who were there and what they wore, critics were pro-
nouncing judgment on the singers, from Caruso down
to the least important member of the cast. Grave questions were propounded and gravely answered. How
did this Carmen compare with other Carmens the town
had seen? Was Fremstad as good as Calvé? No, said
Blanche Partington in the *Call;* Fremstad was " a Teu-
ton of the Teutons " and " temperamentally at war
with the role." The *Examiner* agreed: " Fremstad's
' Carmen ' was inclined to be dutchy." There was less
difference of opinion about Caruso. Caruso was mag-

nificent. San Francisco had never heard a more adequate Don José. Ashton Stevens did, however, point
out that Caruso's Don José "sounded better than it
looked." It was Caruso who "lifted the large audience
to an enthusiasm that was denied the unfortunate
'Queen of Sheba' opening. . . . This fat little man
with the chins is pretty much the Conried season."

Not long after midnight the fat little man dropped
into the Palace bar and sipped a pony of cognac with
other male members of the cast. Some had been longer
at the bar. The success of the evening's performance
was so often toasted that several of the celebrants decided to make a night of it. Inquiries were discreetly
made, addresses written down, and presently a hack rattled away through the deserted streets. One of the
group, Alfred Hertz, remained behind. He was to conduct *Lohengrin* on the night of the 18th and he must
get some sleep. He ascended to his sixth-floor room and
went virtuously to bed.

There were other celebrations. Up on Nob Hill,
Mesdames Sembrich and Eames were entertained in
the big wooden mansion of James Ben Ali Haggin on
Taylor Street. Whether or not the guests were privi-
leged to see the famous stables in the rear, where the
Haggin racehorses were sumptuously housed, is not
known. Here and there all over town lights burned
uncommonly late as guests in hotels and restaurants
and scores of houses lingered over post-opera suppers,
exchanged last bits of gossip, tossed off final opinions
of the performance and performers, said their belated
adieux and went off sleepily to bed. *Carmen* was exciting — especially with Caruso! — but it was also ex-

hausting. And these suppers lasted so long — just *look* at the time! It would be nice to sleep late in the morning. . . .

3

AT THIRTEEN minutes past five on the morning of the 18th — only an hour or two after late celebrants had dropped off to sleep — the steamer *Argo,* proceeding through the dawn ninety miles north of Point Arena, was suddenly jolted so violently that her captain thought she had rammed a raft of logs.

A second later the Point Arena lighthouse, a massive cone of masonry, was demolished as if by a single shattering blow. At near-by Alder Creek, the land at the west end of a bridge was wrenched so far to the right that the approach missed the bridge entirely; a section of the bridge itself toppled into the creek.

The earthquake rift moved southward " veering to the left or right according to the resistance of the soil," but keeping the same general direction. It was really a slipping of the earth's surface, more than two hundred miles long; a horizontal movement of up to twenty feet, with a corresponding vertical rise or fall that in places formed cliffs a dozen feet high.

Near the Gualala River the rift toppled and split huge redwoods and virtually wrecked the town of Fort Bragg. It then slipped out to sea, followed the Sonoma coast past Fort Ross, throwing down everything movable in that and other towns. Across Bodega Head,

326

into the sea again, on to Tomales Bay, the rift progressed, while the accompanying earthquake shook
Marin County as if it were in the grip of a giant.

At San Rafael, fifteen miles north of sleeping San
Francisco, United States Circuit Judge Morrow heard
his bedroom clock strike five. " The morning," he
later recalled, " was bright and clear, and the air fragrant and balmy . . . birds were unusually busy and
through the open window came the message of the
early dawn promising a pleasant day." Fifteen minutes
later the hotel at Marshall's Station was wrenched from
its foundations and tumbled into Tomales Bay. At
Point Reyes the train for San Francisco awaited the
signal to leave. Five fifteen approached; the conductor
climbed on board, watch in hand. The train suddenly
jerked violently to the east and toppled on its side. A
brick chimney crashed through the roof of the station.

At near-by Olema a number of extraordinary things
happened. In the barn at Skinner's dairy the routine
morning milking was going on. The farmhouse stood
north of the barn; both structures faced the county
road. At the roadside in front of the house stood a row
of tall cypress trees; between the trees and the house
was a rose garden. A little beyond the house and farther up the road were a row of eucalyptus trees and
some raspberry bushes. Along the east wall of the barn
were a number of windows and under each was a pile
of manure. The earthquake struck violently, throwing
both cows and milkers to the ground and causing the
animals to stampede. The men made their way outside
and found that a drastic realignment of landmarks had
taken place. The cypress trees and the rose garden had

moved away from the front of the house and now stood in front of the barn. The clump of raspberry bushes had slid down from the north and occupied the space vacated by the roses. The eucalyptus trees had marched to a position opposite the barn and in the process one had shifted from the foot of the line to the head. The piles of manure before the barn had each moved some sixteen feet south of the window to which it belonged.

At the Shafter ranch near by, the rift passed through the corral, opening a gap directly beneath one of the cows. The animal fell in head-first and the ground closed again, leaving only its rump and tail visible. The seaside village of Bolinas, a few miles farther south, was roughly treated; the Flagstaff Inn there, built partly over the water, was shaken into the surf. The rift there left the land again, passed the Golden Gate and San Francisco several miles out to sea, and regained the shore at Mussel Rock. Following the scarred trail of other ancient fault lines, it crossed the southern peninsula, where it snapped the pipes that connected San Francisco with its reserve water supply (thereby sealing the doom of the city) and all but completely wrecked the stone quadrangle of Stanford University. Throughout Santa Clara Valley buildings were demolished and trees leveled. The rift entered the hills beyond, following up valleys, over ridges, through stands of giant redwoods. There century-old trees, five feet or more in diameter, were snapped like matches. In the mountain canyons, still damp from the spring rains, the jolting of the earth brought other perils:

The rift crossed Hinckley's Gulch at right angles. This is a narrow gorge about a hundred feet deep, in which stood the large Loma Prieta sawmill. The gorge was filled by landslips from both sides. The mill was completely buried, with nine millhands, and a redwood tree over a hundred feet high was set erect and unhurt over the place where the mill stood. The bodies of six men were recovered. One of these, the foreman, was found erect, smothered in mud, but standing with extended arms and limbs in the act of running from the mill. With him, equally erect and in the act of running, was the body of a Siberian mastiff. Their position marked the meeting point of the two walls of the canyon.

Miles beyond the southern end of the Santa Cruz mountains the rift became less easy to trace. From the Pajaro River " a series of short breaks creep off to the southeast, ending two miles southwest of San Juan, the last act being the final, almost complete wreck of the beautiful and venerable Mission of San Juan Bautista."

4

BACK AT the Palace, Alfred Hertz, who had retired comparatively early, was awakened to find the room tossing in long, jarring movements of surprising vigor, with everything movable dancing about the floor. Creaking timbers, cracking masonry, and shattering glass and the crash of falling objects made a din so terrific that Hertz thought he must be in the midst of a major explosion. He leaped from bed and made his way to the door. There he heard Robert Blass, the American basso in the adjoining room, shouting at the top of his ample lungs: " Earthquake! "

All over town that word was rising above the tumult. An earthquake of unprecedented violence was giving the " joyous and breezy town a jolt that will live in history." The quotation is from David Starr Jordan, Stanford University's president. He added that its effect was " a greater destruction of the results of human effort than was ever known before in the records of the world." The damage was city-wide and impartial. Half a thousand cemetery monuments were shaken down. All fell in the same direction, toward the east or slightly north of east. Brick chimneys toppled by the dozens in every block, crashing through roofs and ceilings, sometimes falling on the occupants before they could leap from their beds. Plaster showered down from tens of thousands of ceilings, pictures were shaken from walls, the stocks in stores were tossed in heaps on floors.

This was the milder sort of damage and it was universal. More serious destruction was widespread: fronts of buildings fell to the sidewalks; houses on hillside lots left their foundations and slid into the streets; here and there badly constructed buildings, both brick and wood, collapsed into rubbish heaps. Those who rushed to the streets found evidences of the tremendous stresses exerted by the undulating earth. Street-car tracks were bent into horizontal snake-line curves or raised or depressed in a series of humps and dips; pavements were broken in long fissures from which water from broken mains geysered upward; undulations appeared where pressure caused sections of sidewalk to buckle and arch upward; in the downtown area stone and brick cornices had fallen, breaking through sidewalk wells into basements, spilling out into the middle of the streets and rendering them impassable.

To no one was the full extent of the damage at once clear. During the first minutes each was fully occupied with his immediate problem. Each faced the emergency in his own way, his impressions and behavior determined by his temperament or training. Standing in the doorway of his Palace room, Alfred Hertz, opera conductor, listened with professional interest to the weird medley of sound. " It has always seemed extraordinary to me that even in that moment I was conscious of sound effects. In operas such elementary catastrophes are invariably orchestrated FFF, while musically speaking, the earthquake gave me the sensation of an uncanny *mezzo forte* effect, something comparable to the *mezzo forte* roll on a cymbal or gong. . . ."

Hertz, who liked to sleep late, had given orders that the windows of his room be tightly curtained against the morning sun. The instructions had been so faithfully followed that he found the room in complete darkness, for the shock had put the electric lights out of order. He found an overcoat, raced through the corridor, and joined a concerted rush to the ground floor. But Hertz was still capable of surprise. " I could scarcely believe my eyes when I saw an old Chinese servant quietly and calmly cleaning the easy chairs and carpets of the lobby, as if all this was just a daily occurrence."

Less calm was Caruso, who reached the lobby at that moment, spied Hertz, and rushed to his side. " Caruso . . . embraced me hysterically, and crying like a child, repeatedly insisted that we were doomed. . . ." Tenor and conductor clung together, both expecting annihilation, then bolted outdoors. Hertz continues:

" The street presented an amazing series of grotesque sights. The majority of people had fled from their rooms without stopping to dress, many of them a little less than naked. But excitement was running so high that nobody noticed or cared.

" The weather was beautiful but extremely cold. After standing for perhaps half an hour on Market Street, I felt so chilly that I took the suggestion of our first cellist, that we get something to warm us up at a nearby saloon. Before we realized what we had done, we found that we had consumed a whole quart of whiskey, and while under ordinary circumstances such an amount of alcohol might have killed me, this actually gave me sufficient courage to climb back to my room and get some clothes."

In the darkness of his curtained room Hertz found the clothes closet and selected a costume by touch alone. When he emerged he saw that he was wearing full-dress trousers, a gray vest, and a brown coat. " I did not take the time to put on my shoes, and only when I was downstairs again did I realize that I had forgotten to take any socks." He made other discoveries. He had brought away an empty Eau de Cologne bottle, leaving behind his watch and pocketbook and all his other possessions. The litter on the floor of his room prevented him from closing the door. " In spite of this I took my key along. Later a friend in Paris had this key mounted and framed for me. I still have it in my library. . . ."

Other members of the troupe fared no better. The opera stars were treated to a show as bizarre as any in their repertory, and far more realistic. Scotti, who had quarters near Caruso, awoke feeling seasick, lay listening to the clamor, tried to snap on his light, then groped over the unstable floor to the door. In the hallway he saw Martino, Caruso's valet; then Caruso himself burst out of his room and fled downstairs. Scotti tossed on some clothes and followed. In the lobby he was joined by Madame Sembrich and others of the company. All had on only what they had managed to snatch up in their flight; there were notable gaps in their costumes. Madame Josephine Jacoby appeared in her nightgown, wearing the slippers she had worn as Mercedes the night before. She reported her amazement upon awakening to find that her bed was teetering from side to side and that " the ceiling never seemed to stay in one place." In the lobby she too saw Caruso, sitting like one dazed on a little trunk. She recalled how Alfred Hertz, " taking an inventory of our people," missed Fred Rullman, who was in charge of a ticket agency. Hertz, fortified by his visit to the bar, went upstairs and banged on Rullman's door. The latter had been among the celebrants the night before; he had slept peacefully through the earthquake. Still another member of the company gave little evidence that he shared the general panic. " Plançon," stated Madame Jacoby, ". . . appeared in top hat . . . and with his inevitable boutonniere. His *sangfroid* was marvelous." But he may not have been

333

as calm as he appeared. Other eyewitnesses reported that Plançon had forgotten to dye his beard — which he did every morning — and that it was a bright green.

Opera stars and other Palace guests presently picked their way through the streets to Union Square, three blocks away, where one would at least be in the open and so out of the way of collapsing buildings. There Scotti joined another group of Metropolitan artists, who had fled from the new St. Francis, facing the square. The united group were not reassured by the arrival of Caruso wearing a towel about his neck and carrying a framed portrait of Theodore Roosevelt. Still fearing the worst, Caruso insisted that he must get out of town at once. He asked Scotti to return with him to the Palace while he packed his trunks. Scotti refused and Caruso set off alone. At the hotel, according to Scotti, he engaged in a fist-fight with one of the Chinese servants.

Meantime Scotti was searching for someone to transport them to the home of Arthur Bachman, whom he and Caruso knew. Wagons were few and many wanted to hire them, but by bidding three hundred dollars Scotti engaged a vehicle and driver. His and Caruso's trunks and those of one or two others were put on board and they jolted through the broken streets to the edge of town. Caruso refused to sleep beneath the Bachman roof and passed the night under a tree in the yard. Hertz found refuge in an abandoned street-car; his rest was broken by the roaring of unfed lions and tigers in a near-by menagerie.

Next day a group of the opera people made their way to the Ferry Building, where a launch had been

*The Grand Court, about 1905, after the former carriage driveway
had been made into a Court Lounge*

Ruins of the Grand Court

Market Street in Flames. The Palace at the extreme left

The Palace Meets its End. The Burning of the Hotel on April 18, 190

engaged to take them to Oakland Pier and so to a train for the East. Scotti recalled that after they had boarded the launch the party saw Caruso on the dock arguing excitedly with several policemen who, unaware of his identity, barred his way. But the tenor still carried his portrait of Roosevelt, inscribed to Caruso himself. This proved an acceptable passport; the officers stepped aside and the tenor scrambled aboard.

Caruso reached New York six days later, with badly shaken nerves but otherwise sound. Asked about his experiences, he shouted dramatically: " Give me Vesuvius! "

5

PALACE GUESTS were sure it would take several days to clear away the litter within the hotel and perhaps a week before service could be restored to normal. The big building had received by far the most thorough shaking of its career and of course it had not come through unscathed. Fallen plaster, cracks in the interior walls and marble-paved floors, broken glass in quantity — this and other damage was everywhere visible. But it was also clear that no major structural harm had been done. Whereas all over town buildings had collapsed, chimneys and cornices and façades had fallen into the streets, foundations had sunk and walls been shaken from the perpendicular, the Palace had come through admirably. After a third of a century the foresight of the builders was amply justified. The superficial damage could be easily repaired. Fundamentally the big structure was as sound as ever.

The period of excitement passed. As early as six o'clock taut nerves had begun to relax and all over town citizens were rationally surveying the damage and laying plans for its repair. But just when confidence was begining to reassert itself, foreboding news began to sweep through the shattered streets. The earthquake had occurred at thirteen minutes after five. Early as that was, many families were already up, particularly in the district of small wooden residences south of Market Street. There the first shocks had upset stoves on which early breakfasts were being prepared, strewing burning wood over the floors. More often than not the families had rushed at once into the streets. Not all of them returned in time to put out the blazes. In the first half-hour after the quake fifty-seven fires were reported. Watchers on Nob Hill and on the heights of the Mission district presently saw smoke spiraling upward from a dozen places on the flats below.

Well before seven o'clock a Palace guest, C. K. Harley, thought he saw smoke in the vicinity of his iron and metals business on Harrison Street. He set off toward the spot, and on his way he came to a wooden building, burning briskly. Several fire engines and their crews stood idly by. The fire mains had been broken; the engines had pumped only a few moments before the water had failed. Harley regarded the scene while its implications sank in. He hurried on to his place of business, gathered up the office records, and carried them out of reach of these ominous, unattended fires.

All over town men were setting off on similar errands, for few now doubted that a major catastrophe was in the making. It became a question of rescuing what could be carried away from the sections already threatened and of hoping the destruction could somehow be kept within bounds.

Meantime rescue work got under way. It was carried on under difficulties, for not only was the water system useless, but transportation and communication had been put out of commission. No street-cars were running, the telephones were dead, gas and electricity had been turned off. Police and firemen, augmented by volunteer workers, set about rescuing those trapped in fallen buildings, transporting the injured to emergency hospitals and the dead to improvised morgues. By mid-morning detachments of troops had hurried in from the Presidio and taken over the patrolling of the streets. Fire lines were set up and citizens were ordered from the downtown area, where dynamite squads were preparing to combat the fire by blowing up buildings in its path.

Noon passed and hope of saving any part of the business district began to be abandoned. The smaller fires south of Market Street had by then merged into one giant blaze. It had already consumed more than a square mile of territory and was nearing the big buildings on the south side of Market Street. Among them was the Palace.

Within the hotel a determined struggle had been going on since mid-morning. Here again the foresight of those who had planned the building was demonstrated. Facilities for the quick discovery of fires and for their prompt extinction had been provided when the hotel was built — by watchmen, by automatic indicators, by scores of fire plugs and thousands of feet of emergency hose. There remained a third possibility of danger: failure of the city water supply. This, too, had been foreseen and provided for. The Palace had its own 675,000-gallon reservoir, under the grand court, supplied by its own wells and distributed through the building under pressure provided by its own pumps.

With such a system at hand, the personnel of the Palace felt they could cope even with the situation then confronting them, for the efficiency of the apparatus had not been impaired by the earthquake. As the wall of flame neared Market Street the attention of onlookers was attracted to a welcome sight: jets of water could be seen issuing from hoses on the Palace roof. The roof was kept wet down to prevent its catching fire from the hot ashes and burning wood raining down on it.

Hope that the fight might be successful was sharpened when it was decided to dynamite the Monadnock Building, a new seven-story structure directly across Annie Street. Two attempts were made, but the charges were inexpertly laid and not nearly powerful enough. The steel-frame building was hardly damaged. An hour later the buildings across Jessie Street were a mass of flame, and hope of saving the hotel waned.

Then, in the early afternoon, came the final adverse turn of fortune's wheel. The hotel's big reservoir was pumped dry, the hoses became useless, and nothing remained but for the defenders to call off the fight and make their way through the hot streets to safety. They were the last to leave the hotel; everyone else had long since gone.

At half past two John P. Young, editor of the *Chronicle*, stood with two friends at the corner of Market Street and Sansome. " The fire was then burning in the south of Market district nearly to the waterfront, and had made its way westward in the business district north of Market. . . . The Wells Fargo Building and other large structures on Second Street were aflame, and the Grand Hotel had commenced to burn." The group, stated Young, could see no evidence of life in or near the Palace.

It was true. The Palace, for the first time since its building a third of a century earlier, was deserted, abandoned by all save one last, sinister guest. Then, in late afternoon, the latter began stalking through the corridors, the lobby, the banquet halls, mounting stairways, entering the hundreds of rooms. Trailing his scarlet robe, he advanced inexorably, permeating every corner of the structure, silently at first, then more boisterously, until presently the grand court vibrated with an immense humming roar. Floor by floor, room by room, the flames laid waste the chambers where presidents and royalty had stayed, where actresses and prima donnas had received adulation, where belles of fashion had held court. Within an hour the fire was complete master of the hotel; each of the numberless bay windows of its great façades cast a ruddy glow, visible to thousands of citizens back beyond the fire lines.

It is impossible [continued Young] to state with positiveness whether the fire which destroyed the great hostelry, once the glory of San Francisco, attacked it from the east, but it seemed to our little group that it surrendered to the assault from that direction. It is not improbable that the inroads made much earlier in the morning, and which the force of the hotel had battled with for several hours, were greater than were supposed, and that the fire had eaten its way unnoticed to the lower floors; but from whatever point it came, when it disclosed itself to those on the street, the hotel presented the appearance of being afire in every part. . . . The spectacle was one calculated to inspire awe despite the fact that all around it were structures which had already succumbed to the destroyer. . . .

Driven back from the widening area of flames, crowds watched the destruction from surrounding heights: the Potrero and Mission hills, Twin Peaks, and, closest of all, Nob Hill, the great wooden mansions of which were presently to provide new fuel for the gigantic bonfire. Those on Nob Hill saw the fire cross Market Street, envelop the big buildings about the Third Street intersection, then move on toward the center of the shopping district.

Looking closely, they observed a curious thing. The Palace was virtually surrounded by flame and was itself burning. But on a pole above the Market Street side a flag continued to fly. Now and then smoke rolled up and obscured it, then the atmosphere cleared and the watchers could see it still in place. The spectators, heartened by this little drama, took to cheering each time it reappeared. The flames burned through the roof and poured in greater volume from the upper windows. At last one leaping tongue, higher than the others, shot up the pole and closed about the flag itself. In an instant it had vanished and onlookers saw only the blackened pole.

This destruction of the flag was perhaps a fitting symbol of the hotel's end. There had always been something theatrical about the Palace and it seemed proper that it should have been permitted to make a good exit.

BIBLIOGRAPHY

THE OLD PALACE HOTEL was the delight of newspaper men for the thirty-one years of its existence. So conspicuous was it in the life of San Francisco and the Pacific Coast that almost anything that happened within its walls was good " copy." Thus a great amount of material accumulated in the files of the city's newspapers covering the period from 1875 to 1906, awaiting the eye of research.

Credit is due, therefore, to the *Alta California, Bulletin, Chronicle, Examiner, Call,* and *California Spirit of the Times;* to the weekly *News Letter, Wasp,* and *Argonaut;* and to *Frank Leslie's Illustrated Weekly.* The *Western Hotel Reporter* was also consulted upon occasion.

Most of the material used in the preparation of this volume, including newspaper and magazine files, books, pamphlets, manuscripts, and illustrations, was made available through the resources and facilities of the following: the San Francisco Public Library; the library of The Society of California Pioneers, San Francisco; Bancroft Library, Berkeley; the California State Library, Sacramento; the San Mateo County Library; and the Redwood City Public Library, Redwood City.

The assistance of persons who had first-hand knowl-

343

edge of the old Palace, either as guests or as employees, is gratefully acknowledged. In a number of instances material was supplied by correspondents, through the offices of friends. Among individuals, thanks are due to Alfred Hertz and C. K. Harley for their reminiscences of the earthquake and fire; to John C. Newlands, Herman Riedel, George Fields, Miss Mabel R. Gillis, and Miss Caroline Wenzel and the staff of the California Section of the State Library, Dr. Margaret H. Smyth, and Edwin Grabhorn for illustrations; to Douglas S. Watson, O. W. Shannon, Frank Martin, George Kennedy, and Ferdinand H. Friche for personal recollections; and to Anthony Sotomayor, Miss Muriel Harmon, George Ezra Dane, and Robert Littler for courtesies rendered.

Following is a list of the more important books consulted:

CHAMBLISS, WILLIAM H.: *Chambliss' Diary; or, Society As It Really Is.* Chambliss & Company, New York, 1895.

ELDREDGE, ZOETH SKINNER: *History of California.* The Century History Co., New York [1915].

FROUDE, JAMES ANTHONY: *Oceana or England and Her Colonies.* Charles Scribner's Sons, New York, 1886.

GLASSCOCK, C. B.: *The Big Bonanza.* The Bobbs-Merrill Co., Indianapolis [1931].

GRANT, JESSE R.: *In the Days of My Father, General Grant.* In collaboration with Henry Francis Granger. Harper & Bros., New York, 1925.

GREELY, MAJOR GENERAL ADOLPHUS W.: *Earthquake in California, April 18, 1906.* Special Report of Major General Adolphus W. Greely, U.S.A. Government Printing Office, Washington, 1906.

Bibliography

GREEN, FLORIDE: *Some Personal Recollections of Lillie Hitchcock Coit*. Grabhorn Press, San Francisco, 1935.

HAMMERTON, J. A.: *Stevensoniana*. Edited by J. A. Hammerton. John Grant, Edinburgh, 1910.

HARPENDING, ASBURY: *The Great Diamond Hoax and Other Stirring Incidents in the Life of Asbury Harpending*. Edited by James H. Wilkins. The James H. Barry Co., San Francisco [1913].

HITTELL, THEODORE H.: *History of California*. N. J. Stone & Co., San Francisco, 1898.

JORDAN, DAVID STARR: *The California Earthquake of 1906*. Edited by David Starr Jordan. A. M. Robertson, San Francisco, 1907.

KEEP, ROSALIND A.: *Fourscore Years. A History of Mills College*. Mills College, 1931.

KEY, PIERRE U. R.: *Enrico Caruso. A Biography*. In collaboration with Bruno Zirato. Little, Brown & Co., Boston, 1922.

LANGLEY, HENRY G.: *The San Francisco Directory*. Henry G. Langley, San Francisco, 1875.

LENG, JOHN: *America in 1876*. Dundee Advertiser Office, 1877.

LEWIS, LLOYD, and SMITH, HENRY JUSTIN: *Oscar Wilde Discovers America: 1882*. Harcourt, Brace & Co., New York, 1936.

LLOYD, B. E.: *Lights and Shades in San Francisco*. A. L. Bancroft & Co., San Francisco, 1876.

LYMAN, GEORGE D.: *Ralston's Ring*. Charles Scribner's Sons, New York, 1937.

MORROW, WILLIAM W.: *The Earthquake of April 18, 1906, and the Great Fire in San Francisco* . . . Personal Experiences, etc., San Francisco, 1906.

NEVILLE, AMELIA RANSOME: *The Fantastic City*. Houghton Mifflin Co., Boston, 1932.

PIPER, R. U.: *An Examination of the 'Marriage Contract,' and the 'Dear Wife Letters' and Other Documents Connected with the Sharon-Hill Case in California.* Chicago, n.d.

STETSON, JAMES B.: *San Francisco during the Eventful Days of April, 1906.* Personal Recollections. Murdock Press, San Francisco [1906].

SWISHER, CARL B.: *Stephen J. Field, Craftsman of the Law.* The Brookings Institution, Washington, 1930.

TILTON, CECIL G.: *William Chapman Ralston, Courageous Builder.* Christopher Publishing House, Boston [1935].

WAGSTAFF, A. E.: *Life of David S. Terry.* Compiled and Edited by A. E. Wagstaff. San Francisco, 1892.

YOUNG, JOHN P.: *San Francisco. A History of the Pacific Coast Metropolis.* The S. J. Clarke Publishing Co., San Francisco [1912].

INDEX

i

Index

Index

iii

Index

v

Index

Index

Index

A NOTE ON THE TYPE

THIS BOOK is set on the Linotype in Baskerville. The punches for this face were cut under the supervision of George W. Jones, the eminent English printer and the designer of Granjon and Estienne. Linotype Baskerville is a facsimile cutting from type cast from the original matrices of a face designed by John Baskerville, a writing-master of Birmingham, for his own private press. The original face was the forerunner of the " modern " group of type faces, known today as Scotch, Bodoni, etc. After his death in 1775, Baskerville's punches and matrices were sold in France and were used to produce the sumptuous Kehl edition of Voltaire's works.

This book was composed by the Plimpton Press, Norwood, Massachusetts, and printed and bound by The Haddon Craftsmen, Scranton, Pennsylvania.